Religion in Europe at the End of the Second Millennium

A Sociological Profile

Religion in Europe at the End of the Second Millennium

Andrew M. Greeley

Transaction Publishers
New Brunswick (U.S.A.) and London (U.K.)

This book is printed on acid-free paper that meets the American National Standard for Permanence of Paper for Printed Library Materials.

Library of Congress Catalog Number: 2002073212
ISBN: 0-7658-0131-0
Printed in the United States of America

Library of Congress Cataloging-in-Publication Data

Greeley, Andrew M., 1928-
Religion in Europe at the end of the second millennium : a sociological profile / Andrew Greeley.
p. cm.
Includes bibliographical references (p.) and index.
ISBN 0-7658-0131-0 (alk. paper)
1. Europe—Religion—20th century. I. Title.

BL695 .G74 2002
306.6'094'09049—dc21 2002073212

As a starting point, I offer the following basic principles which might be regarded as vital to them. [theories of religion and social change]. The social significance of religion (i) can rise and fall in any social and economic context -pre-industrial, industrial, post-industrial; (2) does not decay automatically or irreversibly with the growth of human knowledge, rationality or technology; (3) does not decay automatically or irreversibly with industrialization or urbanization; (4) is not to be measured by unity of religious belief or uniformity of religious adherence in a given nation/region; (5) can be challenged by fundamental social and economic change, and can suffer short to medium-term decay, but can adapt to the new context and can show significant long-term growth; 6) can change the ways, or the balance of ways, in which it arises from one social and economic context to another.

(Brown 1992)

Contents

Introduction

I propose this brief book as a summary portrait of the condition of religion in Europe in the last two decades of the Second Millennium. I have decided to write it because the survey data exist to attempt the project, because it seems to be a useful project, and because it would seem no one else intends to do it. Most European sociologists of religion have focused their intentions with single-minded enthusiasm, on the decline of religion and have, it seems to me, paid little attention to the situations in which religion has not declined, to say nothing of those countries where there is evidence of an increase in religious faith—though by now it ought to be evident that such increases have occurred during the last two decades. Religion must decline, you see, because it *ought* to decline. Secularization has become a dogma.

Most sociologists of religion–for example, Bryan Wilson (1965, 1968, 1975, 1982) Steve Bruce (1992, 1993, 1995, 1996), Karel Dobbelaere (1987, 1989), Thomas Luckmann (1976), the early Peter Berger (1969), Tschannen (1991)—describe a general decline in religious faith and practice in Europe. The destruction of the "sacred canopy" by religious pluralism, the Enlightenment, the French Revolution, the discoveries of science, the rise of socialism, urbanization, industrialization, modernization, the influence of Marx and Freud, the increase in educational attainment—all have tended to diminish the power of the churches and to demystify the human condition. Moreover, the fact that the churches were usually on the wrong side in the political and nationalistic revolutions of the nineteenth and twentieth centuries has weakened their hold on the loyalty of their members. The decline is established especially by measuring church attendance in survey data, by "census" statistics (counting those in church), and by diocesan reports from the last century. Religion has not disappeared, but it has little influence on the life of its members. The churches draw fewer and fewer people into their weekly service and convince fewer and fewer of the existence of a transcendental order. In this perspective, the high levels of religious practice in the United States are viewed as another example of American exceptionalism.

Other scholars however (Warner 1993, Stark and Finke 2000) propose a different paradigm which emphasizes the advantages of religious pluralism. In situations where religions must compete in an open marketplace, religion tends to flourish. In markets dominated by monopolies, however, religious practice wanes. They also see a "demand" for religion that is caused by a need for an explanation of human existence.

Social historians in their descriptions of religion, especially in the late medieval and early modern eras, force one to question whether, save in some times and some places, religious practice was ever all that intense: Bossy (1985), Carroll (1992), Christian (1981), Flint (1992), Gentilcore (1992), Ginzburg (1983), LeRoy Ladurie (1975), Obelkevich (1979), Rubin (1991), Schneider (1990), Sommerville (1992). Whether LeRoy Ladurie's *Montaillou* was any more Christian or even Catholic than modern France surely must be open to some question. The golden age of religion never existed.

Casanova (1994), however, has argued that religion still influences important political and social issues. Jagodzinski points out that there is a correlation in Europe between religion and social attitudes and behaviors. Both Solidarity and the American civil rights movement establish that conservative religious impulses, even in the West, can create profound political transformation.

I believe that such words as modernization, secularization, globalization, and so on (to say nothing of "post-modernity") are labels under which we subsume a wide variety of contrasting and contrary phenomena which are ill served by being lumped together. They may be useful hooks for undergraduate instruction and dinner party conversation, but when they become reified so that they are taken as dynamisms which actually exist in the outside world, they are an excuse for not thinking, indeed a substitute for thought. One who uses such words as if they were realities with an existence of their own may sound profound but actually reveals himself to be shallow and superficial, someone who, for the sake of a convenient labels, loses all sense of the complex realities of social life.

In the words of Sewell (1992),

> Sociology's epic quest for social laws is illusory, whether the search is for timeless truths about all societies, ineluctable trends of more limited historical epochs, or inductively derived laws of certain classes of social phenomena. Social processes are inherently contingent, discontinuous, and open-ended. Big and ponderous social processes are never entirely immune from being transformed by small alterations in volatile and local social processes. "Structures" are constructed by human action, and "societies" or "social formations" or "social systems" are continually shaped and reshaped by the creativity and stubbornness of their human creators.

In fact, if one looks at Europe with a relatively open mind, prepared to be surprised by its complexity, one discovers a wide variety of religious phenomena. In some countries, religion has increased (most notably the former communist countries and especially Russia) in others it has declined (most notably Britain, the Netherlands, and France), and in still other countries it is relatively unchanged (the traditional Catholic countries), and in yet other countries (some of the social democratic countries) it has both declined and increased.[1] A single, one-directional model does not begin to cope with the variety of religious phenomena in Europe.

In my experience, it is assumed in the sociological profession and in the larger academic and media worlds that religion is moribund in Europe. Although I have been skeptical of the "secularization" model since the publication of my *Unsecular Man* in 1972, I was astonished to discover, when studying data from the International Social Survey Program 1991 module on religion, that in most European countries the majority of people believe in God and in life after death. However, reviewers summarily and angrily rejected research notes reporting these findings.

It is not my intention to wage war against "secularization" in this volume. It is patently a useless theory because it says too much and hence fails to subsume a wide variety of interesting data. As it is said in the mother tongue *qui nimis probat, nihil probat*.[2] My much more modest goal is to present a picture, a sketch perhaps, of European religion at the end of the Second Millennium (which ended on December 31 of the year 2000), a picture which, to mix the metaphors, might serve as a benchmark for subsequent studies and a corrective for those who thought, as I once did, that Norway, for example, was a godless and irreligious country. In some instances, I will analyze data in search for explanations. Why has belief in life after death increased among young people in seventeen out of the twenty-four nations in the 1998 International Social Survey Program study?)

My elementary argument is that the state of religion in Europe is a complicated matter. Most of my work in this book, therefore, will be descriptive and documentary. Since the data sets that I will consider span twenty years, I will also be able to note changes that have occurred in some European countries, changes in both directions. I will hint delicately that if, a couple of hundred years after Voltaire, most people in the European countries believe in life after death and God, then the demise of religion has been a very slow process. However, my main task will be to say simply that this is the way it is in Europe now: belief in God and in life after death, belief in superstitions and magic, convictions about the relations between church and state, attitudes about religion and science, and the effect of religion on the lives of people.

I will not apologize for the heavy reliance on statistics in this book. It is essential on such a complex subject to present as much precise information as possible. Data from probability samples do not make for easy cocktail party chatter, but they are a lot more reliable than the repetition of cliches about "what everyone knows." Nor do I apologize for the large spread sheet tables. If one wants a picture of religion in twenty-four European countries at the present time, there is no other way to present the data. The reader is welcome to inspect the tables in detail or take my word that I'm interpreting them accurately. Since one of the goals of this project is to provide a benchmark for measuring change in the years to come, it is essential that the present situation be portrayed with as much precision as possible.

I will rely on two different projects for data, the European Values Study and the International Social Survey Program. The former is a European group that was set in motion by a Dutch family foundation with a quietly Catholic orientation. It has carried out surveys in 1981, 1990, and 1995. Its weaknesses are many—lack of any clear theoretical orientation, poor question selection and wording (nothing in 1981 about the role of women), abysmal archiving, an anal-retentive attitude towards data. At this writing (autumn of 2000) the data from the 1995 project have yet to be released for general use. Moreover, the scholars who shape this study have been unable to resist the temptation to fiddle with the wording of questions and then compare the responses as though the questions were the same at both points in time. Thus, in one volume they constructed an index of religion—designed, of course, to show its decline—which contained an item about membership in religious organizations. They did not bother to tell the reader that the wording of this question had been changed in 1990 from the 1981 wording. Nonetheless, the European Values Study has the advantage that it has been conducted twice and provides the opportunity to compare changes and continuities over time on such matters as belief in God and in life after death.

The International Social Survey Program modules on religion (1991 and 1998) have the advantage of much stricter social science controls, probability sampling, superb archiving, immediate release of data, and concern for continuity of questionnaire design. Its most serious defects are that it is limited to a fifteen-minute module and that questionnaires are developed by discussion and consensus. While this is the only way an international project (involving now almost forty countries) can be carried out, it often gives members who have little knowledge about or interest in the subject under discussion (especially when it is religion) an opportunity to weaken questionnaire designs created by a drafting committee.

The International Social Survey Program was convened in 1984 by four survey centers from Germany, the United Kingdom, the United States, and Australia. They agreed that they would develop a fifteen-minute questionnaire which they would add to one of their surveys every year on a mutually agreed subject with a questionnaire they had worked out together. Each country would commit itself to a representative probability sample of at least a thousand respondents and data from the surveys would be made available to the whole world immediately after they had been properly archived (at the Zentralarchiv of the University of Cologne and more recently also at ASEP in Madrid). There are now survey centers from thirty-seven nations which participate in the study, including most European nations and Chile, Brazil, Mexico, Venezuela from Latin America; Japan and Bangladesh from Asia; and South Africa. ASEP of Spain now helps in the mammoth archiving work. There are no central funds. Each research organization funds all of its own costs. Unlike most international studies, the participating centers do not retain control of the data.

In the 1998 religion survey, all European countries were included except Finland, Estonia, Lithuania, Romania, Croatia, Serbia, Macedonia, Belgium, Luxembourg, and Greece (though Cyprus was part of the project). Data are available from the web site of the Zentralarchiv.

The International Social Survey Program regularly replicates previous studies so that time-series analyses become possible. However, there was considerable reluctance to replicate the 1991 study in 1998. The motion in favor of such a survey won by only one vote. Despite the rain forest of European religious variety that I will describe in this book, it is unlikely that there will be another International Social Survey Program religious module any time soon. All the more reason why, it seems to me, the present religious situation in Europe should be documented now.

In conclusion, my own theoretical suspicion (not unlike that of Rodney Stark is that there is a need or in his words a "demand" for religion which affects a considerable proportion of humankind—a yearning for meaning and belonging, for something in which to believe to which to belong. (Greeley 1972). This need results ultimate from two incorrigible human ailments—life from which we eventually die and hope which raises the possibility that death is not the end. A certain proportion of the human race, it would seem, can do without answers to such questions, a larger proportion is content with raising such matters only occasionally, a majority needs answers fairly often, and some—the God-haunted—are fascinated by such matters, perhaps to the point which seems to others who do not share that inclination like obsession.

Religion generally becomes more important to people as they grow older, both because they are faced with the question of whether to pass on a religious tradition to their children. Hence the propensity of some of the "modernization" theorists to cite lower levels of faith and practice among younger people as a sign of religious decline gratuitously ignores the possibility that the age correlation is a life-cycle matter and not a sign of social change. In fact, one must follow birth cohorts through the life cycle to determine whether they are in fact any less religious than their predecessors. Such an analysis requires at least twenty years of data at frequent interludes. It cannot be done in the present study. However, the research done in the United States (particularly with the NORC's General Social Survey) favors the life-cycle explanation: The young are less religious not because they represent permanent social change but because they are young.

However, it is fair to consider educational attainment (net of age) as a measure of a possible modernization effect. In this volume I will consider the possibility that those who have completed university education might be less religious than the rest of the populations which I am studying. To anticipate, they are generally either not less religious or only marginally so.

Patently, religion in Europe has changed enormously between the end of the First Millennium and the end of the Second. In my judgement the change has been an improvement, not because superstition has been eliminated (it has not, as we shall see), but because freedom has replaced compulsion. However, I suspect that if a time machine would permit International Social Survey Program interviewers to return to 1000 A.D. and wisdom to fashion questions appropriate for respondents of that era, a distribution of respondents along the religious continuum described in the previous paragraph would not have much changed.

I wish to acknowledge help from Wolfgang Jagodzinski who coauthored a version of chapter 10 and Conor Ward who was co-author on a version of chapter 9. I also am grateful to Rolf Uher, Eckhardt Mosemann, and Michael Hout for their help.

AG
Grand Beach, September 8, 2000

Notes

1. Ireland, as usual, goes it own unique way.
2. "Who proves too much, proves nothing."

1

The Persistence of God

Introduction

Despite some theologians, God is not simple. Should there be a God, He has a great deal of explaining to do about the complexities of the world that he has created, even if he has demonstrated, as Einstein once observed, a considerable understanding of higher mathematics. On the other hand, a Creator whom creatures could easily grasp intellectually would probably be no God at all. So when one is asked whether one believes in God, one might answer with a number of counter-questions such as when and what kind of God and with what kind of confidence and with what sort of relationship, if any. One could easily (and honestly) say, "Well, I believed with absolute confidence yesterday, for most of the day, and I think by this afternoon I will again, but this morning I have very strong doubts."

Against the background of a very strange God (to say the least) and the mutability of human responses to the God question, a simple survey item about the respondent's belief in God, can provide only a rough cut of the nature of the respondent's faith. As we shall see later, when the researcher asks the question of what God is like the nuances of faith become even more complicated. Thus, those who don't believe in God, or are not sure they believe, are likely to have a more gracious (and arguably more orthodox) image of God then those who do believe.

In this chapter, we will consider six different ways of manifesting belief in God—an answer to a simple question about belief, scores on scales measuring the quality of belief, the conviction that God is concerned personally with each of us, interaction with God in prayer, belief that God works miracles, and religious experiences in which one may encounter God. In some countries, we will see, more people believe in miracles than believe firmly in God or in God's concern for us as persons. The reader will have to draw his own conclusions about which measure is the most satisfactory or whether one must resign oneself to thinking that all are useful in describing the vagaries of human convictions about God.

The Persistence of God

In the first column of table 1.1 we observe the answers of respondents in various countries to question 19 about which statement best describes their beliefs about God. Only in the Czech Republic and East Germany is there less than majority belief in God. More than nine out of ten believe in the deity in Cyprus, the two Irelands, Poland, and Portugal. More than eight out of ten believe in Italy, Spain, and Austria. Six of the top eight countries are predominantly Catholic, one is Orthodox, and one (Northern Ireland) is more Protestant than Catholic but heavily Catholic. It might be argued that in these Catholic countries religion has long enjoyed a monopoly, though not one that has been free of conflict or oppression or anti-clericalism. Certainly there is not, however, the kind of religious competition which those who support theories of religious pluralism would think necessary for the health of religion. Moreover the Lutheran monopoly in the Scandinavian countries has not produced such high levels of belief in God.

In the next three countries—Switzerland, Slovakia, and Latvia – the level of belief in God declines into the 70 percent range. Each of the countries is partially Catholic and partially Protestant. In none of them, however, has the religious pluralism produced results similar to those in Northern Ireland. However, it may be that decades of socialist rule have had some effect on religion in Slovakia and Latvia and, indeed, all the other countries except Poland.

In the next two countries on the list, West Germany and Britain, approximately two-thirds of the respondents believe in God. These two countries—often studied by sociologists—represent perhaps the weakly believing populations who still cling to God but without all that much fervor. They also are the mean for belief in God in the International Social Survey Program sample. The remaining eleven countries, with the exception of France and the Netherlands, are ei-

Table 1.1
Belief in God in Europe

Countries	Belief in God	Theist	Not Atheist or Agnostic	God who is concerned	Pray several times a month	Religious Miracles	Religious Experience	Atheists
Cyprus	96%	85%	96%	71%	55%	89%	10%	1%
Ireland	95%	80%	95%	76%	84%	72%	13%	2%
Poland	94%	78%	94%	73%	79%	60%	16%	2%
N. Ireland	92%	79%	93%	73%	70%	68%	26%	3%
Portugal	91%	78%	95%	74%	62%	79%		2%
Italy	86%	73%	91%	56%	65%	69%	31%	4%
Spain	82%	65%	85%	44%	48%	46%	19%	9%
Austria	80%	52%	87%	41%	51%	65%	17%	6%
Switzerland	73%	45%	83%	49%	52%	60%	23%	4%
Slovakia	72%	57%	80%	57%	52%	53%	26%	11%
Latvia	71%	39%	80%	46%	35%	35%	15%	9%
Britain	69%	50%	76%	37%	37%	42%	16%	10%
W.Germany	65%	45%	78%	37%	41%	39%	16%	11%
Hungary	65%	51%	75%	29%	37%	30%	17%	13%
Slovenia	62%	39%	73%	27%	32%	53%	15%	17%
Bulgaria	60%	35%	75%	37%	26%	29%	16%	17%
Norway	59%	44%	77%	36%	29%	40%	16%	10%
Netherlands	57%	42%	70%	32%	39%	37%	22%	17%
Denmark	57%	34%	70%	38%	21%	25%	15%	15%
Sweden	54%	26%	65%	23%	20%	27%	12%	17%
France	52%	39%	63%	29%	30%	37%	24%	19%
Russia	52%	32%	63%	29%	18%	38%	13%	19%
Czech	46%	31%	66%	23%	26%	32%	11%	20%
East Germany	25%	17%	36%	14%	14%	39%	10%	51%

ther Scandinavian or former socialist countries. In the Netherlands religion diminished when the tri-polar social structure of society collapsed and the Vatican, utterly unsympathetic to the problems of Dutch Catholicism virtually drove many Dutch Catholics out of the church and away from religion. The constant struggles in France between clericals and anti-clericals over the past two centuries may have taken its toll on religion. Since the failure of the pietistic revivals in the Scandinavian countries in the middle of the last century, devotion in these countries has not been fervent. Only in East Germany and the Czech Republic do a majority of the respondents say that they don't believe in God. In East Germany the intense and efficient pressure of an anti-religious socialism seems to have succeeded in crushing religious belief. In the Czech Republic, a long tradition of anti-religious sentiment, represented by the "Free Thinkers, " is more likely the explanation than socialist pressure: 40 percent of the Czechs say that they never believed in God and still don't.

God is still alive and well, then, in most of the Catholic countries (and Northern Ireland), alive but perhaps not well in the mixed Catholic and Protestant countries, and weak in the Scandinavian and onetime socialist countries. It must be noted, however, that there have been considerable changes in the former socialist countries in the last decade that we will examine in subsequent chapters.

The second measure of belief in God (in the second column) is based on question 18. The item is most unsatisfactory in its wording both because it hardly represents an ordered scale and because the meaning of individual items is obscure. However, it survives in questionnaires because it has been often asked and no one has devised a better item to measure the gradations of religious faith. In fact 98.4 percent of the respondents are able to place themselves somewhere on the "scale."[1]

The "theists" are those who say that either they believe that "God really exists" or that while they have doubts, they do really believe in God. When they are compared to those who say flatly that they believe in God because that is the only choice the item gives them, the percentages decline somewhat, generally between fifteen and twenty percentage points. Those who are certain about God (even with some doubts) are a majority only in the Catholic countries (including Slovakia and Hungary). The proportion of "theists" declines sharply from 50 percent in England to 17 percent in East Germany.

However, the picture changes somewhat if one adds in the third column those who choose the middle two items in the scale—those who believe in God some of the time or in a "Higher Power"[2] (caps in questionnaire) to those who are relatively certain or absolutely certain. They choose a middle ground between certainty on the one hand or agnosticism and atheism on the other, opting for the lukewarm instead of the hot or the cold. In effect, they repudiate the agnostic and atheistic responses in the last two items on the scale (which are, curiously enough, the first responses offered in question 18).

When respondents are permitted to take into account their uncertainties, in all but the top three countries, they are more likely to admit some kind of faith in God than they were when they were asked the more simple question about believing in God. Indeed, only in East Germany does this tentative belief fall below three-fifths. In all other countries, the respondents overwhelmingly reject the atheistic and agnostic response to the God hypothesis. Better perhaps, in line with Pascal's wager, to be safe than sorry.[3]

The results are very different, however, when a statement of the orthodox Christian belief is proposed to the respondents (question 22a). They are much less likely to agree that there is a God who is personally concerned with each of us. Indeed 87 percent who are "theists" believe in a concerned God, as do 13 percent who opt for the middle ground and 2 percent of the atheists and agnostics.

Thus the fourth column in table 1.1 might specify the maximum of orthodox theists in Europe, a majority in the Catholic countries of Ireland, Poland, Portugal, Italy, and Slovakia, as well as in Cyprus and Northern Ireland. The proportions who believe in a concerned God are in the 30 percent range in Britain, West Germany, Norway, Denmark, and generally lower in the former socialist countries. Thus to the question as to whether Europeans believe in God, one could reply that most of them do, but only a minority believes that he is concerned about them.[4] Do they then believe in God *really*? They say they do and we must believe them. However, most of them cannot accept what might be considered the God of the Books. Whether their ancestors ever did is not a question which one can answer with any great deal of confidence, since their ancestors were never given a chance to answer a battery of questions and would not have known what to make of many of them.

Do they believe enough in God to engage in dialogue with him several times a month (question 31) through prayer (column 5 of table 1.1)? Here the proportion of orthodox declines even more. A majority in Cyprus and the Catholic countries (except Spain and France) do pray at least several times a month. The majority in the other Western European countries do not and neither do those of the former socialist countries, except Slovakia. In those heavily studied countries, Britain, the Netherlands, and West Germany, the proportion of prayers are 37 percent, 39 percent, and 41 percent—perhaps a higher proportion than one might have expected from reading the secularization literature about these countries.

To believe in religious miracles, one need not, perhaps, believe in either a God who might be concerned or a God to whom it might be appropriate to pray. Perhaps a Higher Power of sorts is responsible for miracles. However, a belief in religious miracles (question 20d) does raise some questions about one's doubts concerning God. Who, it might be asked, is the God who is doubted. It is therefore somewhat surprising that (the sixth column in table 1.1) in thirteen countries the proportion of people who believe in religious miracles is higher than that of those who pray regularly and those who believe God is concerned—Italy, Spain, Austria, Switzerland, Britain, Slovenia, Norway, Sweden, France, Russia, the Czech Republic, and East Germany. In seven countries more people accept miracles than are "theists"—Italy, Austria, Sweden, Slovenia, Russia, the Czech Republic, and East Germany. Indeed in East Germany more people believe in miracles (39 percent) than believe in God (25 percent). Who, one again wonders, is the God in which they do not believe.

The penultimate column in table 1.1 reports the proportion of respondents in each country who report a "a turning point experience" (question 23), an event which might represent some experiential contact with God. Seventeen percent have had such experiences, a percentage that does not vary across age cohorts. A higher proportion is reported in Denmark and France and a lower in Cyprus, East Germany, the Czech Republic, and Russia. Later in this chapter we will consider other items which might hint at contacts with the transcendent.

Finally in the last column we observe that atheism is not a popular religious position in Europe. Only in East Germany of the former socialist countries do more that half of the population report flatly that they do not believe in God. Atheist percentages are low in the Catholic countries and above the 13 percent average only in France, the Scandinavian countries, the Netherlands, and many of the former socialist countries. Still, after East Germany the highest atheism rate in Europe is in the Czech Republic (20 percent) followed by Russia (19 percent). The materialists did not drive God out of Europe.

In summary, the various columns in table 1.1 should not be taken to indicate either inconsistency or hypocrisy in belief in God. Rather, they indicate that the word "God" is fraught with many different meanings. One responds to the word in the context in which one encounters it. Yes, I believe in God. Well, I tend to think of him as a person, but not always. I am not an agnostic or an atheist, but I don't pray all that much and I'm not convinced God is concerned about me, but miracles do happen."

The nuances with which one might express such opinions vary but not randomly. The greatest levels of confidence exist in the Catholic countries except for France. The lowest levels in Scandinavia, the Netherlands, and the former socialist countries except for Poland and Slovakia. Britain and West Germany are usually in the middle. More briefly, the International Social Survey Program countries are generally moderate theists but not intensely so, save in Ireland, Poland, Italy, Spain, Cyprus, and Portugal.

Is God Dying?

Has belief in God declined through the years? Systematic cross-national research with (more or less) the same questions began in 1981. Thus, given the limitations of this project, we will be measuring change only during the last two decades of this millennium. Given the different question wording in the European Values Study and the International Social Survey Program one will be able to judge statistical significance only within the boundaries of a specific project. Thus to say that belief in God has decreased during the last years of the second millennium, one would need significant declines in a given country in both projects. There is no such decline in table 1.2.

In the European Values Study project there was a decline in belief in Spain (from 91 percent to 86 percent) and in the Netherlands from (71 percent to 65 percent) and an increase in Hungary from 55 percent to 65 percent. In the International Social Survey Program project there was a significant increase in Russia from 48 percent to 62 percent and a decline in Germany from 67 percent to 61 percent. In the International Social Survey Program, however, there is a decline neither for Spain nor for the Netherlands. Hence, one can assert cautiously that there is no strong tendency for belief in God to

Table 1.2
Change in Belief in God by Year and Survey

	EVS	EVS	ISSP	ISSP
	1981	1990	1991	1998
Ireland	97%	98%	95%	94%
Poland			95%	95%
N. Ireland	97%	97%	95%	94%
Italy	88%	89%	86%	88%
Britain	81%	79%	69%	68%
Spain	91%	86%**	79%	81%
Austria			79%	81%
France	65%	62%		52%
Hungary	55%	65%*	65%	66%
Slovenia			61%	63%
Britain	80%	79%	70%	69%
W. Germany	80%	78%	67%	62%****
Russia			48%	60%***
Norway	73%	65%**	59%	58%
Netherlands	71%	65%**	55%	58%
E. Germany			25%	26%

* Significantly higher than 1981.
** Significantly lower than 1981.
*** Significantly higher 1991.
**** Significantly lower than 1991.

be declining in Europe for the last twenty years and some surprising increases in two of the former communist countries.[5]

One can also measure change by considering question 19 which describes one's past religious history. Eleven percent of the respondents said that they used to believe in God, but no longer did while eight percent said they used not to believe but now did. Thus there was a net loss of three percentage points in belief in God. However, birth cohort analysis, shows that the net loss to belief in God has declined substantially across birth cohorts, so that the net loss is only 1 percent in the two most recent cohorts (figure 1.1).

Figure 1.1
Change in Belief in God by Birth Cohort

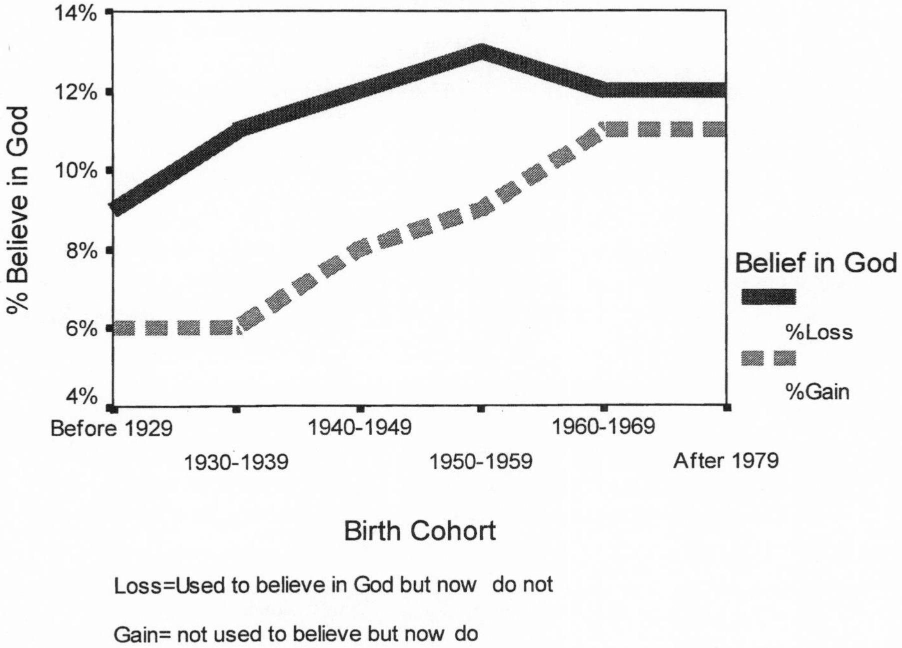

The losses and gains, however, vary greatly among the countries. Losses above the average are in Britain (15 percent), The Netherlands (13 percent), West Germany (13 percent) and France and Norway (10 percent). The most striking increases in belief in God are in Latvia (29 percent) and Russia (21 percent) and Bulgaria (10 percent). God is waning in the social democratic countries in Western Europe and waxing in the former socialist countries in Eastern Europe. Some might suggest that this is merely a temporary change in Eastern Europe. However, that remains to be seen in further studies.

Figures 1.2 an 1.3 show losses and gains in Latvia and the Netherlands (both countries having substantial Protestant and Catholic affiliates[6]) The countries are mirror images of one another with high gains and low losses in the former and the reverse in the latter. There is no reason to suggest that either is the wave of the future. They have had different histories in the last half century. What the next half century will bring is an open question. Latvia could become like the Netherlands or like Ireland.

Figure 1.2
Change in Belief in God by Birth Cohort

Latvia

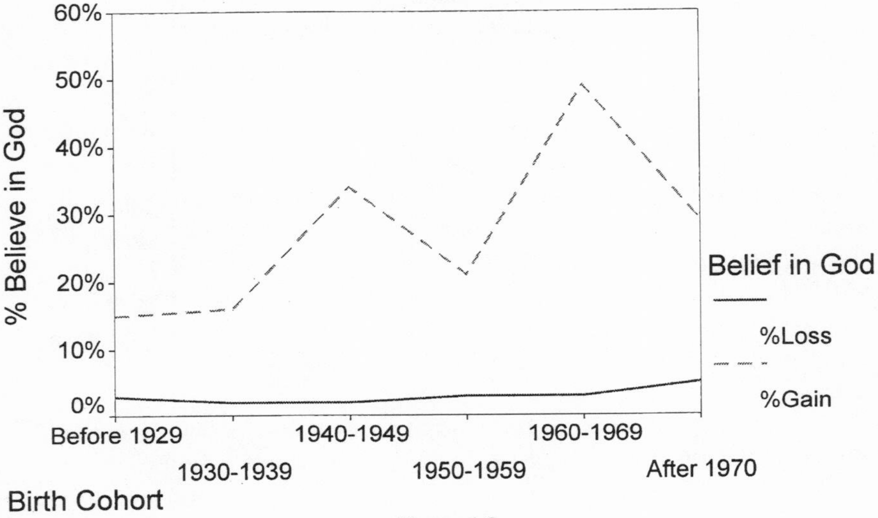

Figure 1.3
Change in Belief in God by Birth Cohort

Netherlands

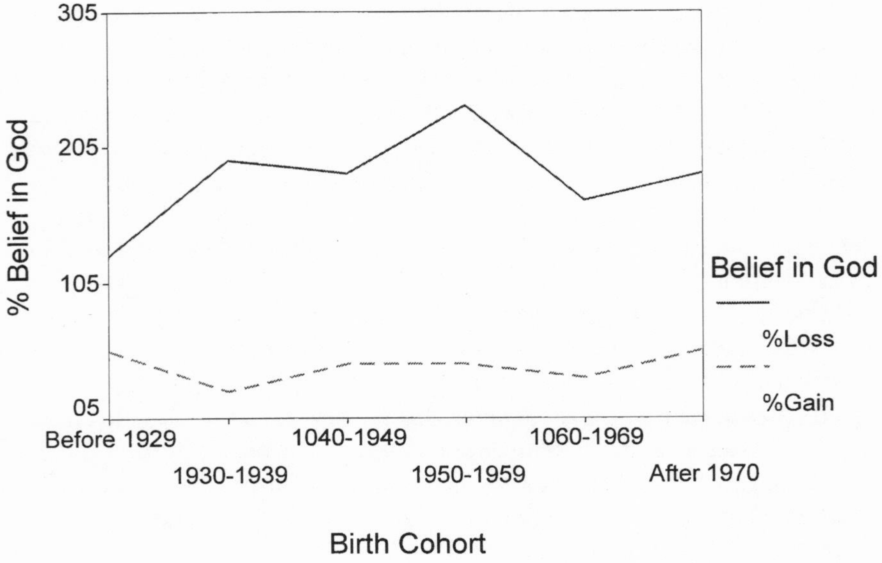

Table 1.3
Changes in Belief in God within Countries

Countries	Net change in Belief in God
Cyprus	1%
Ireland	0
Poland	-1%
N. Ireland	2%
Portugal	2%
Italy	-5%
Spain	-6%
Austria	-7%
Switzerland	-.5%
Slovakia	0
Sweden	-5%
Latvia	29%
Britain	-15%
W. Germany	-13%
Hungary	-5%
Slovenia	-8%
Bulgaria	10%
Norway	-10%
Netherlands	-13%
Denmark	-4%
France	-10%
Russia	21%
Czech	-2%
East Germany	-15%

God continues to survive in Europe, therefore, ambiguously, problematically, uncertainly. Atheism and agnosticism are not yet, not even at the end of the Second Millennium, popular choices.

Does God Matter?

But does God matter? Does belief effect daily life? Such scholars as Karel Dobbelaere and Thomas Luckmann have argued that the churches no longer have an impact on public events. Surely, however, the lesson of Solidarity in Poland would argue caution about such an argument, as to some extent the highly visible re-entry of

Orthodoxy into the public life of Russia and Bulgaria. Jose Casanova (1994) has written about other situations in contemporary Europe where churches have been deeply involved in public events.

The data available to the present analysis, however, enable us only to measure the impact of religion on personal political and social values and behavior. Table 1.4 shows that belief in a God who is concerned personally has an effect on attitudes towards feminism, premarital sex, and abortion (questions 3, 6, and 7) in all countries.

Table 1.4
Effects of Belief in God (Concerned God)
(correlations)

Countries	Equality	Honesty	Volunteer	Feminism	Premarital sex	Abortion	Happy
Cyprus	.00*	.10	.12	-.05*	-20	-.13	.07
Ireland	.05	.11	.00*	-.20	-30	-.23	.05
Poland	.12	.06	.03*	-.13	-.21	-.25	.04*
N. Ireland	.07	.09	.13	-.24	-.38	-.25	.12
Portugal	.13	.00*	.06	-.13	-.20	-.16.	03*
Italy	.09	.02*	.11	-.12	-.24	-.28	.00*
Spain	.03*	.09	.03*	-.19	-.25	-.29	.00*
Austria	.06	.07	.06	-.17	-.10	-.19	06
Switzerlan	.13	.10	.15	-.19	-.29	-.35	.10
Slovakia	.07	.07	.14	-.11	-.31	-.13	.06
Sweden	.08	.15	.17	-.22	-.35	-.29	.08
Latvia	.07	.14	.18	-.10	-.10	-.15	.06
Britain	.05	.09	.13	-.17	-.29	-.38	.05
W.German	.11	.08	.10	-.18	-.20	-.28	.07
Hungary	-.03*	.05	.02*	-.13	-.09	-.32	.05
Slovenia	.10	.01	.14	-.19	-.21	-.26	.04*
Bulgaria	.09	.03*	.12	-06	-.06	-.06	.07
Norway	.07	.12	.14	-.23	-.21	.-50	.07
Netherland	.05	.09	.14	-.29	-.39	-.47	.10
Denmark	.06	.06	.06	-.13	-.20	-.27	.02*
France	.10	.06	.07	-.25	-.40	-.32	.03
Russia	.08	.03*	.02*	-.11	-.10	-.05	.02*
Czech	.00*	.04	.18	-.13	-.26	-.21	.07
E.German	.00*	.09	.11	-.17	-.19	-.29	.08

In most countries, it also has a significant positive effect on beliefs that the government should sustain equality in income, on personal honesty, and on the propensity to volunteer (questions 2, 9, and 16). It also has a significant positive effect on reported personal happiness (question 1) save in Poland, Portugal, Italy, Slovenia, and Russia.

Those who believe God is concerned are therefore less likely to be feminists or to approve of premarital sex and abortion and more likely to believe in income equality and personal honesty and to volunteer. They are also more likely to report personal happiness.[7]

Whether the correlations between belief in God and attitudes and behavior in table 1.4 represent evidence of important religious influence or not will depend on what the reader judges to be important. If, however, there were correlations with, for example, education of the same magnitude, they would not be readily dismissed.

Who is God?

For most humans who have walked the planet, the relevant question probably was not do you believe in God but rather, who is your God and what is he (or she) like. The Jewish and Christian scriptures—particularly Isaiah and St. John—abound in powerful and graceful images of God—God is a mother who loves her children, God is a spouse who has fallen in love with his people, God is love, God is a friend. These images, which seem dominant in many books of the scriptures and in the writings of many holy men and women, seem to have rather little influence on religious preaching today and to have been replaced by harsher images which emphasize the more authoritarian and primitive aspects of the deity. A number of years ago, I devised a series of items to measure respondents pictures of God—four seven-item scales between mother-father, master-spouse, king-friend, and judge-lover (Greeley 1996). In research in the United States, I discovered, not surprisingly, that the scales were tilted towards the harsher images of God. I lobbied strenuously for the inclusion of these items in both International Social Survey Program religion studies. Many of my colleagues thought it was a strange idea. Sociology of religion was supposed to be concerned about church attendance, belief in the Bible, and sexual matters, not vague and poetic issues. It was hard to persuade them that all God-talk is metaphorical and hence poetic. They conceded me the right to add the items to the survey as an "option."

Nine of the European countries, all more or less Catholic, exercised that option. Three of them, however, asked only some of the

Table 1.5
Images of God
%More or at Least Equally

	Mother	Spouse	Friend	Lover	3 or more
Hungary	55%	65%	69%	50%	38%
Latvia	47%	49%	44%	44%	44%
Slovakia	43%	40%	78%	77%	44%
France	43%	50%	81%	81%	51%
Italy	38%	25%	31%	31%	25%
Ireland	35%	40%	47%	48%	35%
Switzerland	35%				
Portugal			89%	87%	
Czech		70%		90%	

Table 1.6
Images of God by Theists by Country

	God as Mother		God as Spouse	
	Not Theists	Theists	Not Theists	Theists
Hungary	59%	53%	38%	31%
Latvia	52%	39%	52%	49%
Slovakia	50%	38%	49%	35%
France	52%	32%	54%	44%
Italy	52%	33%	35%	21%
Switzerland	58%	42%		
Ireland	48%	33%	47%	38%

forced choice items[8] (table 1.5). Of these, the French were the most likely to choose three or more of the gracious images of God (51 percent) followed by the Latvians and the Slovaks. The Hungarians, however, had majority scores on all four items. Only in Ireland and Italy was there considerable caution about such imagery with none of the gracious images gaining majority support. Gracious pictures of God were popular only in Eastern Europe and in France, the least Catholic of the Catholic studies in the project.

I will insist that the picture of God as warm and loving is the more orthodox of the two and leave further debate on the matter to theologically literate sociologists of whom there might be a few in the world. It is fascinating to observe in table 1.6 that those who are not theists[9] in all seven countries are more likely to choose what I claim is the orthodox emphasis on both the image of God as mother and spouse. To the extent that they believe in anything at all, they tend to be more orthodox than the firm believers. The French are more likely than the Italians and the Irish, for example, to picture God as a spouse, *and* the French non-theists still more likely. Perhaps some of those who reject belief in God are in fact rejecting the image that believers propose.

This tendency is apparent in table 1.7 which compares those who choose either the agnostic or atheist items on question 17 with the respondents who do not make that choice. In each country, the atheists and the agnostics have higher scores on the mother/spouse scale than those who profess belief in God.

Perhaps the explanation of this paradox is that many of the atheists and agnostics do not like the God about whom they hear but do like a God they think might be worthy of belief.

God and the Churches

Catholics, Orthodox, and Muslims[10] are more likely than Protestants to believe in God, to be theists, to accept that God is personally concerned with humans and to endorse the possibility of religious miracles (table 1.8). Catholics are more likely than the other three religious groups to pray frequently. (Indeed, the similarity in basic convictions about God among Catholics, Muslims and Orthodox is striking. Might it be, however, that the greater Protestant skepticism is the result of better education? Certainly the predominantly Catholic countries in the sample have the reputation of being a bit "backward."

Table 1.7
Images of God by Agnosticism and Country
% High on Mother -Spouse Scale

	Agnostics	Not Agnostics
Hungary	39%	24%
Italy	47%	14%
Ireland	31%	24%
Latvia	43%	29%
Slovakia	40%	24%
France	42%	29%

Table 1.8
Belief in God by Religion

	Belief in God	Theists	God who is concerned	Pray two or three times a month	Miracles
Protestant (8, 898)	72%	58%	45%	41%	46%
Catholic (18, 393)	88%	68%	56%	63%	63%
Orthodox (3, 055)	88%	62%	56%	41%	62%
Islamic (226)	92%	71%	55%	44%	61%
None (1, 829)	18%	11%	8%	12%	12%

Table 1.9
Differences in belief among four religions
(Regression Equations)

	Belief		Theists		Concerned God	
	Without Education*	With Education	Without Education	With Education	Without Education	Without Education
Catholic	.15	.15	.16	.17	.10	.09
Orthodox	.16	.15	.10	.10	.10	.10
Islam	.18	.19	.20	.20	.22	.21

*Did not graduate from University

Table 1.10
Effect of University on Religious Faith
(Regression Equations)

	Belief in God	Theists	God who is concerned	Pray two or threee times a month
All cohorts	.06	.05	.05	.06
Born after 1955	.02	.01	.01	.02

However, when one runs two dummy variable multiple regression equations (with Protestants as the comparison group) without university education and the second with university education, the results show that the "advantage" of Catholic, Muslims, and Orthodox over Protestants in belief in God is not changed in the least (table 1.9). There remains, therefore, the problem of explaining why

Protestants in European countries are less likely to believe in God than others—as well as the problem of why there is a striking similarity in these beliefs among such disparate groups as the Orthodox, Muslims, and Catholics. However, these questions are beyond the scope of the present profile.

God and the University

University education does not, as we have just seen, account for the higher levels of belief in God among Catholics, Orthodox and Muslims in comparison with Protestants. However, might it not lead to somewhat higher levels of unbelief? Might it not be more difficult for thinking men and women to accept the transcendental, the mystical, the unverifiable? Would not one believe that university graduates would be thinking men and women, less given to religious superstitions? Surely two centuries after the Enlightenment, education should have had some impact on religion, should it not?

Figure 1.4 shows that a negative effect of university education on belief seems to have ended with the cohort born in the 1950s and

Figure 1.4
Theist by Cohort by University

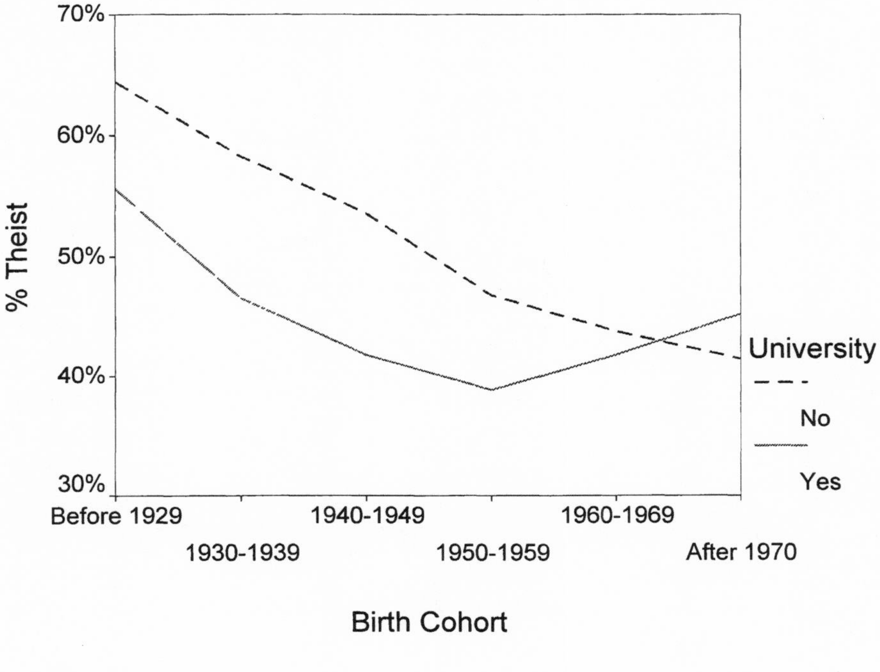

Figure 1.5
Theist by Cohort by University (Since 1955)

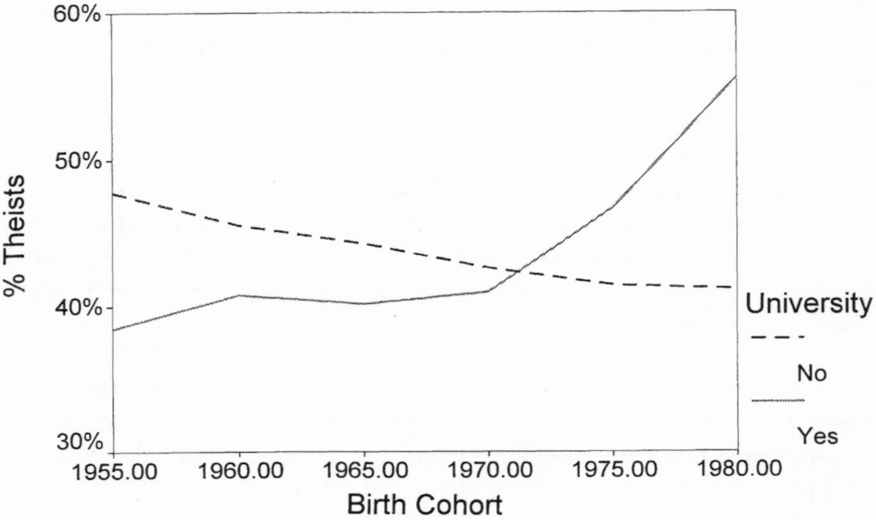

Figure 1.6
Atheism by Cohort by University

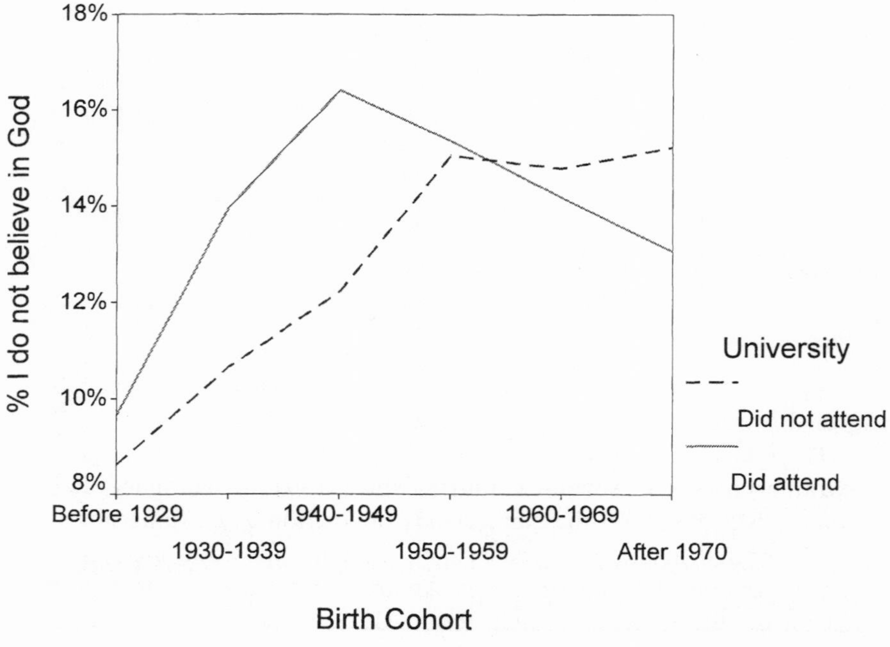

that, in fact, among the most recent birth cohort university graduates are more likely to be theists. Figure 1.5 closes in on the more recent birth cohorts and shows how the earlier pattern has changed in the last two birth cohorts with theism now fifteen percentage points stronger among university graduates.

As for atheists, 13 percent of those who did attend universities say flatly that they don't believe in God as do 14 percent of those who did not attend. However, figure 1.6 shows that in the most recent birth cohorts the university educated are less likely to be atheists.

In some countries, however, significant relationships between cohort and belief for those who graduated from university are quite high: .15 in Spain, .22 in Italy, .23 in the Czech Republic, .36 in Poland, .19 in Hungary. The younger university educated cohorts, in other words, are much more likely to be theists and their predecessors in two Catholic countries and in five former socialist countries. Should these trends continue university education may seem to be a positive asset for religion.

Conclusion

We can derive the following conclusions from this chapter:

1. Europe is hardly godless. In most countries, atheism and agnosticism are not frequent responses.
2. However, the quality of belief in God varies from measure to measure and from country to country. Fervent faith exists only among a minority.
3. Faith is, on the average, strongest in the Catholic countries except France.
4. Faith is weakest in Eastern Europe (excepting Slovakia, Latvia, and Poland) and in Scandinavia and the Netherlands.
5. Faith is in the middle ground in most other social democratic countries (like Britain and West Germany).
6. Communist materialism did not destroy religious faith in Europe. Indeed, there are some signs of its resilience (to be investigated subsequently.
7. Belief in God correlates with a number of important social indicators in most countries.
8. Those who hesitate in belief and even those who don't believe at all have more benign images of God than do those who believe more firmly.

9. As far as we can measure change through the last twenty years or from people's recollection of their religious autobiographies, there has been little erosion of faith in the years before the end of the Second Millennium.

10. No systematic verification can be found for any of the more general theories of the sociology of religion.

11. Three puzzles remain—how to account for the persistent high level of faith in the Catholic countries (besides France); how to explain the possibility of a religious revival in Eastern Europe; how to deal the similarity of faith in God among Catholics, Orthodox, and Muslim and the dissimilarity between these three groups and Protestants.

Notes

1. A sociologist of religion, whose name I do not know since I encounter him only in anonymous reviews, routinely insists that those who do not answer a religious item must be counted as unbelievers. He advances no reason for this argument other than his own inisght.
2. I am at a loss personally to explain the difference between the "Higher Power" and a "personal God." Perhaps the advantage of denying a personhood to God is that God is thereby freed of the limitations we experience in human persons. Whether it also excludes the powers of knowledge and love is not at all clear.
3. I once proposed the Wager to a younger colleague who had blithely informed me that she didn't believe in God. "That's not true, " she responded promptly, "if there is a God, he'll love me like a daughter and will not be angry that I didn't believe in him." I had to admit that her theology was better than that of Blaise Paschal.
4. I mean here a minority of the respondents of the International Social Survey Program sample, from which one cannot estimate to the total European population.
5. Unfortunately four of the former Communist countries joined the International Social Survey Program only after the 1991 study –Latvia, the Czech Republic, Slovakia, and Bulgaria. Hence there is no measure across time for changes in belief in God for these countries.
6. As well as a substantial Orthodox population in Latvia.
7. The highest level of personal happiness is in Ireland where 42% report they are very happy. In the former socialist countries the proportions are very low. Except for Poland (16%) all other countries are under 10%. Russia, Slovakia, and Hungary are tied at 7%.
8. Interestingly enough, the scholars from Britain, the Netherlands, and Germany did not ask the questions.
9. Items 5 and 6 on question 18.
10. Forty percent of the Muslims in the sample come from Bulgaria, 20% from Russia, and 13% from Slovenia.

2

A Rebirth of Hope?

"Religion. . . . Seems to have lost much of the enormous advantage it once possessed as virtually the universal source of consolation, explanation, and hope to men and women trapped in an unchanging order."

—J.M. Roberts,
The Twentieth Century

"If Christ be not risen, " Saint Paul wrote, "our faith is in vain." In six of the twenty-two countries in the International Social Survey Program study of Europe, the majority of people do not believe in life after death: Hungary, Slovenia, Bulgaria, Denmark, Russia, the Czech Republic, and East Germany (table 2.1). Only Denmark is not a former socialist country. More then seven out of ten in Cyprus, the Irelands, Poland, Portugal, Italy and Switzerland believe in life after death, as do more than six out of ten in Austria and Slovakia. In the other countries the majority believe in life after death, though only a bare majority in Sweden and France. In all but one of the countries more people believe in God than in life after death. (Compare table 2.1 with table 1.1.) The exception is France half believe in God and half believe in life after death.

One would think that those who believe in life after death would also believe in heaven, though in given countries the proportion believing in the latter would be somewhat less than those believing in the former. However, this expectation is not confirmed in several countries. Quite the contrary, in a number of them more believe in heaven than in life after death—the Irelands, Poland, Portugal, and, astonishingly, East Germany. In the last-named country 15 percent believe in life after death and 21 percent believe in heaven. What would be the point in heaven if no one has a chance to go there is a difficult question to answer. Perhaps the word "heaven"—even used in a religious context—has a different meaning in some countries.

Table 2. 1
Belief in Life after Death and Heaven by Country

Countries	Life After Death	Heaven
Cyprus	80%	77%
Ireland	79%	86%
Poland	76%	77%
N. Ireland	77%	87%
Portugal	72%	76%
Italy	70%	63%
Spain	55%	51%
Austria	60%	46%
Switzerland	71%	52%
Slovakia	65%	57%
Latvia	52%	33%
Britain	56%	54%
W. Germany	54%	44%
Hungary	33%	32%
Slovenia	36%	33%
Bulgaria	34%	26%
Norway	56%	44%
Netherlands	57%	44%
Denmark	41%	32%
Sweden	51%	28%
France	51%	33%
Russia	39%	32%
Czech	44%	29%
East Germany	15%	21%

Or perhaps in the Irelands and Poland there is a belief that one can go to heaven but what is experienced there isn't life after death.[1]

Has there been a decline in belief in life after death during the last two decades of the second millennium? The rules for interpreting that require, because of the differences in the two survey projects, that a decrease or an increase must be significant within both projects to establish a trend. In fact only in Hungary and Italy are there indications of a long-term trend—an *increase* from 17 percent to 39 percent in Hungary and from 57 percent to 72 percent in Italy. In the European Values Study project there are significant declines in Northern Ireland, Britain, Spain, West Germany, and the Netherlands and a significant increase in France. In the International Social Survey

Program project there is an increase for Slovenia (from 33 percent to 42 percent) and in Britain from 54 percent to 59 percent.

The evidence then is mixed, some decline in belief in life after death, some increases, especially perhaps in Eastern Europe. However, there is no evidence of a systematic long-term (two-decade) decline in the hope of human survival.

When one turns to cohort analysis (in figure 2.1) however, a surprising phenomenon emerges. There is a "U-curve" relationship between belief in life after death and birth cohorts with those born before 1929 and those born in the 1960s and 1970s having the highest levels of belief in human survival and those born in the 1940s and 1950s having the lowest scores. The succession of birth cohorts through the century has witnessed the fascinating story of a decline in hope among those who were the children of the Depression, the war, and the immediate postwar world and then a rebound to a new high among those born in the sixties and the seventies. In a dummy variable multiple regression equation, the first cohorts and the last two are significantly different from the middle three. As the second millennium ground to a halt there was a sudden and utterly unexpected surge of hope in human survival[2]

The secularization theory predicts religious decline. The rational choice theory predicts religious increase where there is competition. No one, however, has suggested that there might be an increase in religious faith in Europe. Indeed, such a suggestion is patently absurd and is normally not even heard when it is made.

Nonetheless, figure 2.1 indicates that belief in a transcendental order has increased among many Europeans born since 1950. If one chooses 1955 as a midpoint year and considers the countries where there has been a statistically significant increase in belief in survival (table 2.3), in twelve of twenty-two European countries there has been a statistically significant increase in belief in life after death since 1955. The twelve countries are societies where such an increase might, on a priori grounds, have appeared the least likely for such an increase to occur—seven of them are former communist countries, three are Scandinavian countries marked by low levels of religious practice, and two are NATO (or EU) countries where religion has thought to have been in eclipse for the last several decades.

Generally, religious faith and behavior increase with age. Hence the findings are exactly the opposite of what one might expect and

Figure 2.1
Life After Death by Cohort

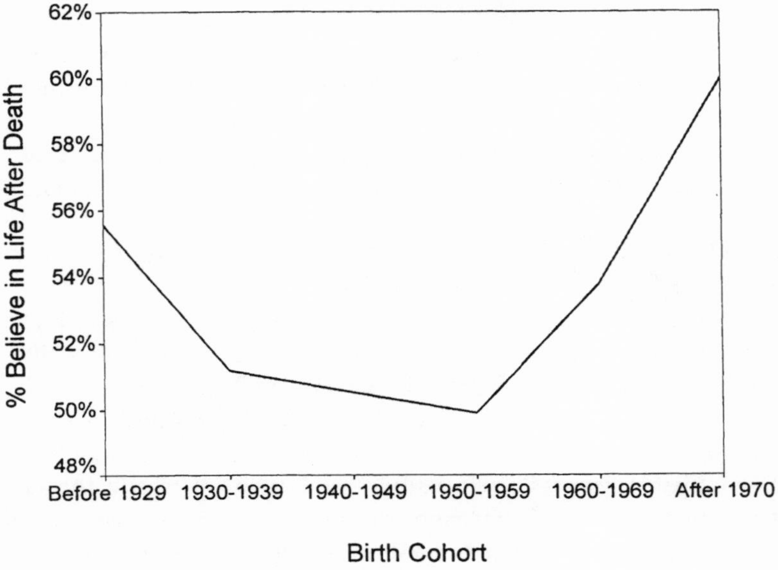

Figure 2.2
Increase in Belief in Life After Death by Cohort and Religion for Cohorts Born Since 1955

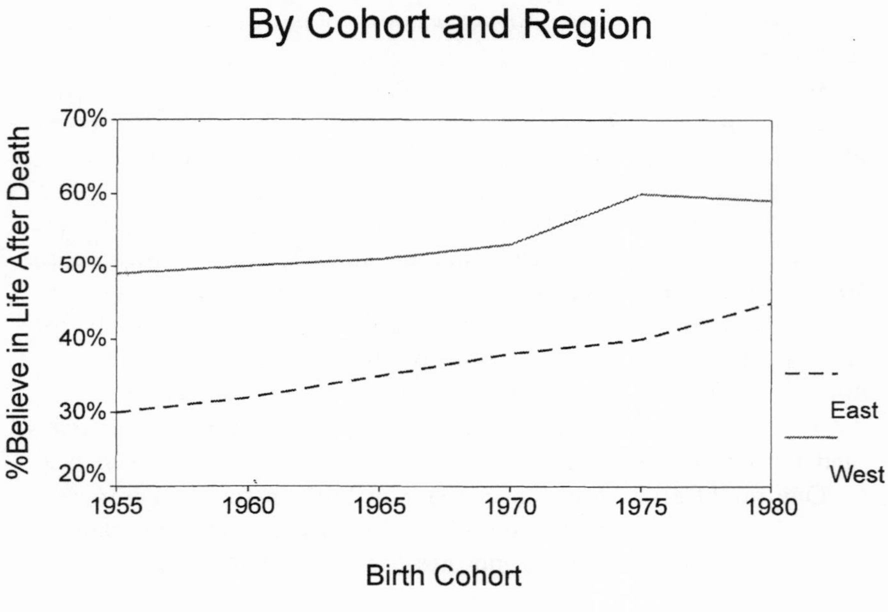

Table 2.2
Change in Belief in Life after Death by Year and Survey

Countries	EVS 1981	EVS 1990	ISSP 1991	ISSP 1998
Cyprus				
Ireland	84%	83%	80%	77%
Poland			74%	78%
N. Ireland	83%	78%**	75%	76%
Portugal				
Italy	57%	67%*	66%	72%***
Spain	67%	51%**		55%
Austria			59%	60%
Switzerland				
Slovakia				
Latvia				
Britain	57%	53%**	54%	59%**
W.Germany	54%	50%**	54%	54%
Hungary	17%	26%*	27%	39%***
Slovenia			33%	42%***
Bulgaria				
Norway	49%	45%	60%	52%****
Netherlands	51%	45%**	52%	50%
Denmark	30%	34%		41%
Sweden	35%	38%		51%
France	41%	44%*		51%
Russia			39%	40%
Czech			48%	48%
E.Germany			15%	15%

*Significant Increase
** Significant Decrease
*** Significant Increase
**** Significant decrease

what one would still observe in many countries—the United States and Britain for example.

One might argue that the increase in faith in former communist countries is in great part a return to religious values that existed before the advent[3] of socialism in these countries. One could also sug-

Table 2.3
Significant Correlations between Birth Cohort and Belief in Life after Death
(For those born since 1955)

East Germany	.16
Hungary	.15
Denmark	.15
Slovenia	.15
Norway	.14
Czech Republic	.14
Sweden	.11
Russia	.11
Netherlands	.09
Bulgaria	.08
Latvia	.06
France	.05

gest that the younger people in these societies might find religion to be a substitute for their lost Marxist faith. Or one might contend that the simple lifting of oppression gave religion a chance to flourish. As valid as any or all of these explanations might be, they can hardly be applied to Norway, Sweden, Denmark, France, and the Netherlands.

Figure 2.3 shows the increase in belief in life after death for the three groups of countries where it has occurred. In all three the process through the twentieth century has been one of decline and the recapture of higher levels—as though the episodes of the middle decades of the century were deviations from a normal pattern. In the Eastern European countries, the increase, starting from a lower level of 40 percent, has through the recent birth cohorts rebounded so that it approaches 50 percent. In the Western countries the more recent cohorts have recaptured the 60 percent level of the 1920s generation. Figure 2.3 zeroes in on the five-year cohorts since 1955 and shows that the increase has been both sharp and consistent across all three groups of countries. The question arises as to whether this is the result of some sort of invisible religious movement which has swept disparate European countries among those who have come of age in the last quarter century.

The average increase in all twelve countries from the birth cohorts born in the late 1950s to those born in the late 1970s is seventeen percentage points. In these countries, belief in life after death is almost half again higher among the later birth cohorts than among the earlier ones, a substantial "revival" of faith in one of the core beliefs that that there is a transcendental order in the universe.

Figure 2.3 shows also that the increase in belief in life after death by year of birth is stronger for those from the former Communist countries (twenty –one percentage points)—than it is for the Western countries[3] (nine percentage points). However, the young people born in the formerly Communist countries in the late 1970s are almost as likely to believe in human survival as were those born in the Western countries during the late 1950s.

Moreover, (figure 2.4) this increase is consistent across all religious categories—correlations of .17 for Catholics, .13 for Protestants, .11 for those with no religious affiliation and .10 for Orthodox. The increase for Catholics is thirty-one percentage points, a finding reminiscent of the Greeley-Hout findings about the increase in belief in life after death among American Catholics. Latvia is the

Figure 2.3
Belief in Life After Death by Countries by Cohort

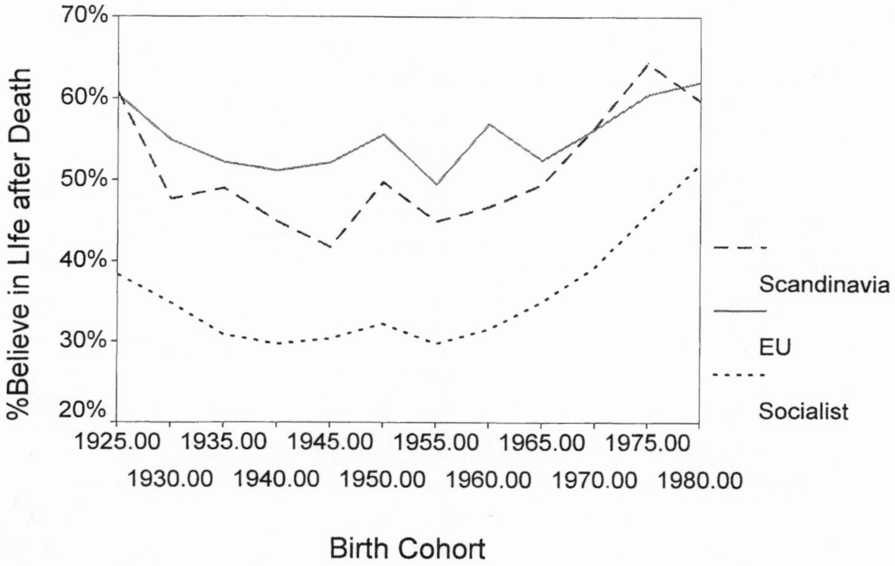

Figure 2.4
Belief in Life After Death since 1955 by Religion and Birth Cohort

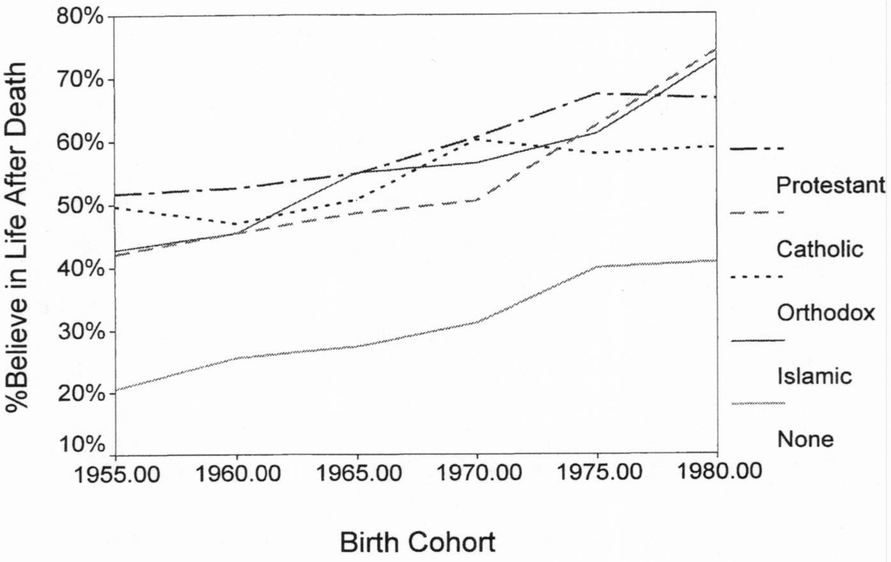

Table 2.4
Countries with a Significant Increase in Belief in Life after Death

	Correlation with Year of Birth*	%Never Believed in God	% "Very Happy"
Hungary	.15	41%	8%
Denmark	.15	45%	32%
Czech Republic	.14	41%	13%
Slovenia	.15	27%	9%
East Germany	.13	53%	9%
Russia	.15	45%	7%
Norway	.14	26%	21%
Sweden	.11	41%	27%
Bulgaria	.08	35%	9%
Latvia	.07	25%	5%
Netherlands	.09	25%	30%
France	.05	28%	17%
All countries		20%	21%

*For those born since 1955

only country (in the whole International Social Survey Program sample as well as among the countries with a significant increase in belief in a hereafter) in which there are enough Catholics, Protestants, and Orthodox to make a comparison. In Latvia there are statistically significant increases among Catholics and Protestants but not among Orthodox or those with no affiliation. For Catholics the increase in belief in life after death is thirty-five percentage points (50 percent to 85 percent) and for Protestants eighteen percentage points (57 percent to 75 percent). In the Netherlands on the other hand a significant increase in belief in life after birth (for those born after 1975) can be found only among Protestants and those with no religious affiliation. That the increase in the belief in life after death generally occurs among those with some kind of formal religious affiliation suggests that it is not merely a "new age" phenomenon linked to a withdrawal from affiliation.

Figures 2.5, 2.6, and 2.7 show the percentages believing in life after death for each of the twelve countries where there has been an

Figure 2.5
Increase in Belief in Life after Death since 1955 by Birth Cohort

Scandinavia

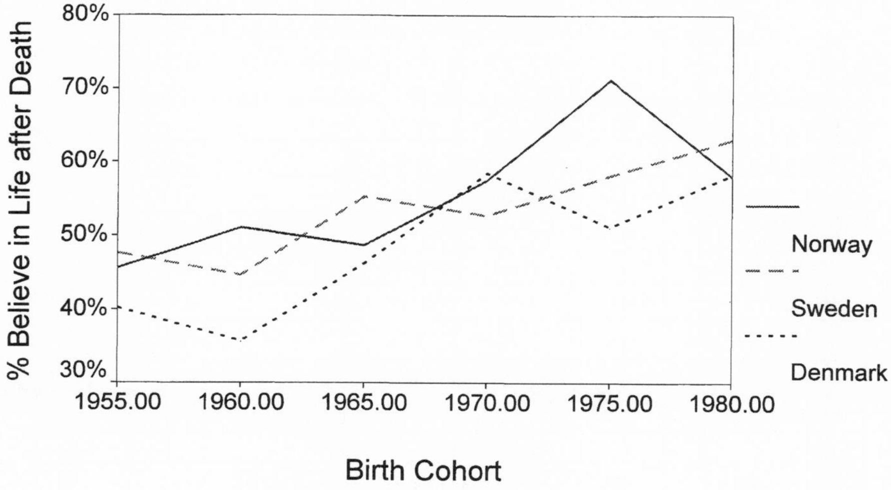

Figure 2.6
Belief in Life after Death Since 1955 by Birth Cohort

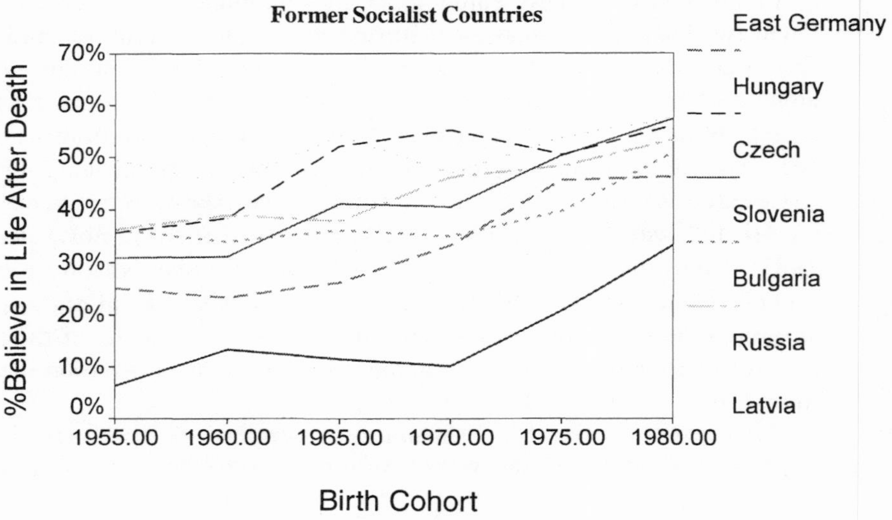

Figure 2.7
Increase in Belief in Life After Death Since 1955 by Country and Cohort

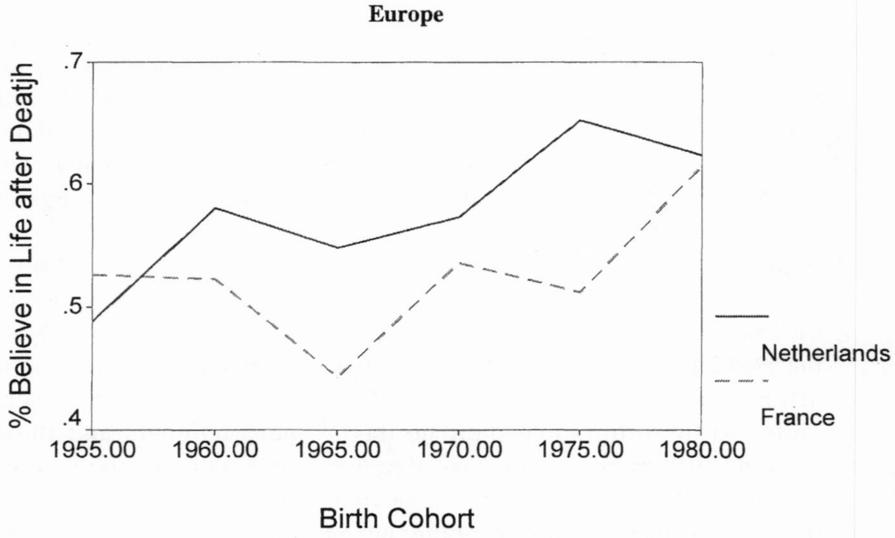

increase. In all three sets of countries there seems to be a convergence towards a common level of belief in life after death among the youngest cohort approximately 60 percent for the Western Countries and 50 percent for the former Communist countries. The only exception among the former Communist countries is East Germany (the lowest line on figure 2.6) where belief in life after death among the most recent birth cohorts has reached only 30 percent. However, this proportion is *three times higher* than it was among previous cohorts of East Germans.

Sixty percent is also the average for the most recent cohort for the whole sample. That three out of five Europeans from twenty-five countries born in the 1970s believe that they live in a transcendental order in which the human person survives death, certainly or probably,[4] raises some question about how "unreligious" Europe has become—or ever will become.

Why, then, is there no evidence of an increase in church attendance which ought to result from an increase in belief in a transcendental order? The answer might well be that young people tend to translate their faith into practice as they grow older and that, therefore, one might, in due course, expect the increase in belief in life

Figure 2.8
Church Attendance by Belief in Life After Death and Age

Total Sample

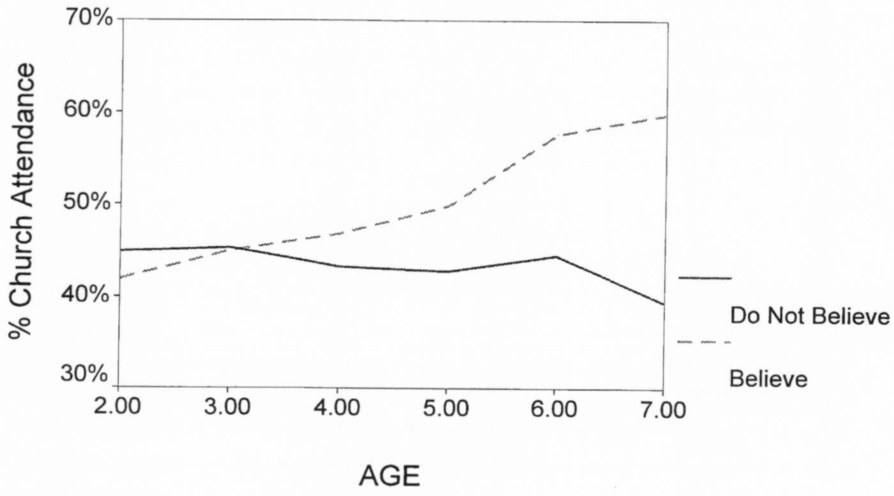

after death in these countries to translate belief into church attendance. Thus figure 2.8 shows that a shift in levels of church attendance happens in Europe only after one's thirtieth birthday. Whether the same shift will occur among the more recent birth cohorts in the ten countries where there has been an increase in youthful belief in human survival, of course, remains to be seen.

How might one begin to explain this increase in faith in a transcendental order in which life continues after death, where there is a place one could call heaven, and in which religious miracles do occur? One could say that the general convergence of the youngest cohort around the same proportion that believes in life after death is enough of an explanation in itself. The former communist countries are merely catching up with the rest of Europe. However, such a possibly elegant outcome does not even begin to suggest what might be the mechanism behind such convergence or why the five Western countries might be involved as well as the former communist countries—or even why at the end of the twentieth century so many Europeans believe in life after death.

The churches cannot be given much credit for the change. As we shall see, confidence in them has fallen in all countries since the 1991 International Social Survey Program study (in those countries which participated in both waves of the study). Moreover, the churches in Eastern Europe have been engaged in little else than enhancing their political power or capturing more.

One might appeal to historical events—the end of the two world wars and the end of memories of those wars, the surge of prosperity in Europe which shaped the world in which the more recent cohorts were born and raised, the end of the Soviet Empire, the alleged rise of post-materialism or post-modernism. However, it is quite impossible to link these factors with the findings herein reported, save in a general and anecdotal way.[5]

Multivariate analysis with the usual suspects offers no explanations. Belief in life after death correlates positively with education, with being a woman, with youthfulness, and with being a Catholic in the countries where there has been an increase in this belief among the younger birth cohorts. However none of these variables accounts in the slightest for the increase.

The International Social Survey Program questionnaires were designed to account for a decline in religion, in the case of the 1998 questionnaire despite clear evidence that no such decline was occurring. Hence there were few variables available which might provide an explanation for the increase in certain religious convictions in some countries. However, one variable (belief in astrology) might measure the contribution of an increase in "New Age" religion and another (belief in a God who cares personally about humans) might be an indicator of an increase in age-old religion. In fact, proportions accepting both notions have increased in the countries where there has been an increase in the conviction that humans survive death.

Together these variables account for about a third of the change. In the former communist countries the correlation between year of birth and belief in life after death was .15. When astrology was added to a regression equation (first to privilege the popular New Age explanation) the correlation declined to .13. The God-who-cares variable reduced the correlation to .10. While both New Age and age-old religion contribute to an explanation of the increase in belief in life after death, the age-old influence, net of New Age is patently the stronger of the two.

In the Western countries there is a similar pattern. The zero order correlation between belief in life after death and year of birth is .09. It is reduced to .07 when the God-who-cares variable is added to a regression equation. The astrology question was asked only in the Netherlands and France among the Western nations. When it is entered into a regression equation for that country, the standardized coefficient for year of birth remains. 07. If one then adds the God-who-cares variable, the standardized coefficient remains the same.

The finding in Eastern Europe that those who believe in a caring God and those who believe in astrology are also more likely to believe in life after death in Eastern Europe is not as impressive as it might first appear. The question remains as to why such young people are more likely than their immediate predecessors to take a caring God and/or the stars seriously.

Could it be that the absence of a belief in transcendental order in the culture of some countries might create a vacuum in which religion, New Age and age-old, might enter? Could it be that there is a "need" for religion in the human species as Rodney Stark has suggested (even without competition among religious "firms"?).

One hint that this might be the case is to be found in the fact that the ten countries in which there has been a significant increase in belief in life after death are also the countries which have the highest rates of respondents saying that they have "never" believed in God (the second panel of the table). Moreover the nine former communist countries also display the lowest levels of personal happiness. Finally, in these countries the correlation between belief in life after death and happiness (.08) is twice that of the whole sample. Perhaps the younger cohorts are reacting against what they perceive as the bleakness of a life without any ultimate explanation for human existence.

In four other countries, there are statistically significant correlations between youthfulness and high scores on the measure of belief in life after death, countries in which there is no U-curve but only an increase in belief in life after death that relates positively to cohort–Switzerland, Austria, Germany and Portugal. In Austria there is a ten-percentage-point increase across the birth decades of the twentieth century and in Switzerland a fifteen-percentage-point increase (figure 2.9). In Germany there is a similar relationship that is obscured by a sudden spike in this hope in the 1930s cohort, perhaps hope of meeting dead parents again in those who were children during the War. However, when that variation is smoothed out by combining cohorts (figure 2.10), the upward trend in Germany is also obvious, with a six-percentage-point increase in hope for human survival. In Portugal (figure 2.11), almost eight out of ten of the youngest cohort believe in life after death.

Figure 2.9
Life After Death by Cohort by Country

Austria and Switzerland

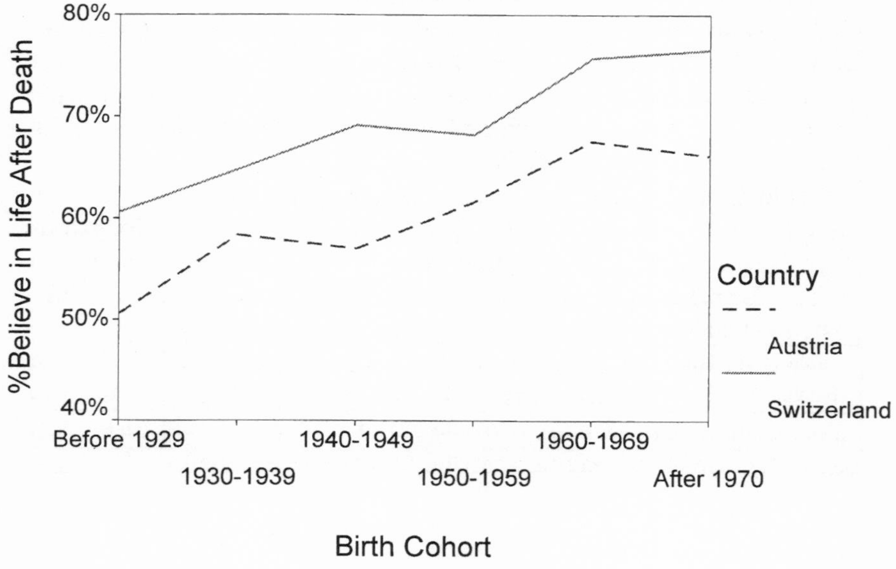

Figure 2.10
Life After Death by Cohort

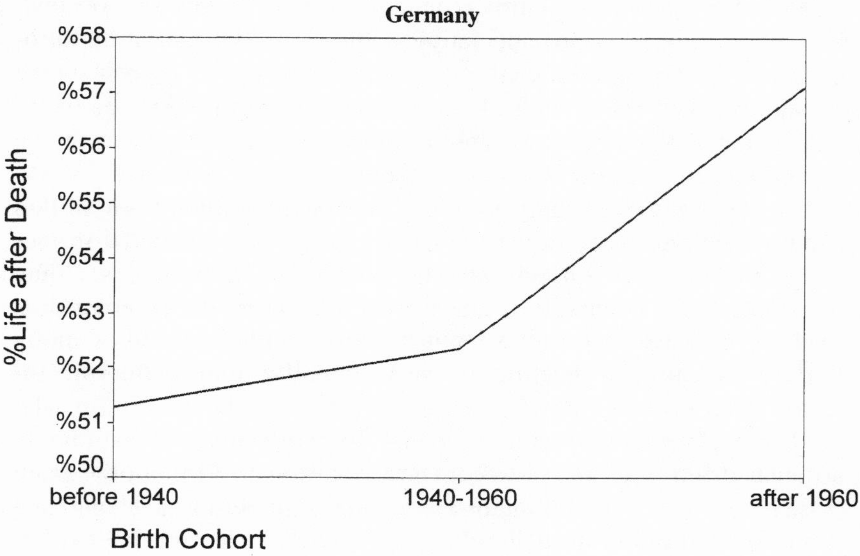

Figure 2.11
Belief in Life After Death by Cohort

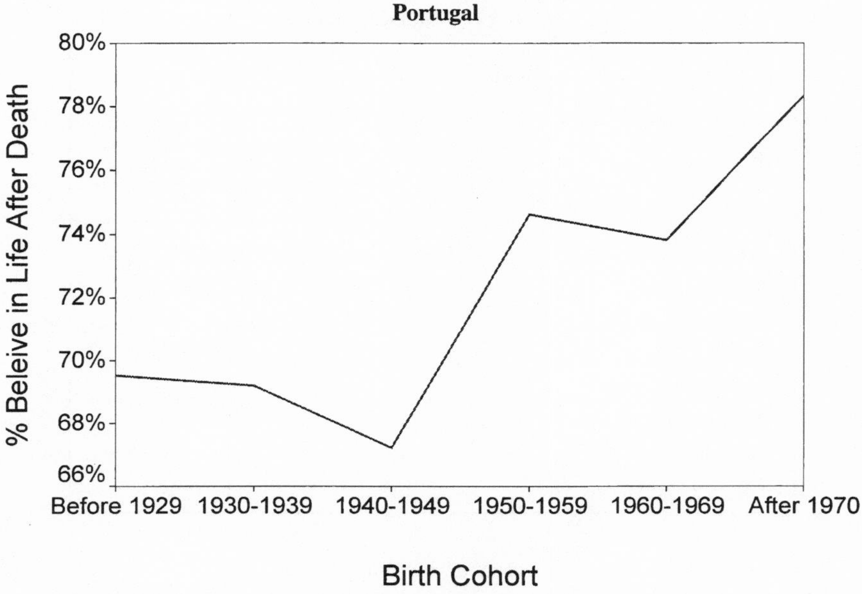

There are, therefore, sixteen nations in the study in which the younger cohorts have high scores on the item that measures belief in life after death. The remaining countries are Catholic (Ireland, Poland, Slovakia, Spain, and Italy), Cyprus, and Britain and Northern Ireland. Perhaps the Catholic countries (though not Spain) have already reached the ceiling on such belief. It may be that the U.K., whose sociologists have so often claimed that there is an American exceptionalism, is, in fact, the exception.

Data in the Values study enable us to consider whether there was a hint in the nineteen eighties of the phenomenon reported in this chapter. Was there evidence in the Scandinavian countries of the beginnings of a U-curve? In fact there were (figure 2.12) indications of an upturn after the 1950s cohort. Thus, it does not seem likely that the findings can be attributed to a systematic flaw in the International Social Survey Program data.

One is tempted to wonder whether the conviction that the human survives death is something in which the youth indulge, but the more mature abandon. Unlike all other religious measures that correlate positively with age, perhaps belief in life after death correlates nega-

Figure 2.12
Life After Death by Cohort

Scandinavia

(Values Study 81-90)

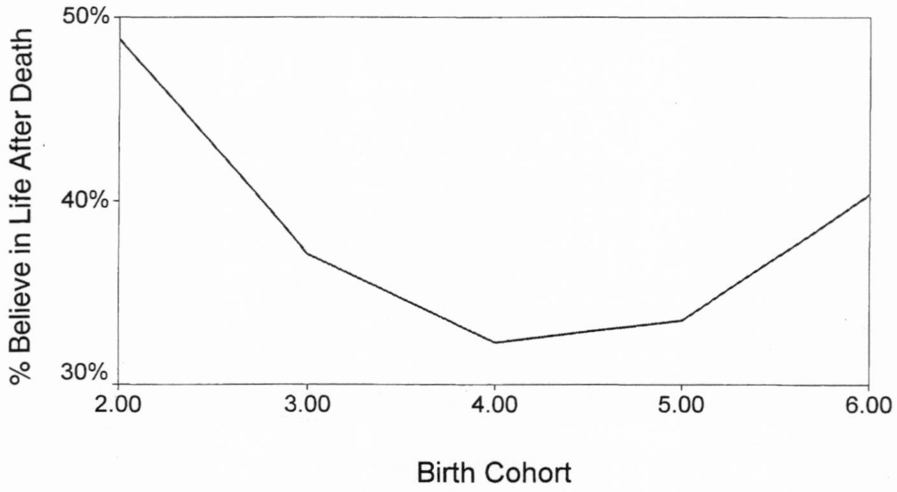

tively. This might partially solve the European problem, though it would not account for the opposite relationship in the United Kingdom and North America. What influence in Europe might explain the U-curves on the Continent, an influence that was not at work in North America?

I find myself leaning towards an explanation which is plausible but which with the data available is impossible to test. The story of hope in the U-curves seems to be a story of the World Wars (or the second phase between 1939 and 1945). Those who were born before the war had more grounds for hope, those born during it and immediately after were affected by the suffering and death of family and friends of their parents, those born since 1960 have grown up in an environment, familial and social, of increased optimism. In Eastern Europe this optimism was delayed until the fall of socialist governments. The war was not fought on American soil and the U.K. was never occupied by foreign armies. Others, I am sure, will have other explanations.

Obviously such explanations must be investigated in further research. One must also wonder whether the cohorts born in the 1980s will continue the upward trend in belief or whether the trend will level off and perhaps even reverse itself. Nor can the findings discussed in this chapter answer conclusively the suspicion that, in general, religion is declining in Europe. All they confirm is that in some countries one form of religious faith and hope is increasing among young people.

By way of conclusion,

1. With the exception of some East European countries, majorities in all European countries believe in life after death.
2. There is no conclusive evidence of a decline in this belief during the last twenty years and some evidence of increase.
3. Curiously shaped U-curves appear in half the European countries indicating that the oldest and youngest cohorts are more likely to believe in life after death than the middle cohorts. The middle 1950s seem to be the turning point. The countries include all the former socialist countries except Poland and Slovakia, the Scandinavian countries, and the Netherlands and France. Increase in belief occurs even among those with no religious affiliations.
4. Four other countries show a systematic increase across cohorts in belief in life after death: Germany, Switzerland, Austria, and Portugal.
5. The countries where there is no increase are Catholic countries with high rates of belief (in excess of .7), Cyprus, and Northern Ireland and

Great Britain. Hence Britain seems to the exception among the twenty-three countries in the sample.

6. Perhaps the trauma of the Second World War caused a dip from the normal rates of hope (70 percent in the heavily Catholic countries, sixties in other countries) in the early and later cohorts.

7. While one must be cautious on such subjects, there does seem to be a relatively consistent demand for hope in Europe—between 60 and 70 percent—departure from which may be unusual.

Notes

1. For which there would be some justification in the Catholic doctrine that life continues to be life.
2. The same finding is produced when a factor made up of heaven, miracles, and life after death is submitted to similar analysis. However, it is more striking to focus on the life after death variable.
3. Even if right-wing governments are in power in these countries at a given time, it is still the case that both the left and the right accept in general the principles of a Social Democratic society.
4. 30% "certainly", 30% "probably."
5. Some scholars cite these events as explanations, secure in the fact that they have resolved the problem, when in fact they have only restated it.

3

Magic, Science, and the Mystical

Religion is one of the ways humankind responds to difficulties of human life—uncertainty, injustice, suffering, death. By its very nature it can provide only problematic solutions because it appeals to a transcendent which at best seems hidden. Thus, religion finally depends on faith not only in the unseen, but in the expectation that the unseen is interested in humankind and capable of taking care of us. Three other ways exist of responding to ultimate questions—magic, science, and the mystical.

Like religion, magic believes in hidden powers. Unlike religion, however, magic also believes that one can control these powers and thus reduce the uncertainties and threats of life—as when one intends to fish not in the calm waters of the lagoon but on the open sea. Religion—as long as it is free from the corruption of magic—cannot promise results. Magic claims to produce results. Magic works, or so it is said.

Science also works. It offers a comprehensive explanation of reality and through its offspring technology proposes scientifically grounded methods for diminishing the uncertainties of human life. Unlike magic, however, science demonstrates a reasonable link between its results and its tools. Magic proposes that if one does the right dances before one ventures out on the waves, the "powers" will guarantee good weather and clear sailing. Water turns a wheel that produces energy that eventually switches on electric lights that illuminate the harbor entrance.

In the Montaillou of Emmanuel LeRoy Ladurie, the priest, one Pierre de Clerg reassured the chatelaine, Beatrice DePlanisoles, that she would not conceive when he deflowered her in front of the alter of their church because he had an amulet which would prevent conception. By the standards of modern contraception, his amulet seems an absurd form of birth control. However, though she later had many children, the Lady Beatrice did not become pregnant as a result of her dalliance with her parish priest.

The mystical disdains all such mediate explanations of reality and human life. It claims rather immediate contact with the Really Real. It *knows* what the Ultimate is like and hence does not worry abut outcomes. All will be well, as the English mystic said, and all manner of things will be well. The uncertainties and travails of ordinary life, while (in Western mysticism) real enough, are only shadows. The mystic encounters the One and understands the Whole and is not afraid.

Magic

The two International Social Survey Program religion modules have items about magic, science, and mysticism. However, perhaps because its steering committee had forgotten about Bronislaw Malinowski, it did not provide items for the latter two in both surveys and recommended the magic items only as "options."

Indeed, the items which seem to me to represent magic, pure and simple and undefiled (fortunetellers, faith healers, astrology, and good luck charms) were advanced as measures of New Age religion. I have never been able to find a definition of the New Age which would permit one to operationalize and measure it. If those who know more about it than I do tell me that these four items do indeed measure New Age attitudes, I will provisionally take their word for it and respond that the New Age obviously believes in and is obsessed by the magical.

The social history literature about medieval religion, previously cited, reports a pervasive belief in magic in Europe of that era. Based in part on older pagan beliefs and in part on the reworking of Christian beliefs, magic was a major component of medieval culture. One might reasonably expect a decline of magic in our more civilized and better-educated populations. At least one might expect it if one believed that science and education eliminate all mystery and uncertainty from the human condition. In the absence of time machines at the disposal of survey organizations, we simply do not know what proportion of the European population of, say, the seventh or the fourteenth centuries actually believed in magic.

Since magic strives to eliminate uncertainties, I would expect to find it strongest among those people and countries in which there are no certainties or near-certainties about the existence or the nonexistence of God.

The first two figures (3.1 and 3.2) offer some confirmation for the first expectation. The highest scores on magic are to be found among those who hesitate between being pure theists and pure atheists and among those who are less than certain about whether God is concerned about them as compared to those who know he is (strongly agree) and those who know there is no one to be concerned (strongly disagree).

Moreover, table 3.1 shows that the countries with the lowest scores on the magic factor are countries where, as we have seen, the proportion believing in God is low—France, the Netherlands, and East Germany—or high—Ireland and Portugal. Among the Western European countries, subscription to magical ideas is highest in countries like Britain and West Germany.

The Irish scores on both sides of the border would be at the very bottom of the list if it were not for their propensity to believe in faith healers—matched only by Slovakia and exceeded only by Latvia. Perhaps the Irish score would be high if such unique Irish magical icons as the holy well and the unfrocked (or drunken) priest had been included (Carroll 2000, Taylor 1995). Who needs astrology when a priest freed from the constraints of ecclesiastical control can use his enormous power to work wonders?[1]

Figure 3.1
Magic by Belief in God

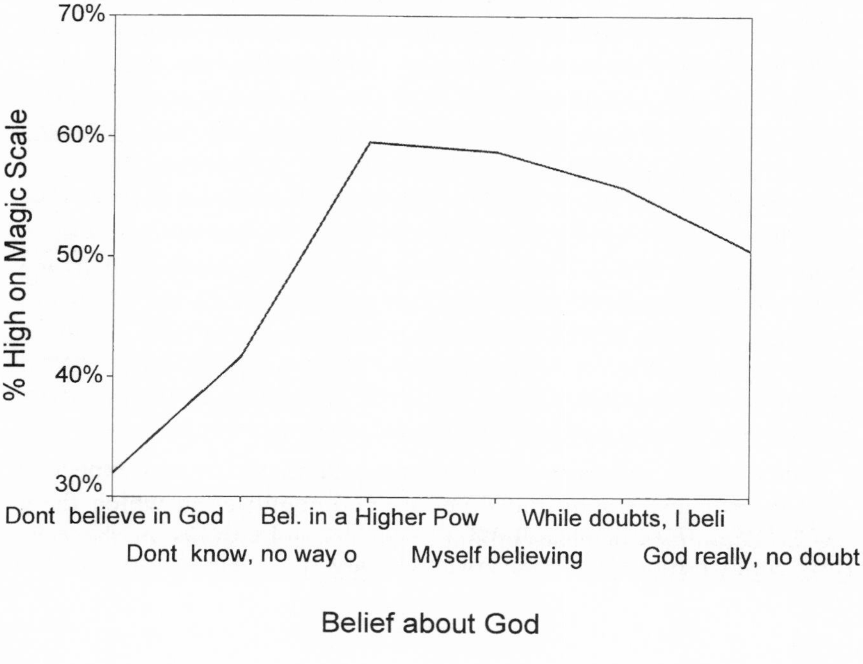

Figure 3.2
Magic By God's Concern

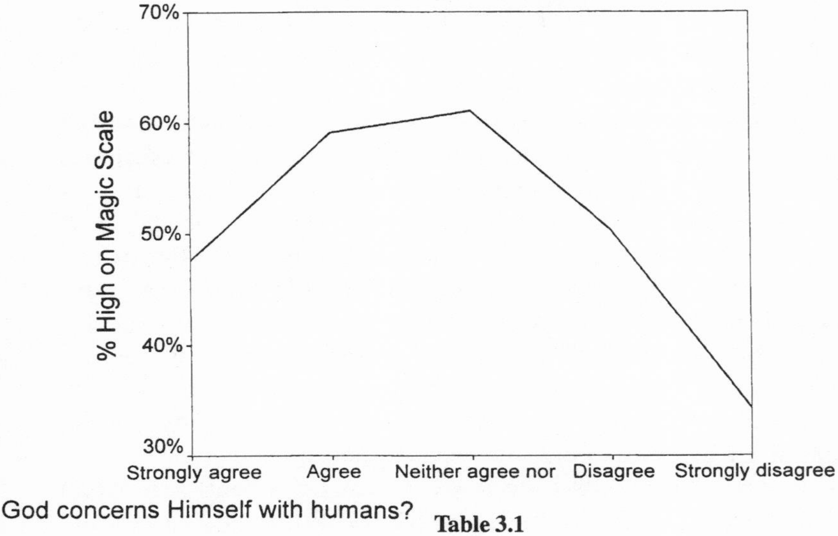

Table 3.1
Magic by Country

Country	Good Luck Charms	Fortune Tellers	Faith Healers	Astrology	Factor
Latvia		80%	81%	66%	.80
Bulgaria	72%	65%	65%	65%	.72
Slovakia	49%	68%	71%	49%	.59
Russia	57%	68%	65%	56%	.53
Czech	50%	71%	62%	53%	.52
Slovenia	35%	55%	69%	41%	.23
Switzerland	40%	48%	40%	47%	.10
Britain	23%	42%	52%	30%	-.04
Austria	33%	27%	48%	38%	-.07
W.Germany	37%	32%	40%	37%	-.08
Hungary	34%	44%	34%	40%	-.10
N.Ireland	23%	33%	70%	19%	-.14
France	24%	39%	38%	41%	-.20
Portugal	45%	28%	36%	30%	-.21
Ireland	25%	30%	70%	19%	-.21
E.Germany	34%	22%	21%	21%	-.33
Netherlands	21%	28%	28%	24%	-.47

This phenomenon raises warning flags about large national sample data sets which strive to analyze major issues of religion and magic (or anything else) across a whole continent or a whole world. The findings of such valiant efforts must be treated with caution by writers and readers alike.

Nonetheless, the highest scores on the measures of magic are to be found in the socialist and Slavic countries of Eastern Europe. Thus 72 percent of the Bulgarians believe in good luck charms (as opposed to 21 percent for the Netherlanders); 65 percent believe in fortune tellers (28 percent); 65 percent believe in faith healers (28 percent); and 65 percent in astrology (24 percent). Comparing Russians with East Germans we see 57 percent versus 34 percent believe in good luck charms; 68 percent versus 22 percent believe in fortune tellers; 65 percent versus 31 percent believe in faith healers; and 56 percent versus 21 percent believe in astrology. Both, however, were once socialist states!

One might have thought that magic would have been popular in the former socialist countries because of the uncertainties of socialist economic and political life. However, since both East Germany and Russia were once socialist and since Hungary (where magic is less popular than in West Germany or Britain) was also socialist, the explanation that the Eastern European magic is Slavic in origins might seem plausible. Indeed one might wonder if the faith in magic in Latvia, Bulgaria, Slovakia, Russia, and the Czech Republic would have been any higher a couple of centuries ago.

On the other hand, it is worth remarking that the fact that half of the Britons, two-fifths of the West Germans, and one-fifth of the East Germans still believe in faith healers. Moreover, similar proportions also believe in fortunetellers. The sociologists who report that religion is disappearing in Britain and Germany, cannot claim that belief in magic is also being "secularized" away, especially since it is more common among younger people in both countries.

Does "secularization," so assiduously celebrated by British social scientists, lead to an increase in magic that does not occur in "unsecularized" countries? In an attempt to answer this question I constructed figure 3.3 which shows the impact of church attendance on belief in magic in Britain and Ireland. There is no difference in acceptance of magic in both countries among those who attend church services once a week or more. However, lower levels of church attendance lead to higher acceptance of magic in "secular-

Figure 3.3
Magic by Church Attendance

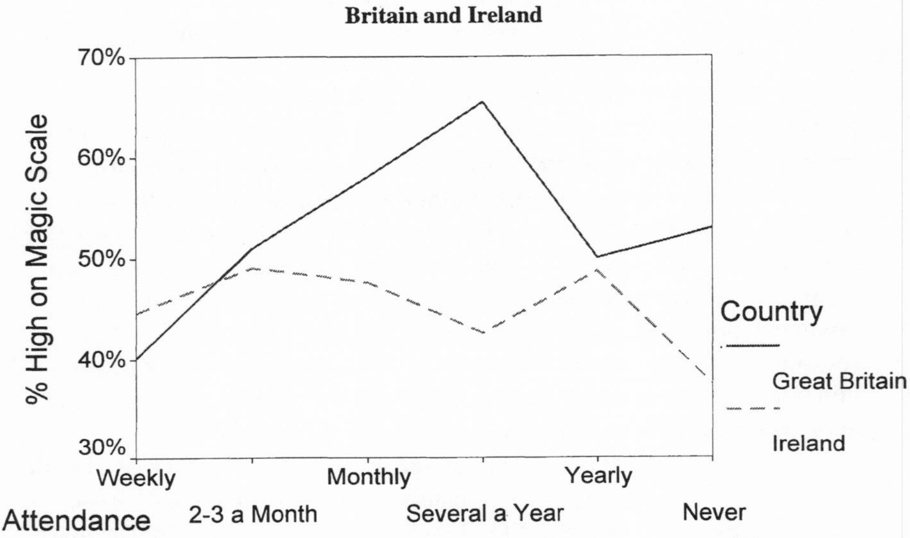

ized" Britain, but not in presumably unsecularized Ireland (the correlation between church attendance and magic in Britain is -.15 and in Ireland .04 (not significant). This comparison between the two countries raises the question of whether religion in a country where it is still strong can fend off the influence of its rival whereas in a country where religion has been badly weakened magic is free to rush in. When British social scientists (e.g., Bruce 1995) celebrate the decline of religion, they should investigate the possibility that magic is replacing it. Everyone, of course, knows that Ireland is a superstitious and credulous country and Britain a civilized and rational country.

To what extent does magic infiltrate religion? Or, to put the matter differently, to what extent does religion, on occasion, seek magic to sustain itself? Table 3.2 strives to answer this question by asking to what extent magic beliefs correlate with religious beliefs. Once again the data force us to a conclusion that it is uncertainty about religion which lets magic take over, more in the Eastern countries than in the Western.

When the issue is a simple yes or no about God (first column) there are strong correlations between faith and magic, especially in the East and in Britain (.33) and much smaller ones in the more

Table 3.2
Magic, Religious Faith, and University
(correlations with Magic)

Country	Believe in God	Certain There is a God	University Grad
Bulgaria	.40	.18	.06
Slovakia	.21	.10	-.06
Russia	.44	.19	-.02*
Czech	.25	.10	-.09
Slovenia	.18	.02*	
Switzerland	.14	-.04*	-.10
Britain	.33	.12	-.06
Austria	.08	.02*	-.04*
W.Germany	.07	-.01*	-.06
Hungary	.14	.00*	-.03*
N.Ireland	.08	.07	-.06
France	.29	.07	-.19
Portugal	.13	.00*	.00*
Ireland	.10	.00*	. 00*
E.Germany	.11	.02*	-.07
Netherlands	.21	.02*	-.04*

*Not statistically significant

religious countries in the West like Portugal and Ireland (.13 and .10) and in the most unreligious country, East Germany (-.11). Again where there is uncertainty (and/or a Slavic culture) magical beliefs flourish. Where there is certainty, either for or against religion, magic is much less successful.

Husband (2000) in his study of the struggle between the Communist Party and the Orthodox Church in Russia observes that among the problems the Party faced was the fact that so much of Orthodoxy was mixed with superstitious practices or with superstition mixed with religion, that it was difficult to extirpate it, no matter what was done to the church organization.

However in the second column of the table when the issue is certainty about God (the last response in question 18) there is much less influence –significant only in the Eastern countries (though not in Slovenia) and in Britain (.12) Northern Ireland (.07), and France (.07). Thus in uncertain countries it is somewhat more difficult for firm theism to exclude some influence of magic from its convictions. Whereas in strongly religious countries (Portugal and Ireland) and in strongly unreligious countries (East Germany and the Netherlands) the firewall between faith and magic is strong and the correlations are either statistically insignificant or, as in Ireland and Portugal non-existent.

Finally, there is some evidence (in the third column) that university graduation tends to exclude magic from a person's worldview but not with very impressive power, except in France. Other factors such as the condition of religion in a country and the cultural orientation of the country (or its former socialist rule) seem to have a greater influence on the power of magic to invade a culture. Britain is, is according to its sociologists, one of the most secularized countries in Western Europe; it is also one that is very prone to magic beliefs, perhaps because there is more religious uncertainty in Britain than in other countries. We will return to this subject in a later chapter.

Magic, then, is alive and well, indeed flourishing in Europe, particularly in Eastern Europe. Moreover it is growing; 40 percent of those born in the 1920s were high on the magic score as opposed to 60 percent of those born in the nineteen seventies (from 60 percent to 80 percent in Eastern Europe). In some countries as religion declines magic increases.

Science

In the 1998 International Social Survey Program module, two items were inserted that purported to measure the respondents' attitudes towards science (question 14). The wording of the questions leaves a lot to be desired, though they were clearly skewed towards eliciting a negative comment on science—presumably so that responses could be then correlated with religion and thus cited to prove that there remained a conflict between science and religion. By opposing science and religion faith in the second item, the question biased the response even more. The majority rejected the first item (60 percent) and a substantial minority rejected the second.

Only in Italy and Portugal did a majority fail to support science on the first item (table 3.3). Only in East Germany did the support go over 70 percent. The other countries are rather narrowly spread between 50 percent and 70 percent. Similarly on the second item Portugal (24 percent), Italy (29 percent), Bulgaria (32 percent), Spain

(35 percent), Norway (36 percent), and Slovakia (39 percent) fall below forty percent. East Germany (72 percent), Sweden (64 percent), France (61 percent), Switzerland (60 percent), Russia and West Germany (53 percent), are above fifty percent. The other nations are spread between 40 percent and 50 percent.

Table 3.3
Science and Religion

Countries	Science Harms %Reject	Too Much Science %Reject	% High on Science Factor	Correlation with Magic	Correlation with Belief in God	Correlation between cohort and Life after death for those who are Pro-science
Cyprus	56%	37%	30%		-.16	-.02
Ireland	52%	41%	32%	.02*	-.12	-.03
Poland	53%	41%	32%		-.12	.10
N. Ireland	52%	41%	30%		-.17	-.06
Portugal	39%	24%	16%	.02*	-.16	.01*
Italy	45%	29%	22%		-.20	.01*
Spain	57%	35%	26%		-.14	.02*
Austria	51%	47%	32%	-.08	-.08	.21
Switzerland	57%	60%	40%	-.04*	-.21	.12
Slovakia	53%	38%	28%	-.08	-.20	.00*
Latvia	56%	50%	21%		-.22	.05*
Britain	50%	50%	37%		-.20	.05*
W.Germany	59%	53%	39%	-.11	-.15	.04*
Hungary	57%	42%	32%	.01*	-.21	.14
Slovenia	58%	40%	47%		-.23	.12
Bulgaria	62%	32%	26%	.09	-.08	.06
Norway	67%	36%	34%		-.16	.02*
Netherlands	62%	53%	42%	-.08	-.23	.06
Denmark	54%	50%	36%		-.19	.16
Sweden	58%	64%	48%		-.23	.19
France	59%	61%	45%	-.08	-.26	.20
Russia	69%	54%	47%	-.09	-.14	.19
Czech	54%	45%	32%	-14	-.17	.13
E.Germany	70%	72%	58%	-.13	-15	.12
Total	60%%	45%	34%		-.21	.11

There is, it would seem, a rather narrow variance among the countries on the scale score. Four of the countries which are more likely to be "anti-science" are Catholic (Portugal, Italy, Spain and Slovakia), but so too are Norway and Bulgaria. More likely to be pro-science are the two Germanys, France, Russia, and Switzerland.

When the two variables are combined in a factor which in turn is converted to a "high" score (over 34 percent), only Portugal (16 percent), Latvia (21 percent) Italy (22 percent) and Spain (26 percent) are notably beneath the average while East Germany (58 percent), Sweden (48 percent), Russia (47 percent), and Slovenia (47 percent). are notably above it. In general, then, some Catholic countries are more likely to be anti-science and some Eastern European countries are more likely to be pro-science. In so far as these admittedly poor measures tap a more generalized attitude towards science, however, most differences among countries exist along a rather narrow range of variability.

However, columns three and four, show that attitudes towards science have far less impact on magical attitudes then on religious faith. (Many countries are excluded because the magic questions were not asked in 1998, the year the science questions were asked.) The largest significant correlations against magic are in some former socialist countries (Russia, Bulgaria, East Germany, and the Czech Republic) where magic is the strongest (excepting East Germany.

In all the countries, science as measured by these two items has a strong negative impact on belief in God—or perhaps those who don't believe in God are more likely to believe in science. Again the range of variance among these correlations is not great. The correlation for the whole sample is -.21. Only France at -.26 is notably above the average, while several Catholic countries, Ireland, Poland, Spain, Portugal as well as Norway and Cyprus are notably below it. The more devout countries seem able to resist both magic and science. Norway's resistance must be explored later.

The final column of table 3.3 is based on figure 3.4. The increase in belief in life after death reported in the previous chapter is specified by the figure as happening among those who were *pro-science*. Among those who were anti-science the very high level of belief in life after death increased only slightly (r=.03). The increase among those who were pro-science was from 35 percent to 50 percent across cohort boundaries (r=.11). The biggest increases have occurred in Austria, Hungary, Sweden, Denmark, France, Bulgaria, and Russia. These

Figure 3.4
Belief in Life After Death by Attitude Towards Science and Cohort

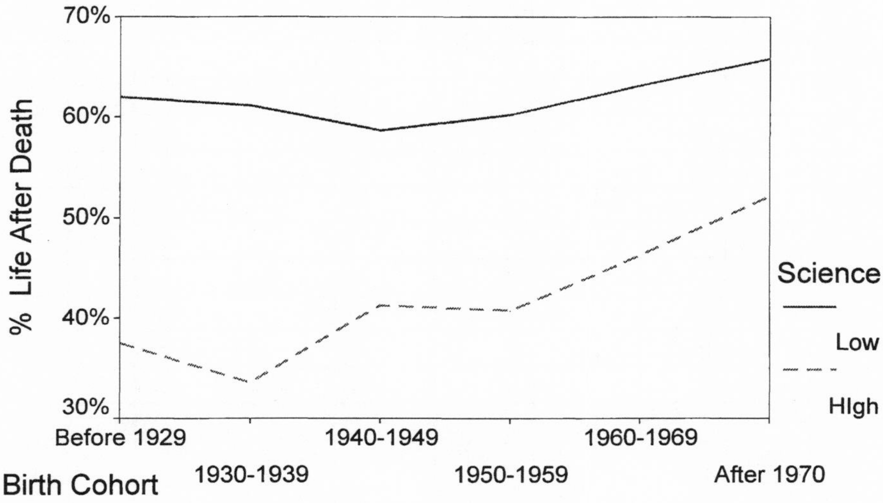

increases are evidence that in some countries and on at least one religious matter, the conflict between science and religion may be ebbing.

The Mystical

In the 1991 International Social Survey Program two questions were asked which might indicate some claim to immediate contact with the transcendent—contact with the dead and the experience of mystical ecstasy. They were banished from the 1998 survey on the grounds that they were silly questions. Too bad for William James! Too bad for Richard Rolle and Meister Ekkehard! Too bad for the ecstatic dimension of religion! Too bad for the 30 percent of the people of England who had had contact with the dead experiences and the 28 percent who have experienced something like William James' experience of ecstasy! Too bad for the researchers who have administered these questions all around the world! Too bad for the sociology of religion when its questionnaires fall into the hands of those who are village atheists with doctorates!

(The responses to the two questions were "Never," "Once or twice," "Several times" and "Often." The percentage in the table represents a combination of the last three responses.)

Table 3.4
Mystical experiences by country

Countries	%Contact with the dead	% ecstasy	%High on Mystic scale	Correlation with Theist	Correlation with Life After Death	Correlation with Frequent Prayer	Correlation with Magic
West Germany	23%	18%	26%	.16	.21	.14	-28
East Germany	17%	6%	14%	.29	.25	.29	-22
Britain	30%	28%	36%	.31	.38	.33	-.29
N. Ireland	17%	24%	29%	.25	.11	.15	-.14
Austria	30%	20%	33%	.14	.21	.20	-.30
Hungary	20%	12%	24%	.19	.24	.27	
Italy	22%	11%	27%	.21	.06	.09	
Ireland	30%	22%	35%	.00*	.15	.13	-.17
Netherlands	24%	19%	31%	.33	.32	.23	
Norway	13%	12%	16%	.29	.22	.23	
Slovenia	32%	15%	33%	.15	.26	.25	-.14
Poland	30%	27%	37%	.02*	.21	.16	
Russia	14%						
Total	23%	17%	29%				

Thirty percent of the British, Irish, Austrians, Slovenes, and Poles report contact with the dead, as diverse a group as one can imagine, save that four of them are from Catholic countries. East Germany, Russia, and Norway are the least likely countries to report such experiences. Poland and Britain have the highest levels of ecstatic experiences, East Germany the lowest.

Is mysticism a substitute for religion in Britain as magic seems to be? Quite the contrary, in Britain mystical experiences happen among the devout and those with a religious affiliation, while across the Irish Sea they are more likely to be divided rather equally among the whole population. In Britain the correlation of mystical experience with frequent church attendance is .27, in Ireland it is .14. In Britain the correlation with denominational membership is .11, in Ireland it is .07. Perhaps in a secularized society, conceding for the moment the claim of British sociologists, the more devout are more open to mystical experiences and/or need them more.

Poland has the highest score on the mystic scale (37 percent), followed by Britain (36 percent), and Ireland (35 percent), Slovenia and Austria (33 percent) and the Netherlands 31 percent. The countries are all Catholic except Britain (and the Netherlands in recent years). The lowest score as one might expect is in East Germany (14 percent). Is mysticism in the Netherlands like that of Ireland or Britain? Is it a response of the devout to the religious crisis in that country or is it more widely distributed in the population? The correlation with no religious affiliation is more like that of Britain -.11. However, the correlation with church attendance is more similar to that of Ireland (.14 compared to .11). In neither England nor the Netherlands can it be said that the mystical has been a substitute for declining religion.

East Germany, however, displays the highest correlation between belief in God and mystical experience (.29) while the lowest correlations (.02) are in Ireland and Poland. Perhaps encounters with the ecstatic are a powerful help to belief in a country where there is little belief and unnecessary in countries where there is overwhelming belief. Correlations are positive in all countries for belief in life after death and frequent prayer. It may be that faith and devotion dispose one to be open to the mystical; or perhaps experiences incline one to be more devout and more believing. (Research by Greeley suggests that the latter might be the case).

Denominations

Muslims and Orthodox (Table 3.5) have the highest scores on both mysticism and Magic, while, among the western churches, Catholics have higher scores than Protestants. Forty percent of those with no religious affiliation endorse magic and 21 percent have a high score on the mystical scale. Hence the absence of denominational affiliation is not an obstacle to either magic or mysticism. The high scores of Catholics and Orthodox probably are the result of the fact that both religions consider the world to be sacramental, that is a place where the sacred is to be found. Such an orientation doubtless opens a person up to the mystical dimensions of life and to the temptations of magic. However, one would have expected that Islam's stern prohibition of idolatry would have impeded its followers from succumbing to the temptation. Since most of our Muslims are from Bulgaria and Russia, where magic is strong, it might be that the Muslims are heavily influenced by the religious atmosphere of the country in which they live.

Those with no religious affiliation are the most likely to be pro-science (51 percent) while Catholics and Muslims (26 percent) trail the Protestants (34 percent) and Orthodox (31 percent). Perhaps the Orthodox sympathy for science is the result of the fact that most of them have lived in once socialist countries where science was heavily emphasized as an alternative to religion. Russia has a much higher score on the pro-science scale than does Cyprus, which was never under socialist control.

The difference between Protestants and Catholics suggests a replay of Max Weber's theories. However, the correlation of .15 be-

Table 3.5
Magic, Science, and Mysticism by religion

% high on scales

Religion	Magic	Pro-Science	Mystical Experiences
Protestant	48%	34%	27%
Catholic	52%	26%	32%
Orthodox	62%	31%	41%
Islam	77%	26%	45%
None	40%	51%	21%

tween Protestants an pro-science is only diminished to .13 when university attendance and propensity to magic are taken into account. Perhaps Catholics because of the strong communal ties of their religion are simply more skeptical to the appeal of science.

Conclusions

Keeping in mind that the indicators on which this chapter is based are thin, one can cautiously propose the following generalizations.

1. Magic is alive and well in Europe and growing.

2. Magic's strongest appeal is in conditions of uncertainty. It's power diminishes among individuals and countries where there is certainty—of either religious belief or non-belief.

3. Magic is strongest in Eastern Europe, perhaps because of the Slavic culture in that region. It is weakest in countries like Ireland and East Germany where strong firewalls of faith or atheism diminish its power.

4. Magic often blends with religion, particularly in countries where people are uncertain about religious faith (Britain).

5. There is limited variability in the pro-science factor, but it is strongest in Eastern Europe and weakest among Catholics. It is inconsistent with magic and correlates negatively with religious faith.

6. However, most of the increase in belief in life after death in our sample is among those who are pro-science, thus suggesting some decline in the science versus religion conflict.

7. A surprisingly high proportion of Europeans report contact with the dead and ecstatic experiences. In secularized countries these reports correlate strongly with church attendance.

8. Mystical experiences are highest in two religious countries (Ireland and Poland) and one secularized country (Britain).

9. Mysticism and religious faith correlate positively in all countries, though it is not clear whether religion predisposes to mysticism or vice versa.

10. Religion correlates negatively with magic.

Note

1. A very sophisticated Irish American cleric remarked to me, "But there ARE faith healers in Ireland!" What do I know?

4

The Churches

Faith, we saw in the first chapter, has survived in Europe, better in some places than in others. Similarly, we discovered in the second chapter that hope has not only survived but in most countries it has increased among the youngest cohorts. We learned in the last chapter that magic survives, flourishes, and increases, especially among people and countries where religion is uncertain. Science is still something of an enemy of religion, but the increase in belief in life after death among the young, we discovered, is happening precisely among those who are pro-science. Mystical experiences are common and reinforce religion or are predisposed to by religion.

In this chapter, we will turn to the churches and will discover that the churches are not doing well, perhaps because they are not doing good. However, as human institutions presided over by human beings, the churches have perhaps never done very well.

Religious Affiliation

First of all, a considerable proportion of Europeans have no religious affiliation, even though in some countries, Scandinavia and Germany, for example, religious affiliation is a formality that seems to many to be required for participation in civic life. You pay your church tax so that when you marry, when you have children, and when you die, the rituals will be performed without undue difficulty. Only in Austria, Northern Ireland, and Italy has there not been a statistically significant increase in those with no affiliation. (The first two columns in table 4.1) The decline in religious affiliation is especially strong in Hungary (22 percent), Slovenia (13 percent) Britain (12 percent) and Ireland (6 percent). In the other countries the declines are only a few percentage points.

Table 4.1
No Religious Affiliation by Country and Year

Country	1991	1998	Second Generation with no religious Affiliation	Loss since Childhood
W. Germany	11%	15%	4%	9%
E. Germany	64%	68%	48%	46%
Britain	33%	45%	9%	33%
N. Ireland	9%	10%	1%	1%
Austria	10%	12%	2%	8%
Hungary	5%	27%	9%	11%
Italy	6%	8%	7%	-1%
Ireland	2%	6%	0	6%
Netherlands	55%	58%	22%	43%
Norway	6%	10%	3%	6%
Sweden		29%	9%	15%
Czech Republic		45%	33%	5%
Slovenia	11%	24%	13%	10%
Poland	3%	6%	5%	5%
Bulgaria	13%	13%	10%	-7%
Russia	68%	35%	31%	-40%
Spain		14%	2%	10%
Latvia		36%	26%	4%
Slovakia		16%	10%	2%
France		47%	14%	31%
Cyprus		0%	0	0
Portugal		8%	1%	6%
Denmark		12%	4%	2%
Switzerland		9%	2%	3%
Total		23%	11%	15%

However, in contrast to these declines, church affiliation has increased dramatically in Russia, from 32 percent to 65 percent. Why Orthodoxy increased in membership when Catholicism lost membership in two other former socialist countries is an intriguing question, especially since Catholicism has lost few members in Poland.

Those with no religious affiliation presently whose parents had no religious affiliation—the third column—(whom we call "second generation" though they may represent many more generations with no affiliation) are especially likely to be found in East Germany (48 percent) and the Czech Republic (33 percent).

Another way of considering the losses for the churches is to compare those who were raised in a denominational tradition but no longer have an affiliation (question 24). Instead of measuring loss through the years, this comparison measures loss across generations. The biggest losses, clearly catastrophic, are in East Germany (46 percent), the Netherlands (43 percent), Britain (33 percent) and France (31 percent). In East Germany, Socialism won its only clear victory over religion. In the Netherlands, the collapse of the tripartite religious pillarization combined with inept behavior from the Vatican created a sudden collapse of religion. In France, the two centuries of wars between the church and democracy may have finally ended in defeat for the church. It remains to be seen what has happened in Britain. On the other hand, the dramatic increase in Orthodoxy in Russia also will require some explanation as this book progresses. Interestingly enough, in the Czech Republic, where as we noted a third of the people are second generation unaffiliated, only 5 percent of the respondents say that they have given up a childhood religious affiliation. Disaffiliation from the church in the Czech Republic is therefore a historic phenomenon and not a recent one, a subject to which we will return in a subsequent chapter.

In table 4.2 we observe that 79 percent of those raised Protestant are still Protestants as are 95 percent of Orthodox, 87 percent of the Muslims, and 85 percent of the Catholics still affiliated with their respective religions. The largest "loss" is among those who were raised in no religion at all: 32 percent of those who were raised in no religion have "defected" to a religious affiliation, 17 percent to Orthodox and 13 percent to either Protestant or Catholic affiliation.

Of the countries where more than 1 percent of the population were those who had moved from no religion to some religion, in both the Germanys 3 percent of the population were "returnees, " in Austria 2 percent, in the Netherlands 2 percent, in Norway 2 percent, in Sweden 4 percent, in the Czech Republic 4 percent, in Slovenia 2 percent, in Bulgaria 9 percent, in Latvia 13 percent, in Slovakia 4 percent, in Denmark 5 percent, in Switzerland 3 percent and in Russia 49 percent. Almost half the Russian respondents had

Table 4.2
Retention Rates of Religious Denominations

Religion Raised in	Current Religion
Protestant	79%
Catholic	85%
Orthodox	95%
Islam	87%
None*	68%**

*47% of those with no religion were not raised in any religion and thus are second generation non- affiliates.
**17% of those raised in no religion have become Orthodox (mostly in Russia). 15% have become Western Christians.

changed between childhood and adulthood from having no religious affiliation to having a religious affiliation (Orthodox). Most of the returnees were in Eastern Europe, especially in Latvia and Bulgaria. A second question arises concerning Hungary and Slovenia in comparison with Russia: why was not Catholicism in these countries able to reclaim nearly as many of the lost as was Orthodoxy in Russia. One possible answer is that many of the Russians were already crypto-Orthodox even if they deemed themselves not to have had any religion when they were young. Another is that Orthodoxy had always been an integral component of the Russian culture in a way that Hapsburg-dominated Catholicism had never been in Hungary or Slovenia (or in Slovakia or the Czech Republic).

Table 4.3 compares the second generation "defectors" (raised in no affiliation and having none now) with the first generation (raised in some religion but having none now), the returnees, and those who have always had an affiliation. Thus half of the second generation are atheists (response #1 in question 18), but almost a quarter of them believe in life after death. More than a quarter of the first generation are atheists but about the same proportion also believe in God in some fashion and a third believe in life after death. The returnees are, as one might expect, much more religious than the "defectors:" 70 percent believe in God (though 11 percent are still atheists), two fifths in a God who is personally concerned and half in life after death. There is no difference among these three groups in university education (17 percent, 18, and 16 percent respectively), though those who always were affiliated were somewhat less likely

Table 4.3
Characteristics of Religious Changers

	2d Generation Defectors (11%)	First Generation Defectors (13%)	Returned Defectors 5%	Never Defected (71%)
Atheist	50%	28%	11%	4%
Theist	2%	7%	24%	42%
Believe	9%	27%	70%	85%
Concerned God	6%	13%	42%	54%
Pray Several Times a Month	3%	13%	29%	55%
Life after death	23%	34%	50%	65%
Age	39.1	43.6	41.2	47.2
University Degree	17%	18%	16%	11%
Gender (women)	46%	47%	48%	58%

to have graduated from university (11 percent) Perhaps for some young people university time is a period in life for religious restructuring. Second generation defectors are, on the average, younger (39.1 years) than either first generation (43.6) or returnees (41.2 percent). Women are less likely than men to be in all three groups and much more likely than those who have never changed their religious affiliation.

There is then some movement back and forth across the line that divides those who have a religious affiliation and those who do not. However, much of the movement back to affiliation is in Eastern Europe where it may be a one-time phenomenon that has resulted from the fall of socialism. On balance, religious affiliation has suffered serious losses, most notably in the Netherlands, East Germany, Britain, and France and some surprising losses in Hungary and Slovenia.

Anti-Church Attitudes

Might the defections be accounted for, to some extent, by people's attitudes towards the churches as institutions? Four questionnaire items (#'s 11, 12, 13, and 17 measure in one way or another attitudes towards the churches. Two of them (the first two columns in table 4.4) ask about general principles—what the church should or

Table 4.4
Attitudes towards Church by Country

Country	%Clergy should not interfere with voting (strongly agree)	%Church should not interfere with government	%Church has too much power	%No Confidence in Church	% High on anti-Church scale	Average number of anti-church responses
W. Germany	44%	42%	47%	37%	57%	1.6
E. Germany	36%	.37%	39.%	55%	61%	1.4
Britain	36%	37%	29%	40%	49%	1.3
N. Ireland	35%	46%	41%	21%	45%	1.4
Austria	59%	53%	38%	40%	53%	1.8
Hungary	51%	51%	16%	29%	36%	1.4
Italy	54%	48%	46%	26%	54%	1.7
Ireland	34%	54%	41%	24%	48%	1.9
Netherlands	39%	44%	23%	39%	44%	1.3
Norway	41%	38%	29%	33%	43%	1.3
Sweden	42%	67%	23%	44%	48%	1.5
Czech Republic	40%	68%	13%	54%	56%	1.6
Slovenia	35%	34%	33%	34%	51%	1.2
Poland	44%	44%	60%	23%	63%	1.6
Bulgaria	63%	87%	9%	47%	53%	1.9
Russia	37%	44%	13%	18%	24%	0.9
Spain	50%	81%	45%	37%	58%	2.0
Latvia	33%	68%	6%	28%	29%	1.3
Slovakia	59%	73%	29%	32%	43%	1.9
France	67%	73%	28%	32%	54%	2.1
Cyprus	50%	82%	70%	25%	75%	2.2
Portugal	70%	79%	27%	20%	38%	1.9
Denmark	76%	78%	30%	28%	36%	1.9
Switzerland	45%	70%	32%	33%	36%	1.5
Average	45%	53%	32%	33%	47%	1.5

should not do. The other two ask about specific situations, the church having too much power and the respondent's lack of confidence in the church. On the average respondents are more likely to take a stand in principle against church intervention in political or governmental affairs than they are to protest against the present situations in their own country. The strongest principled warnings against church interference in government are in some Catholic countries: Spain (81 percent) Portugal (79 percent) France (67 percent); and in some Eastern European countries: Bulgaria (87 percent) Cyprus (82 percent), Slovakia (73 percent), Latvia (68 percent) and the Czech Republic (68 percent); also in Denmark (78 percent), Switzerland (70 percent) and Sweden (67 percent).

Only in Cyprus and Spain, however, is this principle reflected in the complaint above the average that the church has too much power (third column in the table). In the latter country, the memory of the Franco regime and the present reality of the influence of the Catholic secret society Opus Dei might support the complaint. In Cyprus, the memory that its first president was an Orthodox Archbishop might contribute to the unease with church power. The highest proportions objecting to power of the church are in Cyprus (70 percent) and Poland (60 percent), Italy (46 percent), West Germany, and the Irelands (41 percent). In Poland, Italy, and Ireland (until recently) the Catholic Church has tried to exercise political clout in many different ways, particularly on issues pertaining to sexuality. Though principles about the use of power and objection to the church's actual use of power may finally fall on the same factor, it is clear that people react to these questions differently in different countries. Thus 87 percent of the Bulgars do not want the church interfering with government but only 9 percent think the church has too much power.

The highest scores on the absence of confidence (fourth column) in the church are in East Germany (55 percent) and the Czech Republic (54 percent), though in neither country is the church seen as having excessive power. The answer to the question implied at the end of the last paragraph might be that the Bulgars lack confidence (fourth column) in church leaders. Forty-seven percent say they have little confidence in this rather powerless church, seven percentage points more than the British (40 percent) who are hardly suffering from a theocratic regime. Neither are the Swedes whose lack of confidence in the church (44 percent) is notably ahead of the other Scandinavian countries (Norway at 33 percent and Denmark (28 percent). The lowest levels of complaints about lack of confidence in the church are to be found in Portugal (20 percent), Northern Ireland (21 percent), Ireland (24 percent), and Cyprus (25 percent). There are paradoxes in the apparent confidence of both the Portuguese and the Cypriots. The latter score at the top of the list on the first three items and still have confidence in their church leaders, despite their power and the former are also, it would seem, fearful of church intervention in the political world (as they well might be after the long Salazar regime) but also confident in the church organizations.

It might be that in countries like Sweden and Britain and even East Germany the absence of confidence in the church institution is an expression of dissatisfaction with its ineptitude and not with its power. Perhaps the East Germans are distrustful of the West German church leadership which has taken over in the New States. In France, the low levels of complaint about church power and the dissatisfaction with the church might reflect that, despite their opposition to the church intervening in government an elections, the French have a realistic view of how little power the church still has in that (formerly) Catholic country and of how cautious the church organization is about trying to use what little clout it has left.

Obviously attitudes toward the churches in Europe have been shaped by past history and present events in complex fashion. It is a topsy-turvy world in which the highest scores on the anti-church factor (fifth column) are in formerly socialist East Germany (61 percent above the mean) and formerly Catholic France (75 percent) while the lowest scores are in formerly socialist Russia (24 percent), and formerly socialist Latvia (29 percent). Low scores are also found in Denmark and (formerly anti-Jesuit) Switzerland (36 percent) and (formerly quasi-Fascist) Portugal (38 percent). Another way to rank the countries on anti-church attitudes is to consider (in the last column of the table) the average number of complaints (as expressed or implied in the first four columns) against the churches and the clergy.

The highest number of complaints are registered by the Cypriots, and the French, and the Spaniards– 2.2, 2.1, and 2.0 respectively. Close behind at 1.9 are Ireland, Bulgaria, Denmark, and Slovakia, and Portugal. The lowest scores are in Russia (0.9), Slovenia (1.2), Latvia, and the Netherlands (1.3). For the French and presumably the Cypriots, their orientation towards their church and their religion is largely shaped by past history. In Russia, Orthodoxy made the most of the social transformation and emerged as one of the major carriers of the Russian cultural heritage. The Irish are struggling to emerge from the clericalism of an earlier age, as we shall see in a subsequent chapter. (Note that the Irish and the Northern Irish are virtually tied on both summary measures). The Danes patently have nothing to fear from their weak church but they still don't like it much. The Dutch, for their part, living in a secularized society in which the churches were abruptly tossed out of power, have little to complain about. The Portuguese and the Spaniards have not forgotten either Franco or Salazar or the long religious conflicts of the last century. It is worth noting that France, Spain, Ireland, Slovakia, and Portugal are all Catholic countries in which the Catholic Church had considerable power and clerics often dominated government. Moreover, while clerical power is ebbing, it still persists to some extent, save in France, and is nowhere forgotten.

Hence one is not surprised by the finding in table 4.5 that anti-church attitudes are stronger among Catholics than among Protestants (43 percent versus 39 percent.) However, one is surprised to see that the Orthodox are even more likely than Catholics to be high on the anti-church scale (46 percent). Only 37 percent of the Muslims are above the average on the scale and it might be problematic whether it is their own church or the church of the country in which they live, most notably in Bulgaria which is dominated religiously by the Bulgarian Orthodox Church which has never particularly liked the "Turks" in their presence.

Table 4.5
Anti-Church Attitudes by Religion
% High on Anti-Church Scale

Religion	
Protestant	39%
Catholic	43%
Orthodox	46%
Islam	37%
None	68%

The reciprocal interaction between church behavior and attitudes and aspirations of the people in a particular country, particularly when the issue was freedom has generated conflict and classic Clericalism and Anti-Clericalism for two centuries. The fierceness of the struggle has waned, especially since it became evident—to risk a broad generalization—the church had lost the battle. The conflict has not completely disappeared, however, and continues now over sexuality and the rights of women. Religion has survived the conflict, weakened no doubt and perhaps somewhat chastened, but still alive and still teaching doctrines which to some extent are still believed by the majority of people save in East Germany and the Netherlands.

Anti-Clericalism and Membership Loss

Can one find traces of loss in the last couple of decades, first of all by comparing the scores on the anti-church measure in countries which participated in both the 1991 and the 1998 International Social Survey Program projects and then by attempting to relate them to decline in denominational affiliation?

In table 4.6 we observe that there have been statistically significant increases in anti-church scales in four countries, Hungary (from 31 percent to 40 percent), Slovenia (from 46 percent to 63 percent), Ireland from (44 percent to 52 percent,) and Russia (from 13 percent to 63 percent). The Russian case is unique and will be postponed to a subsequent chapter. It occurred during a period when affiliation with Orthodoxy increased. The other three countries, we learned in table 4.1, experienced statistically significant declines in religious affiliation, 13 percent in Slovenia, 22 percent in Hungary, and 4 percent in Ireland. Moreover (table 3.7), in each of these countries there was a notable increase in complaints against the church since 1991—0.1 to 2.1 in Slovenia, 1.1 to 1.7 in Hungary, and 1.1 to 1.9 in Ireland. This change was particularly surprising in the first two countries where one might have expected organized religion to have benefited from the political and social changes in the country, as Orthodoxy did in Russia. Might it be that the increase in complaints accounted for the changes.

Table 4.6
Changing Attitudes towards the Churches
% High on Anti-Church Scale

Countries	1991	1998
W. Germany	57%	57%
E. Germany	57%	67%
Britain	50%	48%
N. Ireland	42%	50%*
Austria	55%	51%
Hungary	30%%	41%*
Poland	65%	61%
Ireland	44%	52%*
Ireland	44%	52%
Netherlands	46%	43%
Norway	42%	45%
Slovenia	46%	63%*
Russia	13%	43%*

*Change from 1991 statistically significant

This model was first applied to Hungary and fit the data perfectly (figure 4.1). In the era of good feeling at the time of the fall of so-

Figure 4.1
No Religious Affiliation By Year and Anti-Church Attitudes

Hungary

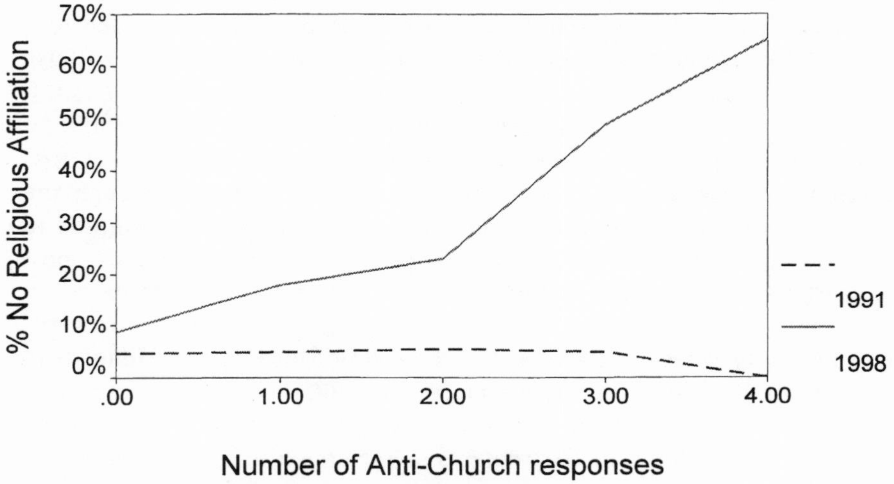

Figure 4.2
No Religious Affiliation By Year and Anti-Church Attitudes

Slovenia

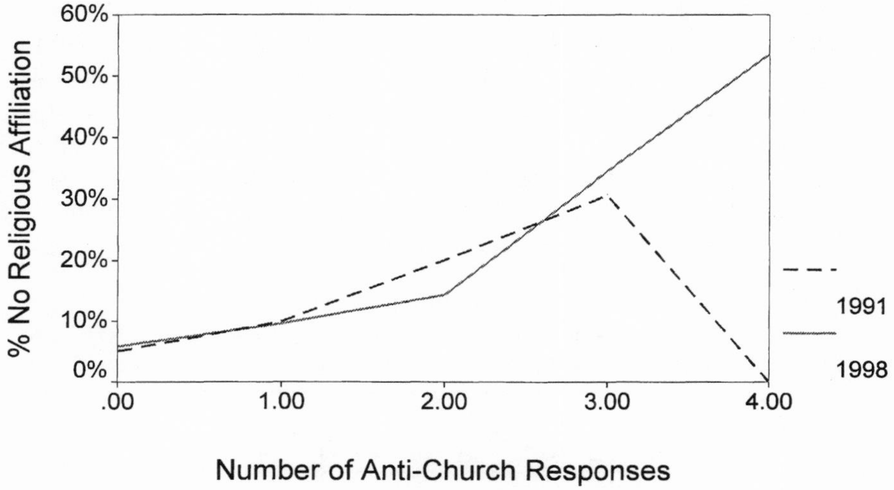

cialism, complaints against the church had no impact on organizational membership. However a mere seven years later, not only had the level of complaints increased, but the impact of complaints on no religious affiliation had moved from a flat line to a sharp upward slope. The perceived abuses of clerical power, as it seems, led to a decline in almost a quarter of the Hungarian people in their willingness to claim church membership—at the very same time Orthodoxy was increasing dramatically in Russia.

A similar model (figure 4.2) accounts to some extent for the loss of the allegiance of one sixth of the Slovene people, though the disproportionate increase in those with no affiliation was limited to those who endorsed all four complaints against the churches, a proportion which increased dramatically in Slovenia during those seven years.

Exactly what the Catholic Church did in Slovenia and Hungary to turn off so many of its members is beside the point. Perhaps many of them were marginal believers who identified temporarily with the church at the time of the social transformation and then deserted it en masse when they discovered, as Borowik and Gabinski have reported, that the Catholic Church in Eastern Europe was primarily interested in reasserting its power, its control, its privileges. As usual when clericalism takes over and threatens what people perceive to be their freedoms, clericalism loses—or wins the way the German panzers triumphed at the battle of Kursk. Clericalism, as the Frenchman said, is the enemy. It always loses because it is an inept, heavy-handed, stupid enemy, incapable of estimating the consequences of its own action or even waiting cautiously and discretely before charging into battle.

The Slovenia model also fits in Ireland, though it affects only a small proportion of the Irish population (figure 4.3). Four complaints against the church had no impact on Irish non-affiliation in 1991 yet

Table 4.7
Increase in Anti-Church Responses by Country
(Mean number of responses)

	1991	1998
Slovenia	0.9	2.1
Hungary	1.1	1.7
Ireland	1.1	1.9

Figure 4.3
No Religious Affiliation By Year and Anti-Church Attitudes

Ireland

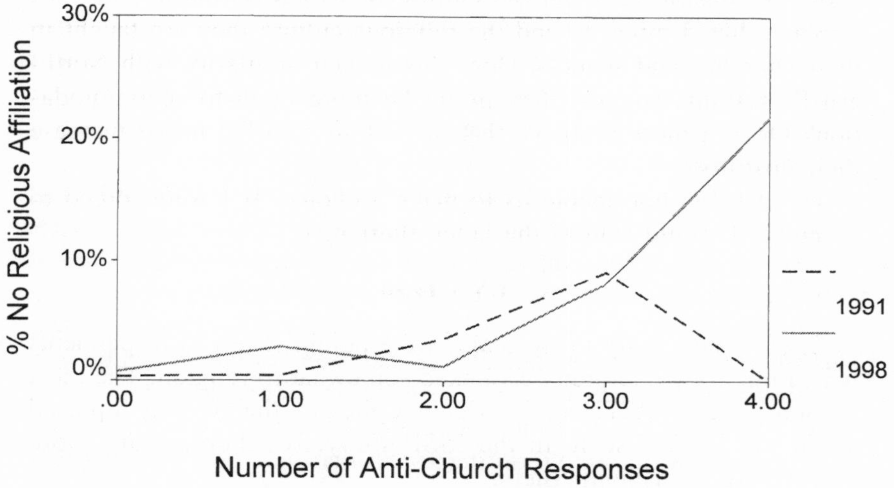

by 1998 almost half of those with four complaints had decamped from church affiliation. Perhaps in each of these countries, the people who were inclined to leave simply became more anti-clerical in seven years. However, even if this were true, it is still the case, that the level of complaints had almost doubled in Ireland.

Do people disaffiliate because they stop believing or do they depart because they feel the church has driven them out? The answer to that question can be obtained tentatively by use of the data available to us. The correlation between year and defection in Hungary is .30. When anti-church sentiment is added to a regression equation, the coefficient with year declines to .21. Loss of faith in God (response #2 on question 19) further declines to .2. Anti-church sentiment rather than loss of faith seems to account in substantial part for the decline in religious affiliation in Hungary between 1991 and 1998.

The same model can be applied with equal success to the correlation of .17 with year in Slovenia. Loss of faith reduces the coefficient to .16. Then anti-church feeling reduces it to .03 and statistical insignificance. In both countries, as the respondents perceive it, the decline of affiliation was a function not of loss of faith but of objections to the ecclesiastical institution.

Figure 4.4 confirms the fact that, while among the first two birth cohorts there were no differences between Catholics and Protestants in anti-church attitudes, beginning with the cohort born in the 1940s, the cohort which would have come of age at the time of Vatican Council II, the level of Catholic complaint diverged and moved higher than that of Protestant complaint so that half of the Catholics born in the 1970s scored high on the anti-church factor.

Did the Council perhaps cause higher expectations and the complaints come from the fact that Catholics are displeased by their failed hopes? Or are they disappointed that the church didn't stay with its old ways? No one should bet too heavily on the second alternative.

Finally, however, while the complaint curve has risen for everyone, there is a declining relationship between complaints and a propensity to leave one's religious heritage (figure 4.5) among the younger cohort, both among those who have more complaints and those who have fewer. While it may be that those who are younger have yet to become angry enough to leave their church (whichever

Figure 4.4
Anti-Church Attitudes by Religion and Cohort

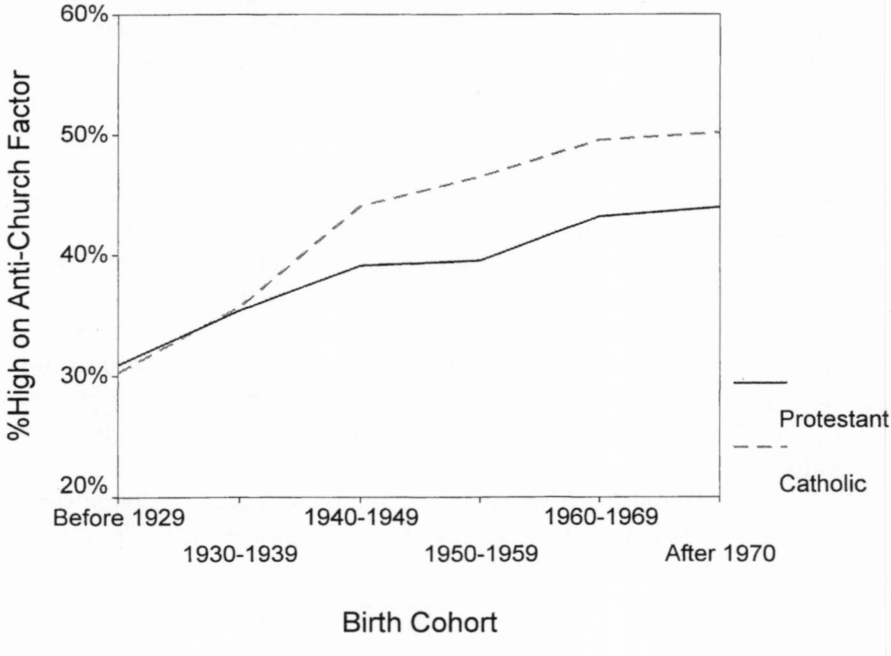

Figure 4.5
Reject Religious Heritage by Birth Cohort and Anti-Church Attitudes

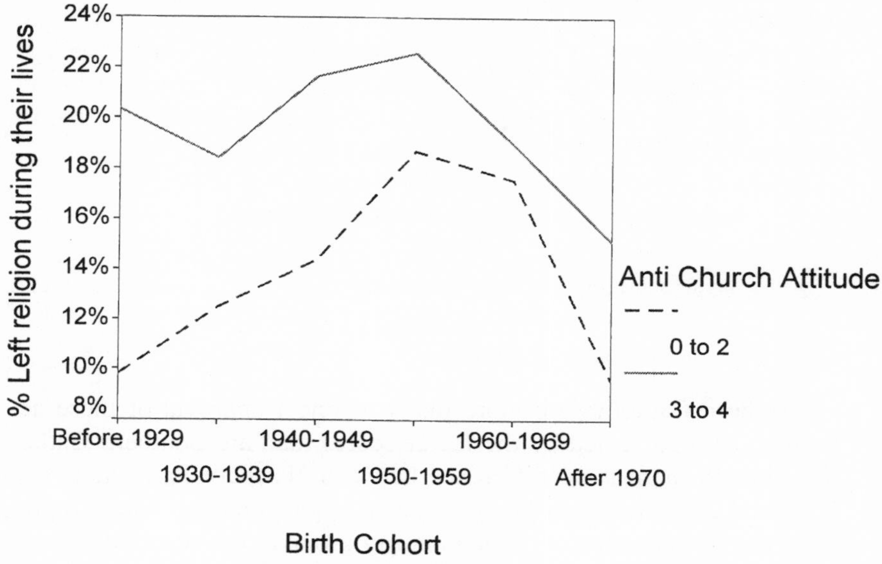

it may be), it may also be that the younger cohort is making a distinction between a religious affiliation they value and institutional leadership they do not like. The propensity to disaffiliate increase from those born between 1930 and 1959 and has since then fell sharply.

Church Attendance

Church attendance is the traditional measure of the sociology of religion. It is usually proposed as evidence that religion is declining, as if that's all religion really is and as if the Council of Lateran IV in 1215 did not impose the Sunday obligation[1] of mass attendance on the Catholic faithful because the fathers of the Council thought that most Christians of the day where not going to church very often. Declining church attendance certainly shows that one aspect of religion is changing. If one aspect changes, then religion is changing. However, a decline in church attendance no more proves that religion is at last giving up as Voltaire and company suggested it should, any more than the increase in belief in life after death discussed in chapter 2 proves that religion is entering a golden age. It seems more likely to be, given the historical benchmark of Lateran IV, that there is an ebb and flow of religious devotion through the decades and the centuries. What is unique about the present time, perhaps, is that obligations cannot be imposed (any more than there is reason to think that the canon of Lateran IV was immediately, if ever, obeyed). Religious leaders will have to find other motives for persuading people to come to church on weekends besides the threat of mortal sin and hellfire.[2]

Table 4.8
Church Attendance by Study and Year
% 2 or 3 Times a Month or More

	EVS	EVS	ISSP	ISSP
	1981	1990	1991	1998
W. Germany	19%%	18%	15%	17%
E. Germany			4%	(flawed)
Britain	14%%	14%%	17%	17%
N. Ireland	51%	50%	56%	51%
Austria			26%	33%**
Hungary	11%	21%**	19%	20%
Italy	32%	38%**	49%	44%*
Ireland	82%	81%	75%	73%
Netherlands	25%	20%*	21%	18%
Norway	5%	5%	10%	7%
Sweden	6%	6%		8%
Czech				12%
Slovenia				23%
Poland			67%	61%*
Russia			5%	5%
Spain	40%	29%*		36%
Latvia				12%
Slovakia				41%
France	10%	10%		13%
Cyprus				8%
Portugal				41%
Denmark	2%	2%		7%
Switzerland				64%

Table 4.9
Church Attendance by Study and Year
%Never Attend

	EVS	EVS	ISSP	ISSP
	1991	1998	1991	1998
W. Germany	23%	23%	21%	20%
E. Germany			60%	flawed
Britain	48%	47%	36%	54%*
N. Ireland	12%	13%	14%	24%*
Austria			21%	20%
Hungary	51%		32%	30%
Italy	22%	16%**	13%	19%*
Ireland	4%	4%	5%	5%
Netherlands	41%	43%	54%	60%
Norway	38%	40%	34%	34%
Sweden	38%	48%		28%
Czech				48%
Slovenia				30%
Poland			3%	4%
Russia			67%	55%**
Spain	26%	30%*		20%
Latvia				33%
Slovakia				24%
France	59%	52%**		50%
Cyprus				15%
Portugal				8%
Denmark	45%	44%		29%
Switzerland				5%

Tables 4.8 and 4.9 measures change in church attendance in the last twenty years by considering two dependent variables, attendance two or three times a month at least and attendance never. While sociologists like to use attendance as a quick and handy measure, they are reluctant to agree on how the question should be asked. Thus the same rule applies in these tables as in previous tables when com-

parisons between European Values Study data and International Social Survey Program data are considered: only when a consistent statistically significant change is found within both studies can one speak confidently about decline (or increase) in church attendance.

In the European Values Study there are significant decreases (table 4.8) between 1981 and 1990 in frequent church attendance in the Netherlands (five percentage points) and in Spain eleven percentage points and significant increases in Hungary (ten percentage points), and Italy (six percentage points).[3] In the International Social Survey Program studies there is a significant decline (from 49 percent to 44 percent) in Italy which still leaves Italian church attendance higher than the European Values Study figures indicate. There is also a significant decline in Poland (from 67 percent to 61 percent) and a significant increase in Austria from 26 percent to 33 percent. The 1998 Spanish proportion (36 percent) is midway between the two estimates of the European Values Study

The Hungarian increases are part of the unique religious events in Eastern Europe. The Italian increase in the European Values Study must be viewed with some skepticism as must be the Austrian increase in the International Social Survey Program (though some Austrian colleagues report that it is a real if little understood phenomenon). The decline in the Netherlands is congruent with what we know of the religious collapse in that country. It is possible that Spanish attendance has declined, but not as much as the European Values Study suggests. Otherwise there are no important trends.

The data about those who never attend is (table 4.10) similarly inconclusive. In the European Values Study there is a significant decline of never attendance in Italy and, surprisingly, in France (from

Table 4.10
Church Attendance by Religion

	% Attend 2 or three times a month	%Attend never
Protestant	25%	21%
Catholic	43%	12%
Orthodox	8%	25%
Islam	40%	29%
None	2%	75%

59 percent to 52 percent). In Italy, on the other hand, in the International Social Survey Program never attendance increases significantly (13 percent to 19 percent as it does in the Netherlands (54 percent to 60 percent), in Britain (36 percent to 54 percent), in Northern Ireland (14 percent to 24 percent). On the other hand in Russia the proportion who never attend church has fallen from 67 percent to 55 percent.

The East German data are flawed because in an incredible bungle, those collecting data from East Germany asked attendance figures only from those who reported a church affiliation in 1998, gratuitously assuming that those who no affiliation never went to church—*even though data from the 1991 survey indicated that some of them did.* They also broke the International Social Survey Program rule that repeat questions must be asked the same way at both points in time *and* the rule that no country in the project may unilaterally change question wordings.[4]

A cautious summary of the findings of tables 4.8 and 4.9 would suggest that during the last twenty years attendance seems to have declined in the Netherlands and perhaps in Britain and decreased somewhat in Poland and increased somewhat in Russia and East Germany while the situation in Spain and Italy is inconclusive.

Conclusions

1. With the exception of East Germany and the Netherlands the majority in the countries under study have a religious affiliation. In France and Britain close to a majority are non-affiliates.

2. There have been heavy losses in affiliation in Hungry and Slovenia, apparently because of a surge in anti-church sentiment during the 1990s.

3. There has been an enormous increase in church affiliation in Russia.

4. Forty-six percent of those raised with no religious background now have a church affiliation, though most of them are Russians.

5. Orthodox, Muslims, and Catholics (in that order) are more likely to retain their membership than Protestants.

6. Anti-church sentiments are stronger among Catholics and Orthodox than they are among Protestants.

7. Anti-church sentiments are stronger in 1998 in Ireland, Hungary, Slovenia, East Germany and Russia than they were in 1991. In Hungary and Slovenia, these anti-church feelings and not loss of faith in God accounted for the decline in church affiliation during the decade.

8. In the more recent cohorts the Catholic Church has been the target of more anti-church feelings than the Protestant churches. However, the correlation between anti-church feelings and rejection of one's heritage has declined among the very youngest cohorts.

9. There is as much evidence of increase in church attendance in European countries in the last twenties years as of decline. Decline has occurred in the Netherlands and in Britain, increase in Hungary and Russia.

Notes

1. Not apparently under obligation of grave sin.
2. It is a Catholic urban legend that pastors at Christmas and Easter rail against those who come to church, instead of welcoming them and inviting them to come more often.
3. I personally doubt this finding very much.
4. Among those with church membership the rates did not change from 1991 to 1998—seventeen percent attended regularly and 18% never attended.

5

Trust, Tolerance, and Sex

In this chapter we will consider the effect of religion on trust in other humans, the charge that religion is intolerant and divisive, and the relationship between religion and sexual ethics.

Can You Trust Other People?

In the 1998 religion study, two items were introduced to measure trust in others (questions 10 and 11), doubtless to see whether religion has an effect on trust. It does but only some of the time and in some countries.

In table 5.1 we note that the majority of the people in the sample do not believe that other people are to be trusted and a large minority think that people will take advantage of you. The largest proportions which vote that people are unfair (in the first column) are in Eastern Europe and Latin Catholic countries: Bulgaria (74 percent), Slovenia (71 percent) Russia (59 percent), Spain (57 percent), Cyprus (57 percent Latvia (56 percent), Italy (53 percent), and Poland (51 percent). The lowest votes against unfairness are in Norway (14 percent), Switzerland (17 percent), Austria (19 percent) and Denmark (26 percent) and Ireland (26 percent).

The Eastern Europeans and the Latin Catholics are the leaders (the second column) in judging that other people are not to be trusted. Only the Hungarians (47 percent) of the Eastern peoples score below 60 percent voting against trust. Only the Scandinavians, the Irish (both Irelands), the Swiss, and the Dutch vote lower than average on not trusting.

When the two items are combined in a factor scale, the same pattern emerges—the lowest scores on distrust are to be found in Scandinavia, Switzerland, the Netherlands, Austria, and Ireland and

Table 5.1
Confidence in People in Europe

Country	People not fair	Not to be trusted	% High on Factor Score	Correlation with Life after Death	Correlation with frequent prayer
W. Germany	28%	52%	28%	-.08*	-.12*
E. Germany	24%	63%	30%	-.05	-06.
Britain	34%	50%	27%	-.08*	-.14*
N. Ireland	33%	51%	31%	-.04*	-10*
Austria	19%	50%	21%	-.02	-.04
Hungary	31%	47%	35%	-.01	.00
Italy	53%	63%	56%	-.03	-.04.
Ireland	26%	55%	24%	-.08*	-.01
Netherlands	8%	34%	10%	. 00	-.03
Norway	14%	21%	10%	-.01	-.01.
Sweden	28%	32%	21%	-.05	-.00
Czech Republic	42%	59%	35%	-.06*	-.04
Slovenia	70%	83%	69%	-.04	-.05
Poland	51%	77%	51%	- .02	-.05
Bulgaria	74%	76%	70%	-.12*	-.01
Russia	59%	77%	61%	-.05	-.02
Spain	57%	61%	52%	-.03	-.00
Latvia	56%	78%	58%	-.12*	-.09*
Slovakia	35%	84%	47%	-.10*	-.08*
France	36%	61%	37%	-.01	-.03
Cyprus	57%	84%	63%	-.06	-.09*
Portugal	44%	78%	45%	-.01	-.00
Denmark	26%	34%	21%	-.06	-.00
Switzerland	17%	35%	17%	-.03	.06
Average	39%	59%	38%	-.04*	-.01

*Correlation statistically significant

the highest scores are in the Eastern European countries with the exception of Slovakia and Hungary and East Germany. Scores above average come from the three Latin Catholics, though not from France. Confidence in one's fellows seems to be a phenomenon of Western and Northern Europe.

One wonders about the distrust of others in Eastern and Southern Europe. Perhaps suspicion of everyone was part of the ethos of the socialist cultures with their fear that anyone might be a government spy, though that this would not explain the mistrust of the Cypriots. Maybe the turbulence of Italy, Spain, and Portugal in the nineteenth century and much of the twentieth would account for the high levels of suspicion in these Mediterranean Catholic countries. From the Norwegians and the Dutch who have only 10 percent of their populations above the mean on distrust scale to the Bulgars (70 percent) and the Slovenes (69 percent) at the high end, there is a vast range of unwillingness to trust others.

The Irish, who suffered a long history of poverty, hunger, and oppression, seem singularly mild in their distrust, not the last Irish paradox that we will see in this book.

Since this a book about religion in Europe, one must inquire whether religious faith (as measured here by belief in life after death and relatively frequent prayer), minimizes somewhat this dyspeptic view of other human beings. The answer (fourth column of the table) is that it does in some countries and not in others. Belief in life after death diminishes (though only somewhat) distrust in Germany, Britain, the Irelands, and Switzerland. Belief in life after death also has some effect in Bulgaria, Latvia, the Czech Republic, and Slovakia.

Frequent prayer plays a role in mitigating distrust but only in Britain, Northern Ireland, Germany in the west and in Latvia, Slovakia, and Cyprus in the east. Perhaps it will require many years of a working civil society before the people of certain European countries will have the security to trust others. Spain and Portugal developed such societies in the eighties. The Eastern countries are just now trying to develop them. Only in such contexts, it would seem, is it even remotely possible that religion can overcome distrust and that by only a small amount.

The Intolerance of Religion

Three more questions, to measure hostility to religion (not the churches) were introduced in 1998 International Social Survey Program religion module (question 15), against the strong opposition of the present writer. The first two items are sucker items, designed to draw a stereotyped answer which would be hostile. There are no positive alternatives suggesting that sometimes religion brings peace, not conflict, and that sometimes men and women with strong religious beliefs are not intolerant. I confess that I am ashamed to be associated with a project that asked such loaded questions.

Table 5.2
Hostility Towards Religion in Europe

Country	Religion creates conflict	Religion is intolerant	Want less religious influence in their country	%High on Factor Score
W. Germany	65%	65%	15%	55%
E. Germany	75%	68%	25%	42%
Britain	78%	79%	24%	39%
N.Ireland	70%	76%	52%	30%
Austria	69%	78%	11%	51%
Hungary	45%	48%	11%	71%
Italy	53%	67%	23%	57%
Ireland	56%	73%	37%	46%
Netherlands	70%	78%	18%	47%
Norway	39%	77%	15%	39%
Sweden	43%	69%	12%	43%
Czech Republic	65%	53%	13%	64%
Slovenia	70%	69%	45%	36%
Poland	45%	65%	34%	56%
Bulgaria	55%	46%	11%	68%
Russia	35%	48%	22%	65%
Spain	52%	62%	27%	55%
Latvia	38%	44%	6%	79%
Slovakia	47%	53%	18%	61%
France	65%	69%	14%	46%
Cyprus	61%	43%	26%	63%
Portugal	65%	75%	21%	41%
Denmark	86%	79%	12%	31%
Switzerland	71%	81%	10%	48%
Average	61%	65%	20%	51%

As the first two columns of table 5.2 illustrate, on the average the first two items elicit strong anti-religious responses—61 percent of the respondents agreeing that religion causes conflict and 65 percent arguing that religion is intolerant. However, in the third item, in which the respondent is permitted to say that he wants less religious influence in his own country the average anti-religious responses falls to one third of the first two (20 percent). Unlike the others, it is not a global or philosophic answer but rather one tied to the specific conditions in one's own country. The high scores in Ireland (37 percent) and Northern Ireland (76 percent) are obviously a response to the conflict between Catholics and Protestants in Northern Ireland. The low scores in Scandinavia, the Netherlands, Switzerland, Austria, and West Germany are the result of the fact that in these countries religion has very little influence. The highest score (45 percent, more than twice the average) is in Slovenia where something happened to turn people off during the 1980s. Twenty-two percent of the Russians and 23 percent of the Italians wish that religion would have less influence in their countries, in both of which their respective religions are trying to sustain their traditional power. On balance, the Russians and Italians seem to be saying that religious influence is not too big a thing in their country. In Bulgaria and Latvia, strongholds of criticism of religion in the last chapter, the respondents do not seem to think that religious is too influential in their society.

Twenty-eight percent of the Catholics in the sample wish that religion had less influence in their societies (table 5.3) as do 24 percent of the Orthodox, 23 percent of the Protestants, 19 percent of the Muslims (most of whom, one must remember, live in non-Islamic European societies), and 38 percent of those with no religious background.

Table 5.3
"Better Country if Less Religious Influence"

Religion	
Protestant	23%
Catholic	28%
Orthodox	24%
Islam	19%
None	38%

The three items are, in fact, much ado about nothing, useful perhaps because the third item specifies the high end[1] of religious resentment in Europe at the end of the Second Millennium, on the average only about one-fifth of the Europeans in the sample seriously desire a decline in religious influence. Indeed, only a little less than two-fifths of those without religious affiliation desire to see religion's influence lessen as do two-fifths of the professed atheists. Those concerned about the future of religion might find some reassurance in the fact that, with the exception of Ireland, there is no strong feeling in any of the countries to curtail the power of religion.

Sex and Religion

Sexual morality is not, in the strict sense of the word, religious, though religions usually generate their own ethical codes. One would think, however, that for many religious leaders and preachers, sexual morality is almost the only religious issue about which they are concerned. When the primate of Ireland (not to be confused with the primate of all Ireland) lamented the fact that Ireland had become a post-Catholic country, he was undoubtedly referring to the rejection of much of the traditional sexual code by Irish Catholics. Neither, the Hebrew Prophets, nor Jesus, nor St. Paul denounced sexual sins in any stronger fashion than that in which they denounced all other sins. In their origins none of the religions of the book seemed to have believed that sexual sins were particularly worse than other sins.

However, in recent decades the Catholic Church has expended major effort to re-impose the church's sexual teaching on its faithful—or so it has seemed to many of the faithful. This effort has not been particularly successful, as table 5.4 demonstrates. Only about a tenth of the Europeans in the study think that pre-marital intercourse is always wrong. In Ireland in 1998, 28 percent of the population believe that premarital sex is always wrong (a statistically significant decline since 1991). In Portugal 23 percent believe it is always wrong. In no other predominantly Catholic is the rate of rejection above the 17 percent in Italy. How this dramatic change in attitudes towards premarital sex through Europe and the Western world and in Catholic countries as well as others is a fascinating question, but one beyond the scope of this book.

There also have been statistically significant declines in many countries on the subject of same-sex relations—Britain, Northern Ireland, Austria, Hungary, Italy, Norway, Sweden, Slovenia, and Russia. Majority opposition to same-sex relations as always wrong existed in 1998 only in Portugal (72 percent) Hungary (61 percent), Northern Ireland (59 percent), Ireland, Russia, Latvia (52 percent) Italy (50 percent). To the extent that acceptance of same-sex relationships is declining even in the traditionally Catholic countries,

Table 5.4
Sexual Attitudes by Country and Year
(% Always Wrong)

	Premarital		**Same Sex**		**Extra Marital**		**Abortion (defect)**	
Country	1991	1998	1991	1998	1991	1998	1991	1998
W. Germany	3%	6%**	25%	22%	35%	40%*	11%	12%
E. Germany	2%	2%	26%	27%	44%	42%	8%	8%
Britain	12%	11%	52%	37%*	60%	62%	8%	8%
N.Ireland	31%	22%*	79%	59%*	75%	70%*	26%	23%
Austria	1%	3%*	33%	29%*	46%	41%*		10%
Hungary	14%	16%	77%	61%*	44%	52%**	11%	5%*
Italy	16%	17%	60%	50%*	50%	57%**	16%	11%*
Ireland	34%	28%*	61%	52%*	70%	60%*	44%	37%*
Netherlands	5%	7%**	14%	14%	47%	54%**	9%	7%
Norway	9%	6%*	41%	33%*	55%	55%	10%	7%
Sweden	13%	4%*	60%	31%*	58%	57%	25%	4%*
Czech Republic		3%		24%		37%		11%
Slovenia	2%	3%	46%	39%*	33%	46%**	6%	9%**
Poland	14%	15%	60%	61%	58%	62%**	15%	24%**
Bulgaria		28%		60%		46%		11%
Russia	12%	14%**	57%	52%*	35%	30%*	5%	5%
Spain		15%		30%		61%		16%
Latvia		9%		52%		39%		11%
Slovakia		16%		47%		54%		12%
France		5%		32%		35%		6%
Cyprus		17%		57%		51%		7%
Portugal		23%		72%		76%		14%
Denmark		6%		27%		62%		5%
Switzerland		6%		21%		39%		12%
Average	11%	11%	47%	47%	39%	50%	11%	11%

the Vatican's strictures on homosexuals has won very little support even in the traditional Catholic countries.

There has been, however, a statistically significant reaction against extramarital sex in several countries since 1991. In Hungary, Italy, Poland, Slovenia, and the Netherlands opposition to extramarital sex has *increased* in the last seven years, though opposition has significantly decreased in the Irelands, Austria, and Russia. Perhaps the reason for the increase is fear about AIDS, some of it in countries which perhaps were not aware of the dangers—though it certainly does not seem likely that the Dutch have only recently learned about the AIDS problem.[1]

Only 11 percent of the sample (seventh column) are opposed to abortion when there is a chance of a defect to the child. There has been a statistically significant decline in opposition since 1991 in Hungary (11 percent to 5 percent) Italy (16 percent to 7 percent), and Ireland (44 percent to 37 percent). However, there has been an increase in Poland (15 percent to 24 percent) and Slovenia (6 percent to 9 percent) in the last seven years. The Vatican's fight against abortion has turned the tide appreciably only in the Pope's native Poland, and even there, three quarters of the population do not accept that it is always wrong.

Fourteen percent of the Catholics in the sample (table 5.5) believed in 1998 that premarital sex is always wrong, 45 percent that same-sex relations are always wrong, 58 percent that extramarital sex is always wrong, and 16 percent that abortion when there is a risk of a defective child is always wrong. Opposition to same sex relations has fallen among Catholics but there have been statistically significant increases to opposition to premarital and extramarital sex (from 12 percent to 14 percent for the former and 51 percent to 58 percent for the latter).

Muslims have become less tolerant of premarital sex and extramarital sex, the Orthodox have become more opposed to abortion (5 percent to 8 percent). Those with no religious affiliation have increased their opposition to same-sex relationships (66 percent to 76 percent). It must be remembered that the composition of the Orthodox, the Muslims, and even the "nones" has changed between

Table 5.5
Sexual Attitudes by Religion and Year
% Always Wrong

	Pre Marital		Same Sex		Extra Marital		Abortion	
	1991	1998	1991	1998	1991	1998	1991	1998
Protestant	12%	10%*	47%	38%*	57%	57%	12%	9%*
Catholic	12%	14%**	57%	45%*	51%	58%**	17%	16%
Orthodox	18%	19%	60%	57%	43%	44%	5%	8%**
Islamic	20%	41%**	70%	66%	43%	56%**	9%	12%
None	5%	4%	66%	76%*	34%**	36%	5%	5%

the two studies. The Muslims are mostly from Bulgaria and those with no affiliation are more likely to be from Eastern Europe.

The picture of the so-called "sexual revolution" in Europe is therefore more complex than one might have expected. Yet for all the complexity in the findings (opposition to extramarital sex increasing in some countries and opposition to abortion increasing in Poland and Slovenia), there still is a pattern of greater tolerance for premarital sex and same-sex relationships and of more tolerance for abortion.

(One must note here that I write this section of the chapter as a sociologist and make no judgments of the moral right and wrong of the behavior reported.)

Sex and the Churches

It is often argued that, while there may have been as many sexual transgressions in the past as there are now, men and women in the past at least knew they were doing wrong. People today, it is said, have lost all sense of sin. One is permitted to remain skeptical about such an argument. Given the enormous power of the human sexual drive necessary for the preservation and education of the offspring of the species, chastity has never been easy and it still isn't. The churches face a very difficult problem in trying to impose their traditional teaching in the present era. Longer life expectancy and the decline in infant mortality and maternal birth death rates mean that considerably fewer live births are required to sustain populations—2.2 births as opposed to more than seven in years past. Effective contraception techniques are readily available. It is estimated that a woman now spends perhaps four years of her adult life rather than twenty in the bearing and nursing of her children. Hence jobs and careers are available for women.

The churches have been unable to make effective arguments against pre-marital sex in such an environment. Indeed it often seems that they have not tried to persuade their members so much as to impose by fiat the old rules in the new context. Hence, to the extent that church leaders believe that (one of) their principle mission(s) is to regulate the sexual lives of their members, they have failed badly. Most of the laity seem convinced that the church doesn't know what it's talking about when the subject is the ethics of human sexuality. How this "crisis" will resolve itself in years to come remains to be seen. The efforts of Pope John Paul II to reverse the tide among the

Catholic laity have not enjoyed much success according to the International Social Survey Program data.

Has the so-called sexual revolution led to a decline in church membership and attendance? Or is it something else which accounts for the losses observed (which do not seem at this point to be catastrophic)?

In table 5.6 we say an answer to this question by asking how four variables may relate, net of one another, to a person having no religious affiliation or not attending church or having left the church of his childhood—the feeling that the church has too much power, low levels of confidence in the church organization, sexual beliefs, and loss of faith in God.

Many church leaders, among Catholics most notably Cardinal Joseph Ratzinger, president of the Congregation for the Defense of the Faith, have argued, innocent of any data that the present crisis for Catholicism is the result of the "loss of faith." However, table 5.7 shows that for all three of the dependent variable sex and loss of

Table 5.6
Standardized Correlates of Religious Behavior
(beta)

	No Affiliation	Never Attend	Left Church
Church Power	.07	.06	.06
Confidence in Church	.32	.31	.19
Sex Mores	.14	.10	.11
Lost Faith in God	.09	.10	.11

Table 5.7
Standardized Correlates of Religious Behavior
(beta)

	No Affiliation	Never Attend	Left Church
Church Power	.07	.06	.06
Confidence in Church	.32	.31	.19
Sex Mores	.14	.10	.11
Lost Faith in God	.09	.10	.11

Table 5.8
Standardized Correlates for Never Attending Church by Country (beta)

	Church power	Confidence in Church	Sex Mores	Loss of Faith in God
W. Germany	.06	.27*	.02	.21*
E. Germany	.05	.46*	.10	.05
Britain	.11	.18*	.07	.21*
N. Ireland	.03	.16*	.02	.21*
Austria	.07*	.22*	.01	.12*
Hungary	.03	.31*	.01	.08
Italy	.11*	.13*	.05	.20*
Ireland	.06*	.07*	.00	.15
Netherlands	.12	.15*	.05	.15
Norway	.23	.29*	.08*	.00
Sweden	.11*	.08*	.04	.01
Czech Republic	.08	.32*	.03	.08
Slovenia	.03	.21*	.02	.25*
Poland	.07*	.02	.01	.14*
Spain	.04	.26*	.04	.12*
Latvia	.20*	.15*	.02	.09
Slovakia	.01	.25*	.03	.13*
France	.04	.23*	.07	.12
Portugal	.01	.12*	.12*	.03
Switzerland	.03	.11*	.03	.01

*Statistically significant

faith are relatively minor aspects of disengagement from religion, as is the feeling that the church has too much power. The strongest predictor of leaving the church in which one was raised, of never attending services, and of having no affiliation at all is lack of confidence in the church as an organization. Blaming disengagement and disaffiliation on loss of faith is a self serving response. In fact, the leaders of the churches should look to lay dissatisfaction with them and their institutional structures.

When this model is applied to never attending church among the countries, sex mores are a significant predictor only in the Netherlands and Portugal; the church's power in Austria, Italy, Ireland, Sweden, Poland, and Latvia; loss of faith in God in West Germany, Britain, Northern Ireland, Austria, the Czech Republic, Slovenia, Poland, Spain, Latvia, and Slovakia; and lack of confidence in the church organization in every country except Poland.

The churches therefore have some problems with sexual ethics (most people seem to believe that you can reject the sexual teachings and still be a valid member of a denomination and attend church services), loss of faith, and the perceived abuse of power, but their greatest problem lies within themselves or at least with their members' perception of how much confidence the church organization merits.

Conclusions

1. Most Europeans, especially in Eastern Europe, do not have strong feelings of trust for one another.
2. Religion helps to mitigate this distrust in some countries.
3. While Europeans in general accept the cliches about the intolerance of religions, only a minority wants to see religion have less power in their own county.
4. In most countries, toleration for premarital sex is almost universal.
5. In many countries, there has been an increase in sympathy for same-sex relationships, though only about half of the sample were prepared to say in 1998 that such relationships were not always wrong.
6. Disapproval of extramarital sex has increased in several countries.
7. Only in Poland and Ireland do more than a fifth of respondents oppose abortion in the case of a defective child.
8. Neither loss of faith, nor disagreement with sexual teachings are nearly as much of a problem for the churches as is lack of confidence in church leadership.

Summary of First Five Chapters

Some surprising results emerge from this section of the book:

1. In a majority of the countries there is an increase in belief in life after death among the younger age cohorts.

2. There is a remarkable religious revival going on in Eastern Europe with almost as much variety among the various revivals as there is between East and West.

3. With the exception of France, religious culture seems much stronger in Catholic countries than in either Orthodox (with the possible exception of Russia) or Protestant or mixed countries.

4. Three countries clearly fit the secularization model—Britain, the Netherlands, and France.

5. The competition model perhaps applies to Eastern Europe, though the competition is with a Socialism that has either disappeared or been transformed.

6. Neither model fits the Catholic countries, though I would suggest that my own model of the Catholic Imagination may apply.

7. Neither model fits the increase in belief in life after death.

I will now turn to case studies of certain countries to illustrate in detail the phenomena I have listed:

Ireland because it is the most Catholic country in the West and is likely to continue to be.

Russia because it is the site of the largest religious revival in human history.

Other Eastern European countries because they must no longer be excluded from serious discussion about the sociology of religion.

Norway because it is perhaps not as unreligious as it may seem.

Britain and the Netherlands because the secularization model seems to fit here.

Note

1. In one of the sex studies sometimes, the question might be asked it you thought there was nothing wrong in extra marital sex for your spouse. 48% of men think it is not always wrong in the present sample as do 59% of the women.

changes in attitudes is a warning to the church leadership that such attempts are counterproductive. Since this attitude does not correlate with age (save for the decline among the respondents from the oldest cohort) lagging age contrast will not change the pattern of apparent resentment.

Finally, figure 9.8, the increase in the conviction that the church has too much power in Ireland has occurred especially among the younger two cohorts, in both of which disapproval of church power has attracted a large majority. In the other cohorts (except the oldest) at least half disapprove of the power they perceive the church to possess. It would not be an exaggeration to suggest that the leadership of the Irish church may be faced with considerable resentment among its entire population, especially among those born since 1950.

Religious leaders in many countries respond to similar finding by blaming the laity for succumbing to various vaguely defined cultural trends—consumerism, secularism, materialism, capitalism, individualism, pan-sexualism. Such explanations are attractive because of their simplicity: at any rate, they explain all the variance and are not subject to empirical validation. Moreover, they do not require the insti-

6

Russia: The Biggest Revival Ever?

Introduction

Although the Constitution of the Soviet Union guaranteed freedom of worship, there is little question that religion was repressed if not completely suppressed during the years of socialist rule. The forms of repression changed from outright persecution during the Stalin years, to grudging toleration with considerable civil disability during the more recent years. If one wanted to get ahead in Russian society, one either professed atheism and stayed away from churches or kept one's religious propensities a secret. Seminaries were closed, churches turned into museums or centers for atheist propaganda, the clergy rigidly controlled, the bishops appointed by the state. As we shall see in this report, nine out of ten Russians were not raised in the Orthodox Church and three out of four did not believe in God. Never before in human history has there been such a concerted effort to stamp out not merely a religion but all traces of religion. Such a campaign was, of course, consistent with Karl Marx's conviction that religion was, as he said in his lectures on Feuerbach, the opiate of the people. Atheistic communism thought of itself as pushing forward the inevitable process of secularization in which religion would disappear from the face of the earth, a process which, in perhaps a milder form, is an article of faith to many dogmatic social scientists.

What impact does seven decades of state atheism have on a religious tradition? What is there left to be revived when state socialism finally collapses? A few symbolic appearances by Russian Orthodox clergy in their flowing robes? A few babushkas praying in empty churches? An occasional nod by shrewd politicians to the small number of believers that might still be around?

Russia is the most interesting test case of all in which to examine the issue of whether a long period of enforced secularization will either destroy religion or leave it so enfeebled that it has little resiliency once the weight of oppression is lifted. Were the followers of Karl Marx able to crush or at least fatally weaken a millennium-long heritage which dates back to St. Vladimir of Kiev?

The Soviets from the beginning were determined that they must crush the power of the church and exorcise religious faith which they would replace with "scientific" materialism. However, opposition to religion was not high on their agenda. There was considerable debate within the Party, as Husband (2000) shows in his monographic study of the battle between the Party and the church between 1917 and 1932, whether it might be wise to leave religion and church alone until more basic social and economic changes were in place. In fact, the strength of the pressures varied during the years of the New Economic Plan. The Party did close down most churches and monasteries, arrest and imprison many clergy, and confiscate most church property. It also did its best through, agitation, "cultural enlightenment, " and the campaigns of "The League of the Godless" to convert the Russian people to materialism. By its own admission, the Party's efforts in this direction were none too effective. Religious holidays were still celebrated, religious superstitions were still practiced, children were brought to the surviving priests secretly for baptism.

Both the church and the faithful resisted, the latter by demonstrations, protests and occasional violence. The Party controlled the absolute power of the state, but hesitated, for differing reasons at different times, to utterly destroy Orthodoxy, perhaps because it realized that it could not.

Husband summarizes in the situation in 1933 before the worst era of Stalinism began:

> Citizens used combinations of resistance, circumvention, and accommodation throughout early Soviet society. As economic hardship and social transformation converged, individuals and groups practiced at least one such strategy, and any current position could subsequently be renegotiated. Such experiences during the formative years of the revolution left an indelible imprint. They placed a premium on consensus above competence; rewarded acquiescence more than initiative; and fostered rationalization in place of responsibility. The choice between religion and atheism therefore did not result in a clear victory for either side in the conflict. Rather, this conflict stood at the center of-and served a didactic function ininculcating the behavior of the "new Soviet man." In the end, the relationship

between ideals and observed experience gave rise not to a population intensely religious or materialist, but to a predominant ethos of misdirection and dogged self-preservation.

Conflict between state and church, between materialism and faith continued for the next sixty-seven years, ebbing and flowing as the Russian and the international context changed. Stalin reversed his harsh anti-religious policies when the Germans invaded Russia. Nikita Khrushchev, a village atheist on the subject of religion, however "liberal" he might have been on other matters, passed a new battery of anti-religious laws. Under his successors, persecution languished. Husband's model seems a fair summary of the struggle for seventy-three years and three generations. However, by the 1980s it was certainly reasonable to assume that the accommodation of youngest generation of Russians leaned far away from religious faith and towards materialism. Only 10 percent, as I noted above, claimed to have been raised Orthodox and only a quarter believed in God. By sheer dogged persistence, the "Godless, " it would have seemed, had triumphed.

Data for the 1991 International Social Survey Program religious module were collected in Russia (the Russian Federation) in June and July of 1991 just before the abortive Communist coup.[1] Leningrad became St. Petersburg again and God and Orthodoxy were more fashionable. In the 1994 volume of the *Journal for the Scientific Study of Religion,* I reported that data from the 1991 study suggested a resilience of religion in Russia, especially among the cohort born in the 1970s. In this chapter, I will begin with the 1991 results (which were supplemented by additional questions our Russian colleagues asked) and then ask whether, as many predicted at the time, the results were ephemeral or whether they were replicated and confirmed in the 1998 research.

Data were collected by VCIOM, the Russian Center for Public Opinion Research in Moscow, under the direction of Dr. E. Petrenko with a self-completion questionnaire. The sample was limited to Russians sixteen and older who are permanent residents of the Permanent Sampling Units and was administered in the Russian language. Under those constraints it is a two-stage randomized probability sample of the population. The analysis includes 2,964 respondents. This chapter will consist of three parts. In the first Russia will be compared to East Germany, in the second internal comparisons will be made among various Russian groups, in the third Russia in 1998 will be compared with Russia in 1991.

Russia and East Germany

Despite seventy years of socialism God seems to be alive and well and living in all Russia in 1991 and not just Moscow (though a little more in perhaps in Moscow than in the Far East as we shall see subsequently). Between a half and three-quarters of Russians believed in God, depending on how the question is worded (table 6.1). Two out of five Russians believe in life after death, half of them believe that God is personally concerned with each human. Approximately a third believe in heaven and hell, more than a quarter report that they personally feel very close to God and two out of five believe in religious miracles. On all these items, Russians not only score higher than East Germans at levels of statistical significance (except in the matter of belief in miracles[2]), but the differences are considerable—more than twice as likely for example to believe in both a caring God and in life after death.

Table 6.1
Religious Beliefs in Russia and East Germany in 1991

	East Germany	Russia
God 1[1]	29%	47%*
God 2[2]	39%	74%*
Life After Death	14%	40%*
God Cares[3]	21%	48%*
Heaven	20%	33%*
Hell	7%	30%*
Close to God	16%	28%*
Miracles	40%	40%*
N=	1486	2964

1Response to question in Table 2
2Response to question about how close you are to God which does not choose "do not believe in God."
3There is a God who concerns himself with every human being personally.

Nor is the religious faith in Russia something confined to older Russians. The "U" curve relationship between belief in life after death and age is striking in Russia.[3] As in the other countries, the curve is statistically significant; in logistic regression analysis the bottom of the "U" is significantly lower than either of the top points. Moreover, the "U" curve flattens when belief in a personal and caring

God is taken into account. The older and the younger are more likely to believe in life after death because they are more likely to believe in a God who personally cares about each human.

On two measures which enabled us in the early nineties to simulate time-series analysis there is religious growth in Russia and religious decline in East German (as of 1991). Only 5 percent of respondents in the latter country (table 6.2) say that they did not used to believe in God but now do while in Russia 22 percent have become believers. In East Germany a quarter of the population are former theists who have become atheists while in Russia only 3 percent fall into that category. Thus theists have suffered a twenty percentage point loss in East Germany while they have gained a nine percentage point increase in Russia. Approximately a third of those who were once atheists (by their own admissions) have become theists.

Table 6.2
Attitudes Towards the Existence of God in 1991

	East Germany	Russia
Never Believed	51%	50%
Believed, but Don't	25%	3%*
Don't but Do Now	5%	22%*
Always	20%	25%

It should be observed that this is a personal religious report on the part of each Russian respondent and not merely a global shift in proportions The Russian respondent admits (perhaps the word "claims" should be used) that s/he used to be an atheist and is one no longer. No claim seems inherent in the wording of the question that the respondent pretended to be an atheist but was in fact a secret believer.

Moreover (table 6.3) only 11 percent of the Russian respondents said that their religion was Orthodoxy when they were growing up but two and a half times that many (28 percent) claimed Orthodox affiliations in 1991. One out of six Russians (17 percent) are "converts" to the religion of their heritage. These numbers and those showing the emergence of New Believers (as I will call the atheists turned theist) would seem at least at first glance to demonstrate, after the most serious attempt to obliterate religion in human history, the most dramatic religious revival in human history. Perhaps St. Vladimir

Table 6.3
Religious Practice in Russia and East Germany

	East Germany	Russia
Pray Ever	30%*	25%
Pray Daily	4%	10%*
Attend Ever Now	40%*	32%
Attend Monthly	7%	8%
Attended Young	63%*	27%
Affiliation Now	29%	28%
Affiliation Young	48%	11%
Religious Experience	17%	14%

may have triumphed over Karl Marx after all. In East Germany, however, affiliation with the Evangelical Church has decreased by nineteen percentage points—from 48 percent to 29 percent

In 1991 thirty percent of the East Germans prayed as do a quarter of the Russians, but one out of ten Russians pray every day compared to 4 percent of the East Germans. Two out of five East Germans attend church services and one out of three Russians, 7 percent of the former go at least once a month, as opposed to 8 percent of the latter. But the Russian 8 percent who attend regularly must be compared with the 27 percent who attended at all when they were young and the East German 7 percent with the 63 percent who attended when they were young. By those standards Russian church attendance seems to represent a dynamism which is going up and the East German one that is going down.

Despite their apparent increase in religious faith (and perhaps as a cause of it) Russians are much more likely to be pessimistic than East Germans (table 6.4). 31 percent of the former and only 18 percent of the latter agree that people can do little to change life. Moreover three quarters of the Russians as opposed to only 4 percent of the East Germans believe that life does not serve any useful purpose. The Russians are almost four times as likely to believe that their life is pre-determined (even if they say it is in part determined by themselves) and less likely to believe that one can impose one's own meaning on life. Slavic fatalism seems more than just a stereotype in the data in table 6.4, though whether the fatalism at this time in history is the result of seventy years of horrendous misrule or an

Table 6.4
Attitudes Towards Life in Russia and East Germany in 1991

	East Germany	Russia
Fatalism[1]	18%	31%*
Nihilism[2]	4%	74%*
Predetermination[3]	14%	29%*
Determine Own Fate (Strongly)[4]	26%	37%*
God Gives Meaning[5]	11%	14%
Give Own Meaning (Strongly Agree)	46%	34%

[1]People can do little to change life
[2]Life does not serve any useful purpose
[3]There is little people can do to change the course of their lives
[4]Life is only meaningful if you provide the meaning itself
[5]The course of our Life is decided by God

Table 6.5
Attitudes Towards Religion and Politics in Russia and Germany In 1991

	East Germany	Russia
Support School Prayer	13%	67%*
Ban Anti-Religious Books	41%	75%*
Church has Too Much Power	34%	7%*
Great Deal of Confidence in Church	21%	75%*
Church Should Not Interfere in Vote	77%	55%*
Church should Stay Out of Politics	70%	43%*
Atheists unfit for Public Office	4%	16%*
Believers Should Hold Public Office	11%	25%*

older and deeper cultural propensity remains to be seen. Perhaps both forces are at work.

While they may not be found inside an Orthodox church building all that often, Russians in 1991 had highly favorable views of Orthodoxy (table 6.5). Two-thirds of them supported prayer in public schools and three quarters wanted to ban anti-religious books. The average in favor of such bans in all ISSP countries was 45 percent, the proportion in Poland is the same as in Russia, In the United States and in Britain the proportion is approximately one out of three. Perhaps feelings are intense on the subject in Russia because of all the anti-religious propaganda of the last seven decades.

Moreover in 1991 three quarters of the Russians had at least a "great deal" of confidence in organized religion and only 7 percent thought it had too much power—as opposed to 21 percent and 34 percent on these two issues in East Germany. In confidence in the church Russians were tied with their Polish neighbors and ahead of the rest of the world by a substantial margin—Ireland was in third place with 46 percent. The American rate was 40 percent.

Moreover the Russian rate of 7 percent who think that the church has too much power was the lowest in the world. In Poland (where there is obviously some ambivalence) the rate was 37 percent, in Ireland 40 percent, in the U.S. 23 percent, and in Hungary—the second lowest—14 percent. Finally Russians were less likely to object to church leaders interfering in the political processes and more likely to reject atheists for public office (16 percent versus 4 percent in East Germany). A quarter of Russians believed it would be good for the country if people with strong religious belief held public office. Whether these convictions are a result of a sense of relief over the freeing of religion in Russia or an older and more profound tradition of a closer alliance between church and state than that with which most Americans would feel comfortable remains to be seen. Nonetheless it is a fair summary that of all the peoples in the ISSP, Russians seemed in 1991 the least anti-clerical.[4]

In their sexual attitudes (table 6.6) Russians were tolerant of premarital and extramarital sex, less tolerant of East Germans of the former and more tolerant of the later. They were strongly opposed to homosexual sex—68 percent only somewhat lower than the 75 percent rate in the United States. East Germans, on the other hand, are

Table 6.6
Sexual Attitudes in Russia and East Germany in 1991
% Always Wrong

	East Germany	Russia
Premarital Sex	3%	13%*
Extramarital Sex	47%	38%*
Homosexual Sex	38%	64%*
Abort – Defect	15%*	10%
Abort – Poor	29%*	12%

the second most tolerant of homosexual sex after the Netherlands (16 percent). The Russians are also less likely to condemn abortion than even the East Germans.

It might be said that while socialism did not destroy the Russian religious heritage it may have broken the link between religion and sexual morality. Or the link might have not been as strong in the East as in the West. Or the link might have declined in Russia with modernization even without socialism.

Can one account for the post-Socialism religious revival in Russia as compared with the non-revival or even decline in East Germany? One might not unreasonably speculate that the Orthodox religious culture in Russia was much stronger than the Evangelical (Lutheran) religious culture in Germany. Is it possible to sort out some elements in that culture which might provide a tentative explanation for the differences? Russians are as likely to believe in a God who cares about individual persons as they are to believe in God. In effect, it seems that in Russia there is little difference between a theist and a believer in a personally involved God. Moreover, might it be the strong Russian propensity towards fatalism which, in turn, accounts for the greater need for and belief in a personally concerned God who may, in the end, take care of the troubles which cause fatalism?

Can this model explain why there are so many New Believers and Converts in Russia in comparison with East Germany and why Russians are more likely to believe in life after death?

The regression equations summarized in table 6.7 suggest that such might be the case. Belief in a personal God (combined with the stronger effect for Russians that this belief has on the dependent variables) reduces to statistical insignificance the Russian "advan-

Table 6.7
Models to Explain Differences Between Russia and East Germany in 1991

	Life After Death	New Believer	Convert	God Cares
Simple Correlation	.31	.24	.25	.24
β with God cares (Fatalism)	.17	.08	.13	.16
β with God cares and interaction	.00*	.00*	.00*	.01*

*Not Significant

tage" in these three variables. Moreover a regression equation which takes into account Russian fatalism (in the fourth column) also accounts for their greater belief in a personal God. Hence because they are more fatalistic, Russians are more likely to believe in (require) a personal God and hence are more likely to believe in life after death and to become New Believers and Converts when they get a chance to.

Such an analysis is obviously highly schematic and surely oversimplifies a complex and fascinating problem. Moreover, one could easily rearrange the three variables in the equations in table 6.7 and suggest that it is conversion or new belief which generates both the notion of a personal deity and in turn a higher degree of fatalism. All I propose to suggest with confidence (and cautious confidence at that) is that these are traits of traditional Russian religious culture which seemed to have survived socialism and to have survived them in vigorous health. Russia has not become a profoundly religious society yet. It is, however, a society which was going through in 1991 religious change which in its own way is as dramatic as the political and economic changes.

Thus to the summary question of whether God survived atheism in Russia, the answer must be that She did and is experiencing a wave of popularity seldom seen in the modern world. Moreover, the Orthodox Church is also flourishing, having more than doubled its adherents and apparently enjoying more popularity than any religious institution in the ISSP countries. God is not only alive and well in Moscow, but He might be found, it would seem, even in the churches.

Now one must turn to the question of who the Converts and the New Believers in Russia are and what impact might they be having on Russian society. Are they elderly people returning to a past about which their parents taught them? And are they likely to have a negative impact on the efforts of those who are trying to build a democratic Russia?

Change in Russia

The change from atheism to theism of about a fifth of all Russians (a third of those who were once atheists) reported in the last section is especially likely to happen among younger Russians. The proportion who always believed has declined with age, but this effect has been canceled out by the increase of the switchers among the younger generation so that all age groups under sixty-five are equally likely to believe in God.

When, one might wonder, has the change occurred. In 1991 some 30 percent of Russians under twenty five, 25 percent of those between those between twenty-five and thirty-four, and 20 percent of those between thirty-five and forty-four, reported that they have switched from atheism to theism. For those under twenty-five the change must have been rather recent, within perhaps the last five years. Did it occur at the same time among the older Russians? Was there a period of time before 1991 when a massive number of Russians, who had not previously believed in God, decided that they now believed in God?

It would not be a difficult question to research. One could merely add to the "change" question, a question about how long ago it happened.

The pattern is somewhat different for the conversion to the Orthodox Church. The change has been greater among those over forty-five and in that respect builds on an already existing base of Orthodox affiliations with the result that identification with Orthodoxy correlates positively with age, from a high of over sixty to a low of a little more than a fifth for those under twenty-five. Nonetheless Orthodox converts under thirty-five are twice as numerous as "cradle" Orthodox. For those under twenty-five the conversion must have been rather recent.

Was there a time, one must wonder again, during the middle years of the Gorbachev era when large numbers of Russians rediscovered religion, or their religious heritage, or God and invited Her back to Moscow and everywhere else?

The result in 1991 was a Russia in which atheists and theists were both approximately half the population and Orthodox affiliates a third of the population. From the point of view of the sociology of religion and in particularly of the sociology of "de-secularization" it would be enormously important to know the "when" of the Big Change, and its "why."

Is this remarkable religious growth, recorded in 1991, limited to certain demographic segments (besides age and gender) of the population or is it relatively invariant?

Some Russian regions were more likely than others to register such change. The average in the whole country for New Believers is 30 percent. In the North Central region it is 37 percent, in the Urals

36 percent and in Moscow 28 percent while in the Far East and Kamerovo it is 15 percent.

There were also correlations, though not very large, with occupation, education, and party affiliation (table 6.8). Managerial and professional workers and skilled workers (perhaps social classes which have more of a vested interest in the socialist regime) are less likely than white-collar workers, unskilled workers, and those not in the labor force to be New Believers. A similar pattern holds for conversion to Orthodoxy except that there is a change among the skilled and unskilled workers with the latter being less likely than the former to affiliate with the church, perhaps because of a feeling that they might not be at home there. Those with a tertiary education are less likely to become New Believers as are those with a secondary and a tertiary education to become converts. Finally voters who lean towards the various communist parties are less likely than those who opt for the opposition parties to change from atheism to theism while no such difference seems to affect conversion to Orthodoxy. Both communists and non-communists are equally likely to have switched from non-affiliation to affiliation.

Table 6.8
New Believers[1] and Converts[2] by Occupation, Education and Party Affiliation[3]

	New Believers	Converts
All	30%	31%
Managerial, Professional	24%	20%
White Collar	42%	30%
Skilled Workers	25%	30%
Unskilled Workers	35%	21%
Not Working	34%	37%
Primary	35%	37%
Secondary	33%	26%
Tertiary	26%	23%
Communist Parties	23%	28%
Opposition Parties	34%	27%
Will Not Vote	26%	28%
Don't Know or No Answer	30%	29%

[1]Proportion of all those who did not used to believe in God.
[2] Proportion of those who did not used to be Orthodox
[3]If the next election was held on a multiparty basis which party would you vote for?

Thus, the structural variables of education, occupation, region, and political affiliation have at best only a modest impact on the Russian religious revival.

Both the Believers and Converts are more likely to come from backgrounds where they attended church as a child (table 6.9) and to have Orthodox spouses. They are also notably more likely to have had religious experiences as part of their conversion process. What kind of religious experience, one wonders, and when and where?

Table 6.9
Attitudes Towards Church and State in Russia by Religious Orientation in 1991

	New Believers	Atheists	Converts	Not Orthodox
Church has too much Power	5%	10%	4%	8%
Atheists Unfit for Public Office	23%	7%	6%	15%
Religious leaders should not influence government	38%	50%	38%	45%
Ban Anti Religious Books	80%	68%	83%	72%
Confidence in Church	87%	58%	92%	67%

Since women are more likely to be involved in the change, does the religious affiliation of their spouse have more of an impact on them than does a wife's religion on her husband's affiliation. In terms of raw percentage points, women who are married to Orthodox husbands are forty percentage points more likely to be Believers themselves than are women with spouses who are not Orthodox (though such a phenomenon could be the result of selected recruiting of husbands or negotiations at the time of marriage). Men in a similar situation are only fifteen percentage points more likely to believe in God than men not married to an Orthodox spouse. The differences in affiliation with Orthodoxy seem to follow a similar general pattern.

However, since women are far more likely to be both New Believers and Converts, the proportionate increase which comes to women from having an Orthodox husband was approximately the same in 1991 as the proportionate increase for men from having an Orthodox wife.

The issue, then, becomes why women are more likely to be involved in religious change in Russia than men. To that issue I will turn shortly.

The U-curve with age for New Belief persists regardless of party affiliation or education. (While those with communist voting sympathies and those with tertiary education are somewhat less likely to have changed from atheism to theism, between thirty and forty percent of the younger members of both groups are in the ranks of the changers. Thus there can be no reasonable expectation that education or party politics will affect (at least in the short run), much less diminish, the religious revival in Russia.

Can a model similar to that which accounted for the religious differences between Russia and East Germany also explain, at least to some extent, religious change in Russia. Does the notion that God is concerned personally with each individual and perhaps a religious experience of that God provide a useful explanatory model, especially when family religious situations and sex are taken into account?

The data in table 6.10 suggest that this might be the case. For each of the dependent variables—New Belief, conversion, and belief in life after death—the "Caring God" variable is a very powerful predictor. A religious experience adds some explanatory power to all three models; and for conversion religious background also provides additional explanation. Gender does not add significant predictive power to the three models, suggesting that women are more likely to believe in this caring God and that fact accounts for their greater religious faith. (The correlation for gender with belief in a God who cares is .27.) Such, indeed, is the case: significant correlations between gender and the three variables are eliminated when women's greater belief in a caring God and an interaction between gender and this belief are taken into account.

Table 6.10
Confidence in Institutions in the United States and Russia in 1991

	United States	Russia
Parliament	25%	26%
Civil Service	18%	17%
Courts	27%	24%
Schools	39%	39%
Churches	39%	75%

At the center of the Russian religious revival observed in 1991 lurked the image of a God who cares, doubtless an old image in Russian culture and one which, for whatever reasons, seems to have been rediscovered. Arguably God was alive and well in Moscow (and elsewhere) because She never left.

That fact may raise certain problems and perhaps certain fears about the impact of resurgent religion on the Russian society, polity, and economy. Might it portend an outburst of extreme nationalism, Pan-Slavism, anti-Semitism, and imperialism as a reborn "Holy Russia" resumes its messianic fervor and seeks once more to dominate the Eurasian landmass with its powerful heritages and traditions?

One would have to be blind to history to deny that such strains have been characteristic of Russian religion in the past—though they are by no means the only or even the most important strains in that religion. Faith and affiliation have yet to generate high levels of religious devotion (or they had not done so in the spring of 1991). While God has survived underground in Moscow for seventy years, it does not follow inevitably that She will be seen with quite the same face that she appeared to display in other centuries of Russian history. Perhaps at the present one would have to say that it is too early to know what mixture of the benign and malign may emerge from the reappearance of God in Russia. There is however solid reason for studying its developments carefully.

In fact, one can see in table 6.9 that while there are differences among the four groups, the general similarities are striking. Only small fractions of the atheists and the non Orthodox seemed to fear the church has too much power and majorities of both have high levels of confidence in its leadership. (Seven out of ten Communist-leaning voters expressed a great deal of confidence in the church and only thirteen percent thought it had too much power). Thus Russians who are perhaps closer to the problem than the rest of us are not yet were not worried about the church in the spring of 1991.

Table 6.11
Life After Death, New Believers, and Converts by Religious Background in 1991

	New Believer	Convert
Spouse Orthodox	41%	58%
Spouse Not Orthodox	25%	20%
Attended as Child	47%	50%
Did not Attend as Child	27%	20%
Religious Experience	93%	66%
No Religious Experience	22%	23%

Three-fourths of the New Believers did not think atheists should be banned from public office while half of the atheists do not object to religious leaders trying to influence the government—and 68 percent of the atheists want to ban anti-religious books!

Supplementary questions included by our Russian colleagues confirmed that the young Russians who had converted from atheism to theism and from no affiliation to Orthodoxy intended to raise their children in religion and believed that religion was essential to hold family life together. Other findings from these questions refute the notion that the sudden flowering of religion in Russia is ephemeral. Thus when asked to account for the change in religious belief – which to our Russian colleagues seemed obvious even in 1991 – only 15 percent of all Russians and 18 percent of Russian atheists claimed that there had been no change; 29 percent and 24 percent respectively that the believers had been hiding, and 24 percent and 30 percent, thought that the change was just a fashion. However, two out of the five of the new theists argued that there had, in fact, been a change. If those who think that the new religion in Russia was a fashion are a good indicator of skepticism about its future, then only a quarter of Russians are skeptical (table 6.12).

Table 6.12
Regression Models to Explain Belief in Life After Death, New Believers, and Converts in Russia 1991

	Convert	New Believer	Life After Death
Caring God β	.55	.55	.48
Attended as Child	.13		
Spouse Orthodox	.13		
Religious Experience	.14	.30	.09
R=	.60	.70	.52
R^2=	.36	.49	.27

A mere 14 percent of all Russians and 19 percent of the atheists write off the religious revival as superstition and deceit while more than half of all three groups think, quite correctly, that religion is people's representation of God and the world around them (table 6.13). The most important roles Russians see in religion (table 6.15) morality, peace, charity, culture, helping the poor, spiritual needs are goals which one suspects young American urban professionals would also endorse, though they may perhaps not be rationaliza-

Table 6.13
Explanation of Religious Feelings of Others[1]

	All	New Theists	Atheists
No Change	15%	6%	18%
Were Hiding	29%	40%	24%
More Belief	23%	38%	16%
Fashion	24%	9%	30%
Other	8%	10%	5%

[1]"According to the results of surveys, in recent years more people are calling themselves religious. What can you say about the religious feelings of people around you?"

Table 6.14
Opinions about the Nature of Religion[2]

	All	New Theists	Atheists
God opens Self	12%	23%	7%
People's representations of God and the World Around	56%	58%	51%
Superstitions	9%	1%	12%
Deceit	5%	0%	7%
Other	2%	2%	2%

[2]"What is religion to your mind?"

Table 6.15
Roles of Religion[3]

	All	New Theists	Atheists
Not Interfere with public life	11%	3%	15%
Public Morals	48%	57%	45%
Support Peace	28%	29%	28%
Satisfy Spiritual Needs	38%	47%	34%
Preserve Cultural Traditions	39%	41%	37%
Charities	37%	41%	35%
Help Poor	28%	32%	26%
Spiritual Literature and Art	11%	14%	11%

[3]"What role to your mind should the religious organizations play in public life?"

tions for religion that would have been available in 1910. The question, however, of the roles of religion would hardly have arisen in 1910. Finally (table 6.15) both the New Theists and the Converts agreed in 1991 that meaning and tolerance are the most important functions of religion.

The responses in these last four tables suggest a good deal more sophistication about the religious change in Russia, even in 1991, then outsiders might have been prepared to expect, especially those who think that the Russian revival is a flash in the pan.

It may take many years before the thinkers and the leaders, the poets and theologians, the prophets and storytellers of Russian religion evolve a design for what that religion should look like in the twenty-first century. If they do not learn from the experience of the Catholic Church across their western frontier that (a) the laity are no longer ignorant and docile peasants; (b) it is necessary to pay attention to that laity; and (c) the "good old days" cannot be recreated, they may find that, while the churches are full (or fuller than they were during the socialist years), no one is listening to what they say.

A powerful religious revival seemed to be underway in Russia in the months before the traditional Russian flag replaced the hammer and sickle above the White House. A fifth of the Russian people had moved from atheism to theism and form non-affiliation to Orthodoxy. This change was particularly strong among the young and (relatively) men—though women were still far more religious than men. Much of the change, including an increase in belief in life after death, follows a U-curve pattern with the younger being more like their grandparents than their parents. The change seemed to emerge from a complex mixture of fatalism, religious experience, and a belief in a God who was concerned about individualism. It may also have emerged as recently as the late 1980s. It is too early to say how this remarkable development, unlike anything we know in human history, will play itself out. However, it is not to early to say that anti-religious socialism failed completely to crush out the Russian religious heritage—as it failed in most of its other efforts. The Liturgy is being celebrated again in the Cathedral of the Dormition in the Kremlin and the new Church of the Savior. St. Vladimir has routed Karl Marx.

1998: The Revival Revisited

The 1991 findings encountered some hostility in the profession. How could religion have survived seventy-five years of socialism?

The results made a rapid progress from what everyone knew couldn't be true to what everyone had known all along. The hostility turned from denial of the facts to predictions that the trends reported in the JSSR article would not continue. One scholar even dismissed the findings on the grounds that younger Russians were professing Orthodox affiliation merely so they could have weddings in church – even though the younger converts to Orthodoxy insisted in a supplementary questionnaire that they intended to raise their children in religion. The 1998 study provided an opportunity to determine whether there are any signs of erosion of the religious "revival" in Russia.

In fact, the revival is continuing and spreading upward from the youngest birth cohort to more senior cohorts. Thus in table 6.18 we see that there are significant positive relationships with time for all but two of the variables in the battery. The exceptions are a sharp decrease in confidence[5] in religious leaders (from 74 percent to 30 percent) [6] and a non-significant increase in belief in life after death. Belief in God, Orthodox affiliation, prayer, attendance at worship (Divine Liturgy to the Russians), religious conversion, feeling religious, "turning point" experiences, and the conviction that God cares about humans have all increased significantly. A recent survey by ROMIR reports the same proportion of belief in life after death.

An ISSP question about belief in God provides respondents with four possible answers—I always believed in God, I never believed in God, I used to believe in God but no longer believe in God, I did

Table 6.16
Roles of Religion[1]

	All	New Theists	Atheists
Not Interfere with public life	11%	3%	15%
Public Morals	48%	57%	45%
Support Peace	28%	29%	28%
Satisfy Spiritual Needs	38%	47%	34%
Preserve Cultural Traditions	39%	41%	37%
Charities	37%	41%	35%
Help Poor	28%	32%	26%
Spiritual Literature and Art	11%	14%	11%

[1]"What role to your mind should the religious organizations play in public life?"

not use to believe in God but I do know. The first row in table 6.18 shows that only a quarter of the Russian population has always believed in God while in 1991 twenty percent say that they didn't use to believe in God but do now for a total of 45 percent who believe in God . By 1998 this proportion has increased to 60 percent, a remarkably rapid change in belief. Moreover, in a parallel change only 10 percent were raised Orthodox, 30 percent identified as Orthodox in 1991 and 58 percent in 1968. Whatever final explanation may be adduced for these dramatic changes, on their face they would appear to represent one of the most dramatic revivals of religion in human history. The church and religion had outlasted the party.

Table 6.17 shows that belief in life after death in Russia has surpassed that in Norway and the Netherlands and West Germany and is close behind that in Britain. In a remarkably brief period of time Russia has become one of the most God-believing countries in Europe.

Figure 6.1 and figure 6.2 illustrate the dynamics of the increase. In 1991, the younger birth cohorts were more likely to believe in God and be converts to this belief than the middle aged cohorts. However, by 1998 the cohorts born in the forties and fifties had caught up with them.

In figures 6.3 and 6.4 we note deviations from this pattern. As in the 1991 study the younger cohorts are more likely to believe in life after death than any of the other cohorts. This pattern persists – the

Table 6.17
Importance of Religion[1]

	New Theists	Converts
Completely Necessary	9%	21%
Meaning	64%	55%
Makes Me Tolerant	44%	45%
Care for Poor	13%	12%
Religious Literature	12%	18%
Moral Purification	12%	18%
Success	4%	12%

[1]"What importances does religion have for you personally?"

Table 6.18
Religion in Russia[1] 1991-1998

	Past	1991	1998
Belief in God	25%[2]	45%	60%
Belief in Life After Death		38%	40%*
Orthodox Affiliation	10%[3]	30%	58%
Weekly Prayer		13%	21%
Monthly Worship		4%	9%
Yearly Worship		29%	44%
Confidence in Church Leaders		74%	38%
Atheists become Theists[4]		30%	40%
Feel "Religious"		4%	23%
God cares about Humans		20%	31%
N=	2964		1703

*Not statistically significant
[1] Russian Federation
[2] Always believed in God
[3] Orthodox at 16.
[4] % of those who didn't use to believe in God who now do

Table 6.19
Belief in God in Selected Countries

	% Believe in God
Great Britain	68%
Russia	60%
West Germany	58%
Norway	58%
Netherlands	54%

Figure 6.1
Belief in God in Russia by Cohort and Year

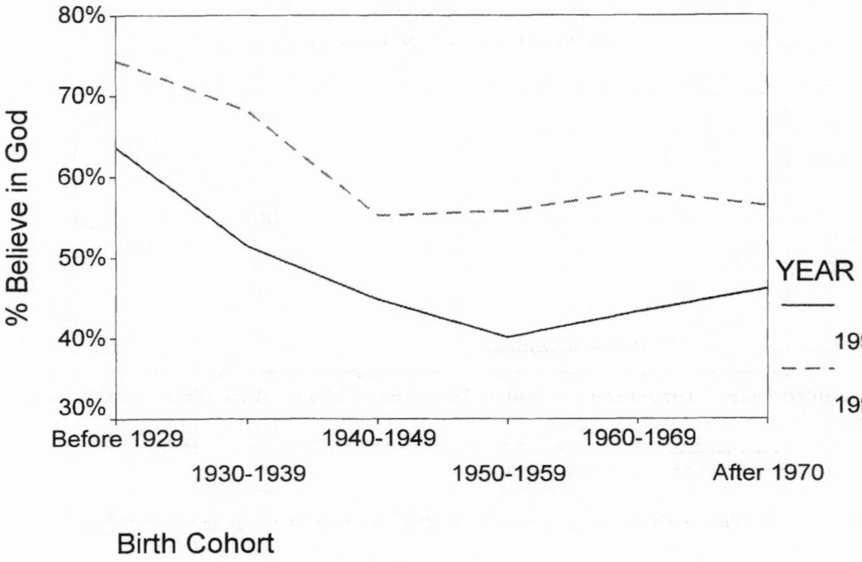

Figure 6.2
Converts to Belief in God by Cohort and Year

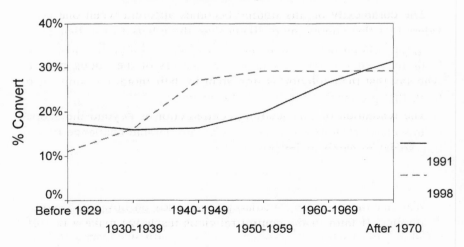

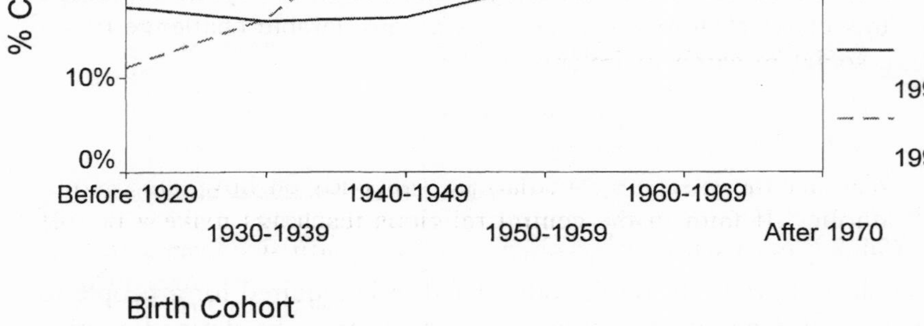

Base= All Russians

Figure 6.3
Belief in Life After Death by Cohort and Year

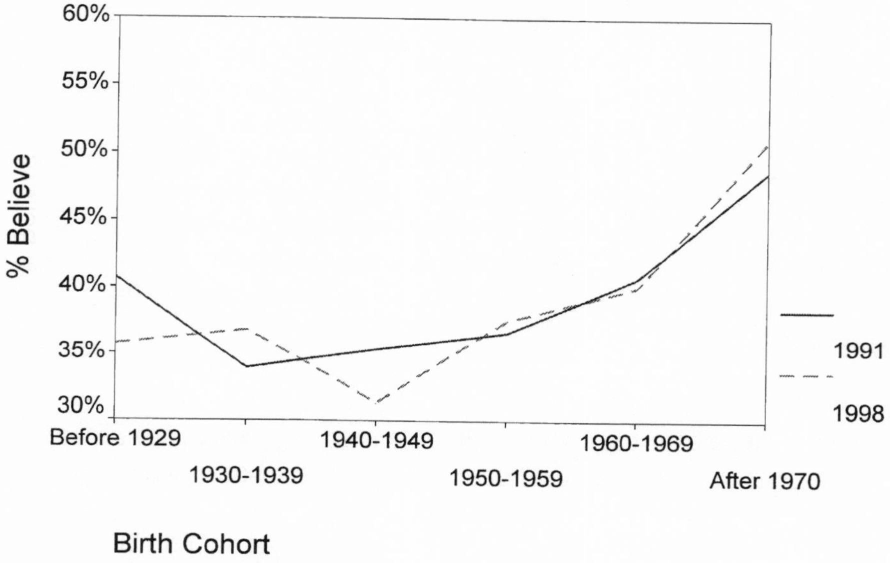

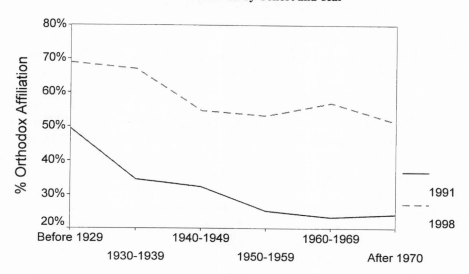

Figure 6.4
Orthodox Affiliation by Cohort and Year

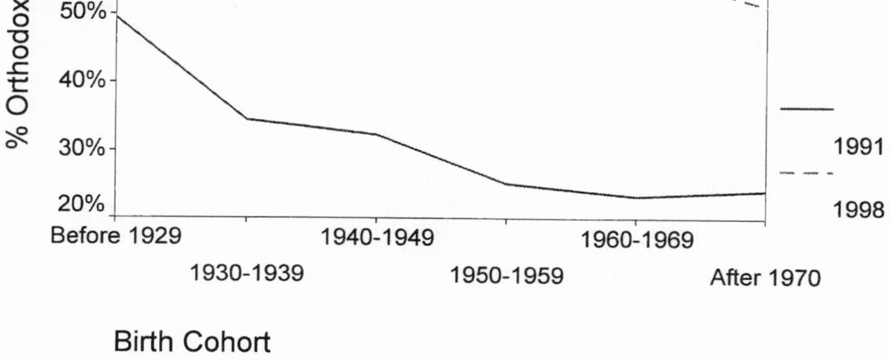

Figure 6.5
Weekly Prayer by Cohort and Year

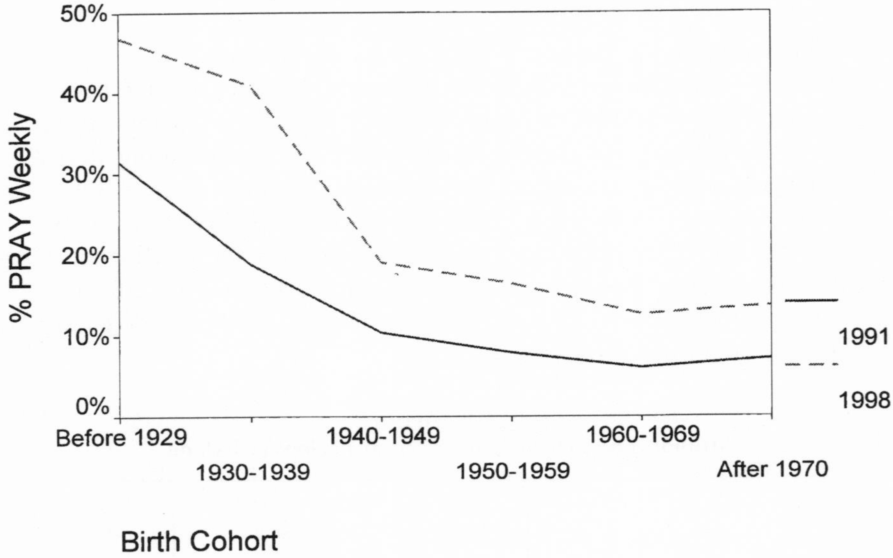

confidence in human survival has not eroded with time among the cohorts born in the nineteen sixties and the nineteen seventies, but it has not spread upward. On the other hand Orthodox affiliation has increased by at least twenty percentage points in every birth cohort.

Weekly prayer has also increased (figure 6.5), especially among the cohorts born before 1940. The increase in participation in the Divine Liturgy has wiped out the U curve which existed in 1991 with a "ballooning" of attendance in all cohorts (figures 6.6 and 6.7). Russians are hardly dashing off to church every week but almost half of them are attending some of the time, presumably at Easter and Christmas.

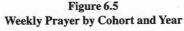

In Cyprus, a predominantly Orthodox country which was never socialist more than 90 percent of the people believe in God—the highest of any European nation in the 1998 International Social Survey Program survey. However, only half of the Cypriots attend Liturgy at least several times a month. It would seem therefore that the link between religious faith and church attendance may be weaker among the Orthodox than among Western Christians. Indeed it was only at the Fourth Council of the Lateran (1215) that weekly attendance was made mandatory in the west and the mandate, according to some historians, was only hortatory and did not bind under pain of serious sin.

The same "ballooning" effect is displayed dramatically in figure 6. 6 which shows the proportion of those who were once atheists who say that they are now theists. Perhaps the religious revival in Russia is merely the reemergence of religion in a country with a long religious tradition. However, figure 6.6 would seem to suggest something else. Men and women have actually gone through a self-perceived religious change experience in virtually all age cohorts. Such a finding suggests that there has been not merely greater ease in admitting religious but an actual change in religious belief, a revival not a reemergence. Probably both phenomena are occurring.

Such a possibility is confirmed by figure 6.7 which shows that in all birth cohorts there is a doubling of the proportion claiming a religious turning point experience. If one enters this variable into a regression equation with conversion from atheism to theism, one can explain the entire increase in conversion from atheism to theism. About a fifth of the Russian people have had this "turning point" experience and it seems to account for the increase in theism in the country. One would dearly love to know more about this experience.

Figure 6.6
Divine Liturgy Monthly by Cohort and Year

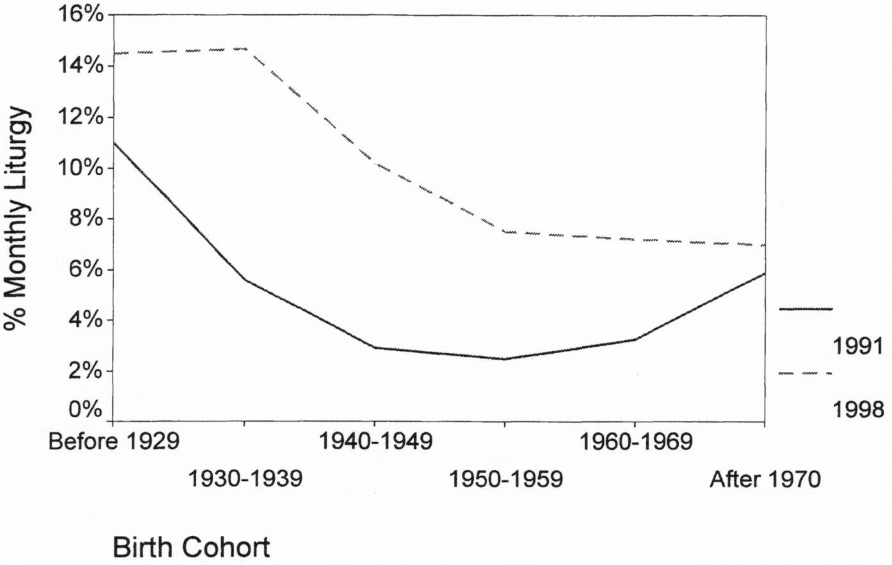

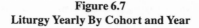

Figure 6.7
Liturgy Yearly By Cohort and Year

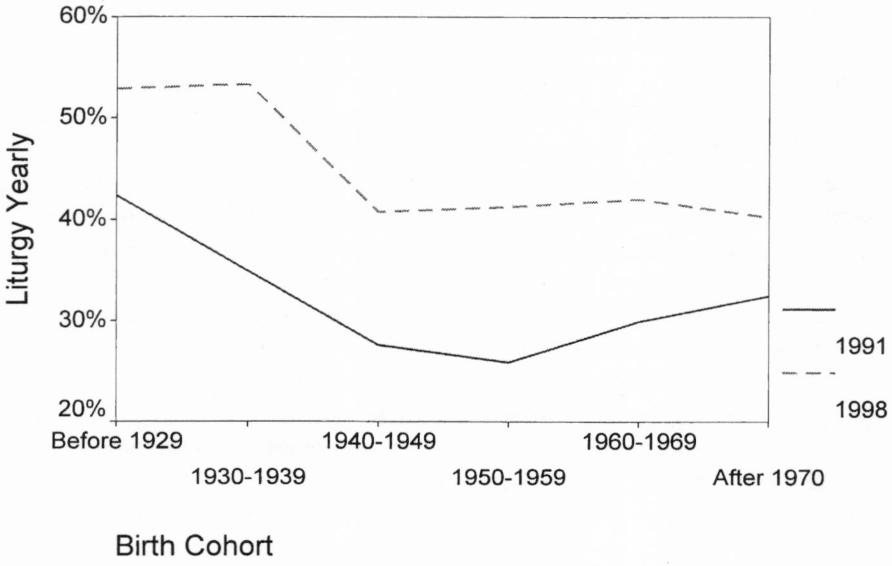

There are also sharp increases in every birth cohort in the proportion reporting that they feel religious (figure 6.8) and that they believe that God cares about humans (figure 6.9), perhaps a surprising finding given the traumas and the chaos of contemporary Russian life. Figure 6.12 illustrates the increase in the HOPE factor (miracles, life after death, heaven) for Russia. It is interesting to note that the nadir of Russian religious hopefulness is among those born during and immediately after the war and who came of age in the nineteen sixties. HOPE increased in each subsequent birth cohort. Indeed, the increase in HOPE can be accounted for in Russia by an increase in the belief that God is personally concerned about each of us as figure 6.13 demonstrates.

Among the criticisms of my earlier work on Russia was the contention that religion in Russia was a cultural phenomena. Religion, pace Clifford Geertz, is indeed a cultural system. When forces which have repressed a cultural system with millennium-long roots in a society are removed that system will tend to flourish again, first among the young and then among everyone. Seventy-five years of generally incompetent socialism was no match for almost a thousand years of art, mysticism, liturgy, monasticism, and the other

Figure 6.8
Conversion From Atheism to Theism by Cohort and Year

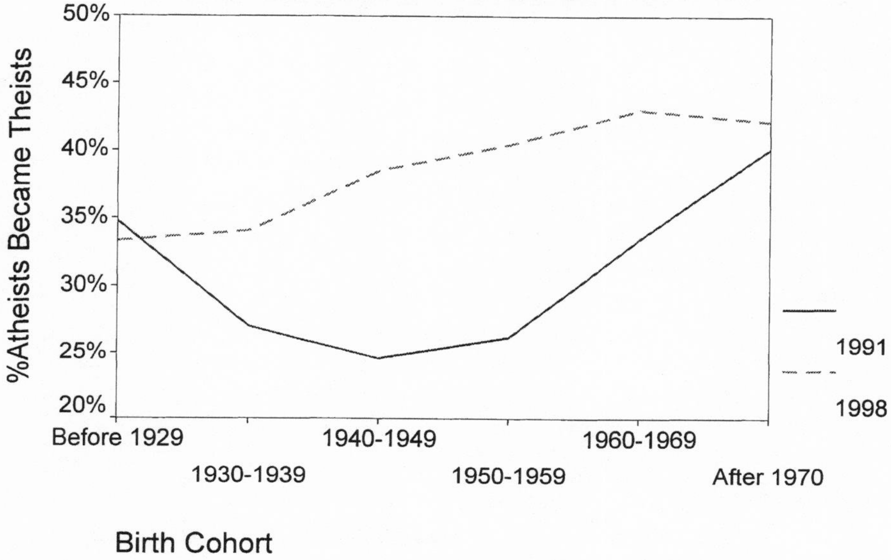

Figure 6.9
Religious Turning Point Experience by Age and Cohort

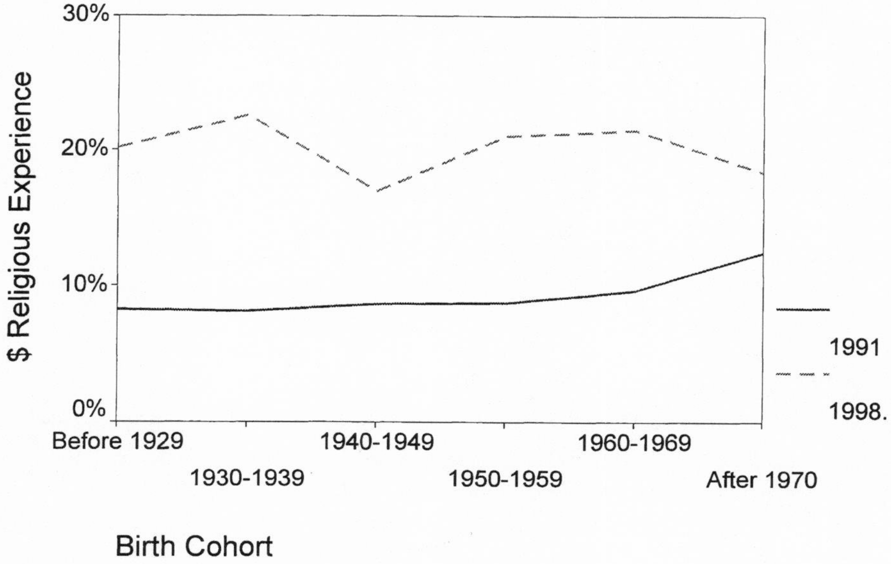

Figure 6.10
Feel Religious by Cohort and Year

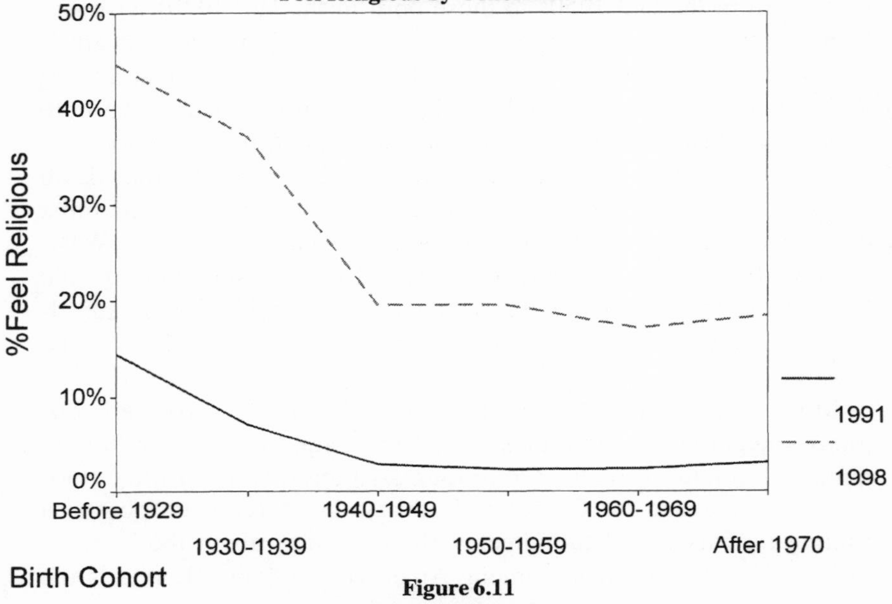

Figure 6.11
God Cares by Cohort and Year

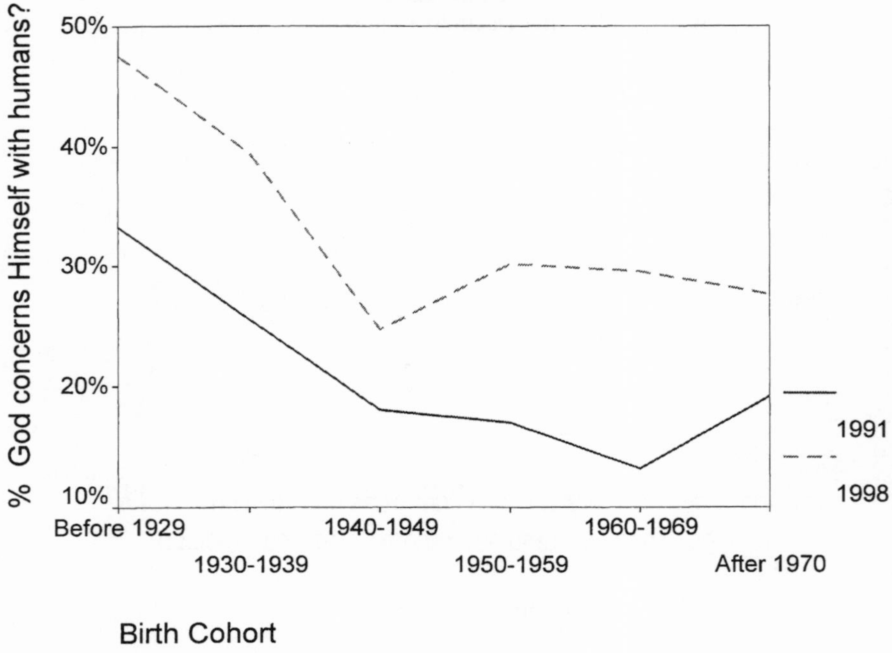

Figure 6.12
Hope by Cohort

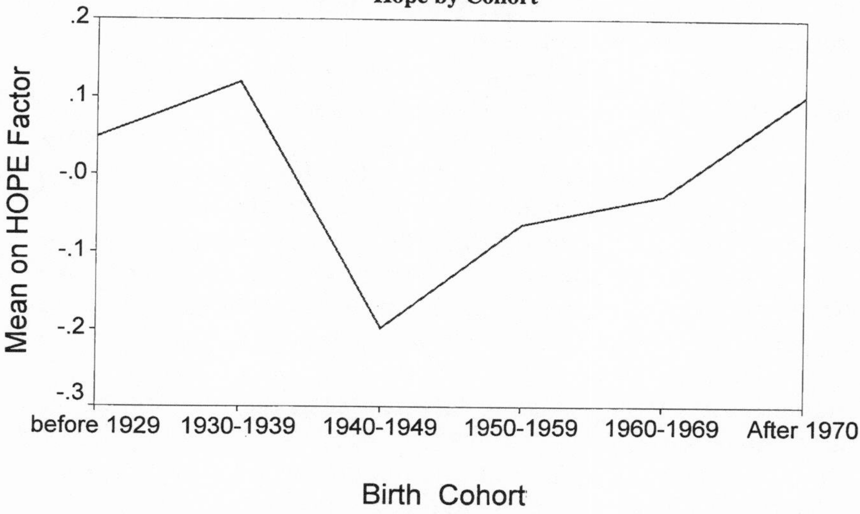

Hope= Afterlife, Heaven, Miracles

Figure 6.13
Hope Factor by Cohort and Theism

Russia

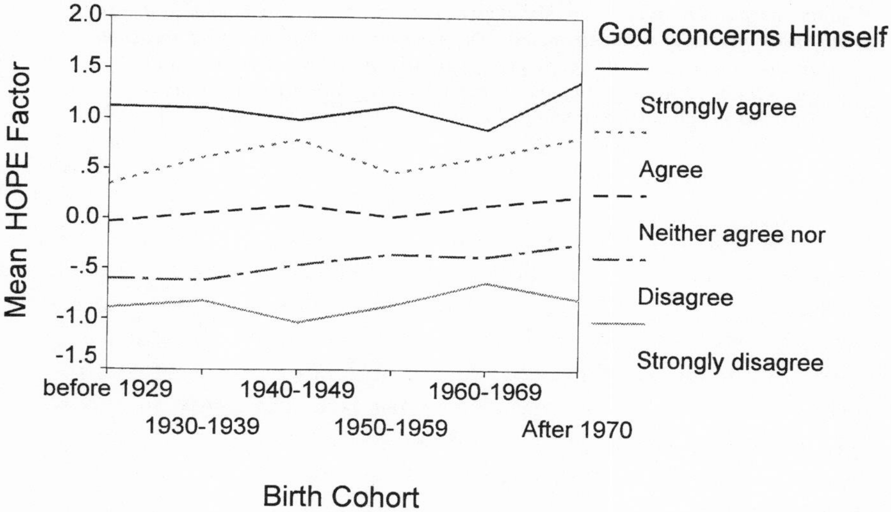

HOPE=After life, heaven, Miracles

sacramental riches of the Orthodox heritage. As Husband remarks, it was precisely the symbols that were most difficult for the party to eradicate. Perhaps we were naïve in our convictions about what religion is to expect that a thousand-year heritage would wither away in seventy-five years of inept socialist oppression.

Two Russian intellectuals, writing in the "Lifestyle" section of *The Russia Journal* on the question of whether Russians have changed since the "social transformation, " advance explanations which are worth pondering. The dramatist Viktor Rozov comments, "Our people are not doomed—the majority have preserved the traditional Russian psychology. Perhaps this is thanks to our religion." And the philosopher Alexander Zinoviev: "Americanization is destructive and disastrous for Russian. . . . The revival of Orthodox Christianity and religiousness is taking place in the context of the rejection of the Americanization."

It appeared in the 1991 data that the turn to religion was especially strong among the young and the better educated who found in religion an energy to hold their marriages together and a heritage which gave direction and purpose to life and could be handed on to one's children.[7] The two quotes may, perhaps, be another way of stating that insight.

Despite seven decades of conflict and accommodation between the Party and religion, Orthodoxy seems to have emerged vigorously from a long period when the most it could do was accommodate. If one had read Husband's monograph before the "social transformation" in Russia one would have thought that there could not be much left after seventy years of such compromise. Perhaps that would have been an underestimation of the recuperative powers of religion.

Nonetheless, one would dearly like to know what went on in the minds of Russians, individually and collectively, during the 1990s. The temptation would be to say that the religious faith they had always professed underground simply emerged above ground when it was able to do so. Somehow the symbols and the practices, including the superstitions, endured in the rich and dense imaginations of the Russian people. However, against that interpretation, we have the testimony of our respondents that their belief in God has actually changed. Some of them seem to be telling us that the events of the last decade and a half did not so much revive and old faith but produce a new faith. Perhaps when it was possible to say publicly that one believed in God, one discovered that one did indeed believe after all.

What would have been the condition of religion in Russia today if the October Revolution had failed or if the Whites had defeated the Reds in the bitter civil war that followed the revolution? Would industrialization and urbanization have taken their toll, as they may have in Britain and the Netherlands. Does the fact that the level of Russian belief in God was similar to that of Britain and West Germany in 1998 suggest that in some respects Orthodoxy may be more or less where it would have been without the socialist revolution, except that now it is free of government control?

The phenomenon of contemporary Russian religion deserves much closer study. No one denies any more that an extraordinary religious phenomenon occurred in Russia at the end of the twentieth century. While surveys may sketch some of the dimensions of the reemergence/rebirth of Russian religion, they cannot substitute for a richer and denser deep description of what is happening. Alas, given the biases against religion and the study of religion in the social science community, it is not likely that this sort of research will occur. In fact, it is not likely that the International Social Survey Program will return to religion in the future.

Is this Russian revival going to ebb in years to come as most sociologists would confidently predict? All one can say on the basis of the data here presented is that it hasn't yet.

Conclusions

1. Religion is stronger today in Russia than it was in 1991.

2. An enormous number of Russian people testify that they have actually changed in their belief in God and in Orthodoxy. In the face of this testimony it is very difficult to claim that that religion has merely reemerged from hiding. The respondents themselves seem convinced that there has been a personal change.

3. While confidence in the church organization has fallen dramatically since 1991, in almost every other measure of religion there has been a "ballooning" phenomenon"—a revival which seemed to have started among the younger cohorts in 1991 has spread upwards to the older cohorts.

4. Russians are not a devout people in terms of church attendance, but even in this matter there has been positive change since 1991.

5. Few Russians seem actively hostile to religion.

6. The Russians who are religious intend to raise their children in religion.

7. Russians want the same things from religion that other peoples want, a binding force to hold their marriages together and a heritage to pass on to their children.

8. In sum, it is time to accept the fact of dramatic religious change in Russia and to abandon efforts to explain it away.

Notes

1. Carried out by VCIOM.
2. In East Germany more people believe in religious miracles than believe in God, a paradox if not a contradiction.
3. In general, religious behavior correlates with life cycle, declining from the middle teens to the middle twenties and than rebounding till the middle forties. The phenomenon depicted in figure 1—the younger being more religious than those older than them—rarely is observed (and does not obtain in the most the ISSP countries). It does therefore suggest not merely an negative age correlation but a real social change.
4. Many Americans would be more comfortable with a Russia which did not retaliate against atheist propaganda of the past by banning it in the present and which had more problems with clergy melding in politics. However, Russians must be permitted to work out their own form of civil liberties and their own notions of the proper relationships between Church and State and religion and society. To judge every policy that they or their leaders pursue by American standards is ethnocentric to say the least, especially when it is done by journalists and Russian experts who could not have been more wrong in the nineteen eighties in predicting what would happen in the then Soviet Union.
5. This decline cannot be explained by a decline in other institutions in Russian society. When the decline of confidence in parliament is entered into the equation the correlation between time and confidence in religious leaders does not change from -.27.
6. Confidence in religious leadership has declined in all ISSP countries in which 1998 data are currently available. Thus in Ireland it has declined from 45% to 28%. Irena Borowik and Gregory Grzegorz have reported in a survey of former socialist countries the churches have busied themselves about efforts to regain their former power and maintain their religious monopolies. There is little effort to address the religious needs, particularly of the younger, college-educated population.
7. The ROMIR study reports that two thirds of Russians believe that a baby should be baptized soon after birth and 7/8 attach importance to a church funeral. More than half think that a wedding should take place in Church. The majority also believe that religion provides an adequate answer to both moral and familial problems.
8. Response to question in Table 2
9. Response to question about how close you are to God which does not choose "do not believe in God."
10. There is a God who concerns himself with every human being personally.
11. People can do little to change life.

12. Life does not serve any useful purpose.
13. There is little people can do to change the course of their lives.
14. Life is only meaningful if you provide the meaning itself.
15. The course of our Life is decided by God.
16. Proportion of all those who did not used to believe in God.
17. Proportion of those who did not used to be Orthodox.
18. If the next election was held on a multiparty basis which party would you vote for?
19. "According to the results of surveys, in recent years more people are calling themselves religious. What can you say about the religious feelings of people around you?"
20. "What is religion to your mind?"
21. "What role to your mind should the religious organizations play in public life?"
22. "What importances does religion have for you personally?"
23. Russian Federation.
24. Always believed in God.
25. Orthodox at 16.
26. % of those who didn't use to believe in God who now do.

This [illegible] earlier days, [illegible] any [illegible] world. The [illegible] ers and workers alike.

Nonetheless, the highest levels of belief in [illegible] magic are to be found in the former [illegible] and Slavic countries of Eastern Europe. Thus 72 percent [illegible] proposed [illegible] percent [illegible] fortune-tellers [illegible] percent [illegible] percent. [illegible] Slovakia [illegible] percent [illegible] have [illegible] fortune-tellers [illegible] percent believe [illegible] and 50 percent [illegible] 41 percent believe in astrology. Here, however, were once socialist states.

One might have thought that magic would have been popular in the former socialist countries because of the [illegible] character of socialist economic and political life. However, since both East Germany and Russia were once socialist and since [illegible] where magic is less popular than in West Germany or Britain was also socialist, the explanation that the Eastern European magic is Slavic in origins might seem plausible. Indeed, one might wonder if the faith in magic in Latvia, Bulgaria, Slovakia, Russia, and the Czech Republic would have been any higher a couple of centuries ago.

On the other hand, it is worth remarking that the fact that half of the Britons, two-thirds of the West Germans, and one-fifth of the East Germans still believe in faith healers. However, similar proportions also believe in fortune-tellers. The sociologists who report that religion is disappearing in Britain and Germany cannot claim that belief in magic is also being "secularized" away, especially since it is more common among younger people in both countries.

Does "secularization," so assiduously documented by British social scientists, lead to an increase in magic? Does [illegible] in "unsecularized" countries? In an attempt to answer this question I constructed figure [illegible] which shows the impact of church attendance on belief in magic in Britain and Ireland. There is no difference in acceptance of magic in both countries among those who attend church services once a week or more. However, lower levels of church attendance lead to higher acceptance of magic in "secular-

7

Religion in the Former "Evil Empire"

Introduction

Besides Russia, eight former socialist countries were included in the 1998 International Social Survey Program – Poland, Hungary, Slovenia, East Germany, Latvia, Bulgaria, Slovakia, and the Czech Republic. The first four also participated in the 1991 survey. Hence one can measure religious change during the 1990s in those countries. For the second four one must rely on the two items which were the basis of the 1991 analysis of Russia, change of belief in God and change in denominational affiliation. In both cases one finds evidence of a religious revival though one not so spectacular as in Russia. It should be remembered that the increase in belief in life after death among the younger cohorts, reported in chapter 2, was found in all eight countries, though it would be difficult to attribute that increase to the fall of socialism since it occurred in many non-socialist countries.

Slovenia

In many ways Slovenia, a new and tiny nation which was able to free itself from Yugoslavia because Croatia was a massive barrier between it and the Serb army, is the most interesting of the former socialist countries outside the Soviet Union. In 1991 there remained a reluctance to ask about church attendance. However, by 1998, atheism had declined from 19 percent to 14 percent, belief in life after death had increased from 33 percent to 43 percent, frequent prayer from 28 percent to 34 percent, and belief in miracles from 49 percent to 58 percent (table 7.1).

Table 7.1
Religious Change in Slovenia

	1991	1998
Believe in God	61%	63%
Atheist	19%	14%*
Caring God	27%	27%
Life After Death	33%	43%*
Church attendance frequent	(not asked)	23%
Church attendance never	(not asked)	29%
Pray several times a month	28%	34%*
Church has too much power	26%	38%*
Confidence in Church	28%	23%*
No religious affiliation	11%	24%*
Heaven	32%	35%
Miracles	49%	58%*

On the other hand, there were significant increases in the convictions that the church had too much power and that the church did not merit confidence while non-affiliation more than doubled (from 11 percent to 24 percent). It would appear that Slovenia is going through a time when it's largely Catholic population is making up its mind how it is going to relate both to its religious heritage and to the Catholic church. Faith and hope have clearly increased with the end of Socialism, but affiliation with the church remains in doubt.

Nikos Tos and Brina Malnar, who direct the International Social Survey Program research in Slovenia (Tos et al. 2000) suggest that the Vatican's decision to impose the "Polish model" on the Slovenian Church assumed that Slovenian Catholics had the same influence in their country as Polish Catholics did. Accepting that assumption and acting on it, the Slovenian Catholic leadership offended and indeed lost many of its initial (1991) adherents.

Hungary

In Hungary belief in life after death (28 percent to 39 percent), a caring God (27 percent to 31 percent), and heaven (28 percent to 36 percent) have increased significantly during the nineties as has frequent prayer (40 percent to 46 percent) (table 7.2). However, just as

Table 7.2
Religious Change in Hungary

	1991	1998
Believe in God	64%%	66%
Atheist	12%	12%
Caring God	27%	31%*
Life After Death	28%	39%*
Church attendance frequent	19%	19%
Church attendance never	32%	30%
Pray several times a month	40%	46%*
Church has too much power	14%	24%*
Confidence in Church	48%	40%*
No religious affiliation	5%	22%*
Heaven	28%	36%*
Miracles	29%	31%

in its neighbor Slovenia, skepticism about the church has also increased and denomination affiliation has declined. The only Catholicism that either country has known is Hapsburg Catholicism. The church has not been linked to the cause of national freedom as it has been in Poland. Rather it stands for oppressive power and foreign power at that.

While both countries are, in most respects, more religious than Russia, they have not experienced the exciting religious revolution that has apparently occurred in Russia, a country in which, like Poland, the church has been on the side of traditional Russian culture. Nonetheless, neither country fits the Orange "secularization" model and both have more believers and more churchgoers than does Britain.

Poland

Even in Poland (table 7.3) there are some signs of an increase in religious faith, though Poland is second only to Ireland as the most religious and most Catholic country in Europe. Belief in life after death has increased from 74 percent to 78 percent, and in miracles from 53 percent to 66 percent. Moreover, while non-affiliation has increased (from 3 percent to 6 percent) and regular church attendance has declined from (67 percent to 60 percent), there has not

Table 7.3
Religious Change in Poland

	1991	1998
Believe in God	94%	95%
Atheist	2%	2%
Caring God	73%	74%
Life After Death	74%	78%*
Church attendance frequent	67%	61%*
Church attendance never	3%	5%
Pray several times a month	79%	78%
Church has too much power	61%	60%
Confidence in Church	33%	40%*
No religious affiliation	3%	6%*
Heaven	76%	78%
Miracles	53%	66%*

been an increase in the conviction that the church has too much power (high, however, at 60 percent) and indeed confidence in the church as an organization has increased from 33 percent to 40 percent. A decline in the Catholicism of Poland after the end of Socialism, which many had anticipated, simply has not occurred. Like other Catholics around the world, the majority of Poles (as we noted in an earlier chapter) do not accept Catholicism's sexual teaching. To the extent that there is a religious revival in Poland, it has been a minor one because Polish Catholicism flourished under socialism. A decade after the fall of socialism, it still flourishes.

East Germany

In East Germany, on the other hand, there is virtually no trace of a religious revival (table 7.4), other than the already noted increase in belief in life after death among the youngest cohorts and an increase in four percentage points in belief in heaven. Atheism has increased, as has the proportion of those with no religious affiliation and confidence in the church has decreased. Paradoxically while only a quarter of East Germans believe in God, two-fifths believe in religious miracles. The question then arises as to who causes the religious miracles if there is no God. Or perhaps the question should be who is the God in whom East Germans do not believe.

Table 7.4
Religious Change in East Germany

	1991	1998
Believe in God	24%	26%
Atheist	49%	54%*
Caring God	14%	16%
Life After Death	14%	15%
Church attendance frequent	(flawed item)	(flawed item)
Church attendance never	(flawed item)	(flawed item)
Pray several times a month	12%	13%
Church has too much power	34%	37%
Confidence in Church	26%	16%*
No religious affiliation	64%	69%*
Heaven	20%	24%*
Miracles	40%	38%

In Russia, Orthodoxy was ideally situated to take religious advantage of the fall of socialism as Catholicism was in Poland. Both religions represented the cultural heritages of their respective peoples. In Slovenia and Hungary, the Catholic Church was at a disadvantage because it did not have an unblemished record in its relationship with the cultural heritages. In East Germany, perhaps the Evangelical (Lutheran) Church did not have the energy to reassert its influence. Even if it did, it is unlikely that the largely atheist people of East Germany would have wanted to or even been able to listen.

The Czech Republic, Slovakia, Bulgaria, and Latvia

Since the four new participants in the International Social Survey Program religion module do not have a 1991 benchmark for comparison, we must infer religious change from the two retrospective items—original religion and belief in God (question 19). Have the people in these countries dramatically increased their religious affiliation and have they moved in substantial numbers from unbelief to belief?

The answer to both these questions seems to be that there has been movement, but not nearly so dramatic as in Russia, in part because the religious situation in these four countries was never as bad as it was in Russia and partly because the Orthodox Church in

Russia held all the cultural cards in a way that was not true in any of these four countries (though Bulgaria is more like Russia than the other three, even if Latvia was part of the Soviet Union for a half century).

Religious affiliation was never so low in these four countries—not nearly as low as the 10 percent in Russia. However, (table 7.5) there has been a a marginal increase in all the countries except the Czech Republic—to Catholicism in Slovakia, Orthodoxy in Bulgaria, and Orthodoxy, Lutheranism, and Catholicism in Latvia. Thus, in 1998, 55 percent of the Czechs, 64 percent of the Latvians, 65 percent of the Russians, 83 percent of the Slovaks, and 87 percent of the Bulgarians reported a religious affiliation.

Table 7.5
No Religious Affiliation by Country and Time
% No Affiliation

	Czech	Slovakia	Bulgaria	Latvia
Raised	38%	16%	19%	39%
Now	45%	14%	13%	36%

Moreover as figures 7.1 to 7.4 demonstrate there has been a net gain in each of the four countries among those who have switched in their belief in God one way or another in the more recent cohorts. In each of the countries those who have changed from not believing in God to believing in God represent in the younger cohort a net gain of ten percent in belief over those who used to believe in God but do so no longer. Thus in 1998 72 percent of the Slovaks and the Latvians believe in God, 60 percent of the Russians and the Bulgarians and 50 percent of the Czechs. The gains in Russia are more spectacular than in the other countries because the original Russian positions were so much lower.

If one adds the 63 percent 1998 belief rate in Slovenia and the 66 percent in Hungary, it becomes obvious that a solid majority of the people in all the former socialist countries except East Germany and the Czech Republic believe in God at the end of the first decade of the great "Social Transformation" in Eastern Europe and that in each of the countries this represents a change from previous times.

Moreover the youngest cohorts in all four countries are more likely (at a significant correlation) to have changed to belief in God in the course of their lives then the older cohorts (figure 7.1) And the younger cohorts (figure 7.2) are also less likely to have defected from the religion in which they were raised.

Figure 7.1
Net Change in Belief in God by Cohort and Country

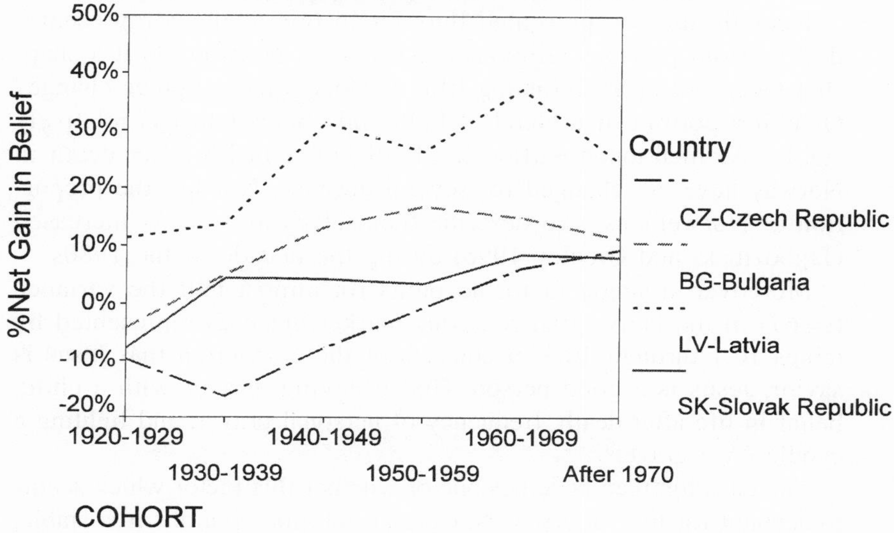

Figure 7.2
Percent Defected From Denomination in which Raised

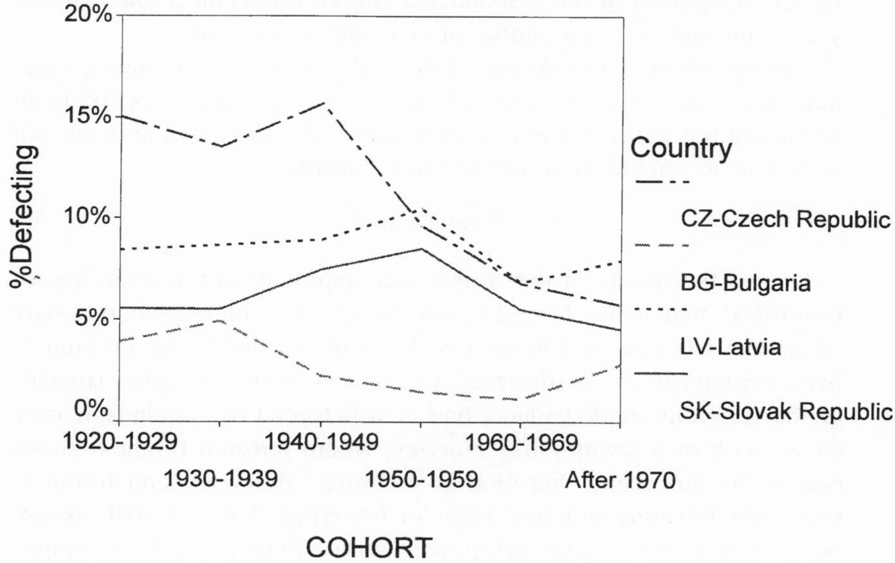

Figure 7.3
No Religious Affiliation in the Czech Republic and Slovakia

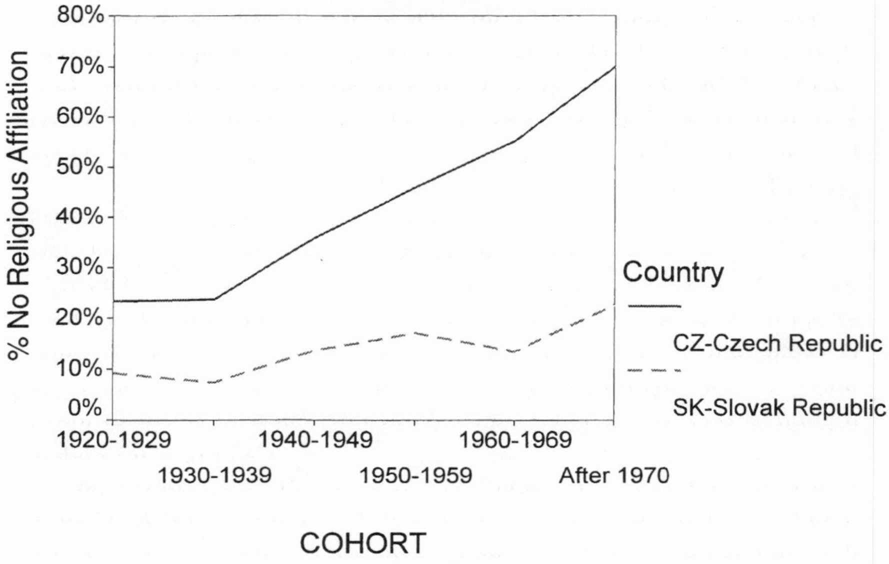

To what extent are these phenomena the result of the decline of Socialism and to what extent do they represent continuity with the past? We do not know how the Bulgarians, the Czechs, the Latvians, and the Slovaks would have answered our questions in 1991.

The Czechs and the Slovaks

The Czechs and the Slovaks are an interesting Central European story. For almost eighty years they were attached as one country, save for a few years during World War II. Catholicism is the dominant religion in both countries. Twelve percent of the Slovaks are Lutherans. Four percent of the Czechs are either Hussites or Brethren. Sixteen percent of the Slovaks have no religious affiliation as do 47 percent of the Czechs. This is a striking difference in religious affiliation between the two people, one country solidly Catholic, the other more irreligious than any country in Europe with the exception of East Germany. They have not always gotten along well with one another, though apparently a majority of both countries would have voted against the split if they had an opportunity to vote on the issue). Yet they share the same language, a similar history, and equal opportunities to dislike the Hapsburgs—though Slovaks thought the

Czechs were the Emperor's agents in denying the Slovaks their national identity and rights.

How can one account for these differences which are presented in figure 7.3? The correlation between country and being Catholic is .31. If one inserts into the regression equation the proportion of those who were raised in no religion, the correlation declines to .13 and to .09 when confidence in church leaders is added. Thirty-eight percent of the Czechs had no religious affiliation when they were young while only 14 percent were without religious affiliation. The differences between the two countries in religious affiliation then are the result of events which happened in the past. As long ago as the late eighteenth century a "Free Thinkers" movement emerged in Bohemia which, given a choice between Catholicism and Protestantism, chose non-belief instead of either, doubtless because of experiences with the Catholic Hapsburg monarchy. Did Socialism lead to secularization in either country. One suspects only marginally. Those who were Catholic in both countries remained Catholic. Those who were atheists or agnostics –34 percent of the Czech's and 20 percent of the Slovaks remained atheists.

Conclusion

One might not be wrong to suggest that, whether by revival or by reemergence, religion in the former socialist countries may well have taken on a pattern like that which existed in 1945 or, in the case of Russia, 1916: Poland and Slovakia very Catholic, Hungary and Slovenia moderately Catholic, Russia and Bulgaria devoutly Orthodox, and Latvia a mix of three religions all strongly adhered to, the Czech Republic "half-Catholic" and East Germany not very religious at all.

This may not seem like a notable achievement until one considers that with greater or lesser skill the various socialist parties in these countries were determined to eliminate religion. It is also not what the "secularization" model would have predicted. Socialism ought to have accelerated "secularization." In fact, it did not do so. Predictions that "secularization" will catch up with Eastern Europe assume that the nine countries we have studied are like Britain and the Netherlands and that Poland and Slovakia will be more like France than like Ireland, Spain, Italy, Portugal, and Switzerland.

The development of religion in the former "evil empire" should be studied in years to come without such assumptions.

8

The Religions of Ireland

"North of the border are the best Protestants in the world. South of the border there are the best Catholics in the world. There are very few Christians in the whole lot of them."

—Frank O'Connor

"Well I don't trust the Prots up here much, but I'll tell you one thing: I trust them more than I do them Catholic fockers down below."

—Northern Irish Catholic with Republican sympathies.

"There is no doubt that Northern Catholicism was a church of the ghetto."

—Fionnuala O'Connor

Introduction

Ireland is the only country in Western Europe of which it may be said that it is still partially colonized, that an important segment of its historical geography is occupied by the military and police power of another country. While it is true that during the late 1990s, Britain began seriously to attempt disengagement from its Northern Ireland colony (and even in the person of Prime Minister Blair apologized for the injustices of the long occupation), it is still reasonable to ask what impact this long and often violent colonization has affected religion on the island. I began to think about this subject when I was asked to explore the possibility that there might be a convergence across religious lines which would help those who were searching for peace in Northern Ireland. Were Protestants and Catholics coming together in their beliefs and attitudes in such a way that religion might be a healing force in Ireland? It was a question worth asking, though there was, it seemed to me, a naïve assumption that denominational members were shaped by their churches instead of vice versa. I indeed found such a convergence, but it was not one that brought much consolation to those who were hoping that religion might contribute to the peace process.

My task in this chapter is to investigate the possible differences between or possibly among the religions of Ireland and ascertain whether there is any convergence taking place in these religions which might underpin any permanent or quasi-permanent solution to the Northern Island problem. I leave it to those who study the same phenomenon from the viewpoint of history or anecdotal comparisons or lived experience—exercises which I do not deprecate—to collect and analyze their own survey data if their impressions seem incompatible with those I find in my data. While I am not unfamiliar with the literature of Irish history, I do not propose to discuss that literature, which is beyond my professional competence, in this chapter. I note that Akenson (1993) discusses differences between Irish Catholics and Irish Protestants, using data from countries to which both groups have migrated and refutes all of the hypotheses about Irish Catholic inferiority that have been popular is Irish historiography.[1]

I propose to work with three data sets, the 1991 International Social Survey Program study of religion, the 1993 International Social Survey Program study of environmental attitudes and the 1990 European Value Study. The data have been collected for these three surveys by reputable data collection agencies. In Ireland by the ESRI and in Northern Ireland by SCPR and British Gallup. All samples were probability samples and all interviews were face to face.

Because the studies in Ireland and Northern Ireland[2] were different projects, they represent valid samples of both regions but when one combines them they do not represent valid samples of the whole island. One can legitimately compare the two regions but one cannot estimate to the whole island, unless one weights for the relative size of the two populations. Moreover sample sizes make it impossible to consider any but the three major religions of the island—Southern Catholics, Northern Catholics, and Northern Protestants. In Ireland in the 1991 study, for example, there were 67 respondents who were not Catholic—30 Anglicans (C. of I.) and 30 with no religious affiliation.

The case bases for the three surveys were as follows:

	Southern Catholics	Northern Catholics	Northern Protestants
ISSP 91	935	275	483
ISSP 93	892	225	411
EVS	2084	160	295

No survey is perfect. Each of the three on which I base this analysis has flaws. The ISSP data are collected in a fifteen-minute module which, in each of the participating countries, is added to another study. The questions are hammered out at frequently acrimonious yearly meetings. I will not attempt to defend the collective decisions of my colleagues, many of whom are neither interested in nor sensitive to religion.

The EVS data set is based on a large mixtum-gatherum of survey items derived from the collective unconscious of the survey fraternity, especially as this fraternity has been shaped by the various Gallup organizations around the world. The study in both its 1981 and 1990 manifestations is utterly without theoretical orientation other than the assumption that religion is declining. (See Whelan et al. 1994 for an intelligent use of the EVS data and Ester, Halman, and deMoor 1993 for a use of the same data which does not inform the reader that the measure of "secularization" changed in the second survey). Moreover, unlike the ISSP data which are available for all users as soon as they are archived at ZA in the University of Cologne, the investigators of the EVS in various countries are notably anal retentive with their data. One does one's best with the data that are at hand. Anyone who insists on better data is welcome to try to raise the money to fund a better project.

Finally, I have no way of connecting the religious attitudes and behaviors which I will report with political unrest in Ireland. Civil unrest and violence is so rare in the countries studied in both the ISSP and the EVS that no thought has been given to concentrating on that subject. Moreover, it does not require many people to launch a riot or a pogrom and not many more to support a secret army. The Irish are not, however, a people who are given to demonstrations in numbers higher than in most other countries. 17 percent of Southern Catholics, 24 percent of Northern Catholics, and 27 percent of Northern Protestants have participated in demonstrations as compared to a 23 percent average in the Values Study. Short of much more elaborate research one can only speculate about the relationship between the findings I will report and possibilities of peace in Ireland. The political surveys indicate that members of all three communities overwhelmingly supported the peace process. There are no data which would enable us to judge whether religion has any impact on the "hard men" (and the "hard women").

There are two issues to be faced in this analysis: what are the religions of Ireland and are the differences between or among the religions diminishing. It would seem at first consideration that there are patently two religions, Catholicism and Protestantism. Catholics in the North and South are led by a single hierarchy, ministered to by priests taught at the same seminaries, and taught by the same religious orders of brothers and nuns and engage in the same kinds of religious devotions. But there is a possibility that after years of repression (seventy-five or three hundred, depending on when one wants to start counting) Northern Irish Catholicism might have diverged somewhat from its Southern counterpart. In fact, the data suggest strongly that the latter is the case: there are three religions in Ireland. In O'Connor's (1993) words "Segregated, shut-in Belfast is a hundred miles and a world away from the fizz and frivol of Dublin pub talk. . . . A minority faith behaves differently."

In the absence of time series data[3] one must approach the issue of the diminution of differences by comparing the young and the university educated in the three populations to see if the differences among them are less than the differences among the total populations. In fact, there is little evidence of a decline in religious differences among the three religions of Ireland, as much as good secularist might hope that such a decline (which they take to be inevitable) might contribute to the peace process.

Survey research often proves that what everyone knows to be true is not true at all. Survey research on Ireland sometimes goes further than that: it suggests that what everyone knows cannot possibly be true is, in fact, true. Thus, for example Ward and Greeley (1990) have demonstrated in an analysis of the EVS data, that the Irish (Ireland in the sense used in this paper) are of the English-speaking peoples the most tolerant of diversity among neighbors and the most likely to approve of homosexual marriage ceremonies. The tolerance of diversity can be explained when one takes into account religion. In England, Ireland, and Northern Ireland, Catholics are more tolerant. Holding religion constant, there is no difference in tolerance among the three countries. One should approach the study of Irish religion with a readiness to be surprised.

Theoretical Orientation

My own approach to the study of religion focuses on the "story" role of religion: a religion is a story (or a series of interconnected stories) which purport to explain the meaning and purpose of life. Religion is experience before it is reflection, poetry before doctrine, story before it is anything else, and story after it is everything else. Religions will vary not only in their basic orientations but in how these orientations adapt to different sets of circumstances.

This approach led me to expect that there would be three religious stories in Ireland—an expectation which nothing in the "secularization" model could have anticipated. It seemed to me that the different social and political environments in which Northern and Southern Catholics found themselves would produce quite different stories, stories which would account, at some level, for the situation in which both groups found themselves and perhaps strengthen the existing differences. I did not expect that either age or education would lead to convergence of these two different religious stories, both Catholic but Catholic in very different environments. Nor did I expect that there would be any convergence in the different Catholic and Protestant stories in Ireland.

ISSP 91: Worldview, Faith, and Devotion

The first two variables in table 8.1, which are drawn from the 1991 International Social Survey Program study of religion, are based on a series of questions about fundamental worldviews:

- There is very little people can do to change the course of their lives.
- The course of our life is decided by God.
- Life is meaningful only because God exists.
- Life is meaningful only if you provide meaning yourself.
- We each make our own fate.

The first three variables cluster on a factor I call CALVIN[4] because it seems to indicate a sense of predetermination or predestination. The fourth and fifth variable cluster on a factor which I name after PELAGIUS,[5] a monk who did battle with Saint Augustine on the issue of whether humans could do good without God's help. Pelagius, who was Irish, held that they could. Southerners are significantly[6] more likely to be PELAGIANS, Northerners more likely to be CALVINISTS. There are no significant differences between the two Northern communities. Among those who have attended

Table 8.1
Religions of Ireland (ISSP)
(% Different from Southern Catholic[1])

	All		Higher Education		Under 35	
	North Cath.	**North Prot.**	**North Cath.**	**North Prot.**	**North Prot**	**North Cath.**
Pelagian	-08%	-15%	-8%	-15%	-8%	-19%
Calvinist	11%	12%	22%	29%	28%	22%
Faith	19%	14%	22%	19%	19%	18%
Devotion	04%*	-31%**	11%	-29%	07%	35%
Superstition	12%	08%	04%	10%	21%	09%
Sexual Morality	04%*	-08%**[2]	-11%	-14%	-04%	-15%
Tough on Crime	-15%*	21%**	00%	.13%	-18%	.19%
Cheat	08%	-12%**	10%	-10%	07%	-16%
Feminism	00%*	-10%**	00%	-08%	03%	=11%
% Very Happy	-07%	00%*	03%	05%	09%	-04%
Hrs Work	-15%	-13%	-06%	-04%	07%	07%
Church-State	00%*	-12%**	09%	11%	07%	18%

*Not significantly different from Southern Catholics
** Significantly different from both Northern and Southern Catholics

university and those under thirty-five, the differences persist. The old battle line between the Irish monk and the African bishop continues in the modern world, most notably, it would seem, along the boundary which separates the Six Counties from the Twenty-Six.

Factor scores were computed for a wide variety of variables in the three studies. Then the scores were dichotomized and the proportions above the means for the three religious groups were calculated. Thus Northern Catholics were eleven percentage points more above the mean on the CALVIN scale than were Southern Catholics and Northern Protestants were twelve percentage points more above the mean than Southern Catholics. Both differences are statistically significant. Thus one concludes that on this scale Northerners, whether Catholic or Protestant, are more inclined to CALVINISM than are the Southerners, but that Catholics and Protestants in the North do not differ significantly with one another.[7]

Then the populations are divided into those who have had university education and those who have not. Far from diminishing the differences between North and South on CALVIN, a university education seems to exacerbate them because such an education leads to a more notable decline in CALVINISM among Southerners than among Northerners.

The three tables in this chapter summarize the differences among the three religions of Ireland. The first two columns present the differences in comparison of Northern Catholics and Northern Protestants with Southern Catholics.[8] The second two columns depict the differences among those who have attended universities. The third two columns represent the differences among those who are less than thirty five years old.[9]

Thus CALVIN wins in the North (and presumably St. Augustine) and the Irish monk wins in the South. Insofar as our measures tap fundamental worldview, Northern Catholics are as pessimistic as their Protestant neighbors, perhaps because the culture of the six county majority has been absorbed by the minority community.[10] The "story" of the meaning of life which Northern Catholics tell is more like that of the Northern Protestants than that of the Southern Catholics.

On matters of religious FAITH (God, heaven, hell, life after death, Bible) Northerners are also substantially more faithful than Southerners. Neither youthfulness nor higher education diminishes these differences. However, Catholics in both regions have higher levels of DEVOTION (prayer and church attendance) than their Protestant counterparts, differences which again are immune to youthfulness and higher education.[11] Protestants are significantly lower than both Catholic groups in their devotions.[12]

Thus, while Northern Catholics are similar to Northern Protestants in their worldview, they are similar to Southern Catholics in both their FAITH and their DEVOTION, perhaps this "via media" is what one would expect from a group which is pulled by two different cultures.

ISSP 91: Superstition and Morality

There were four questions in the 1991 ISSP project which measured attitudes towards superstition and magic—astrology, good luck charms, fortune tellers, and faith healers. As we have seen earlier rates of magic are lowest in countries where religious faith is strong (Ireland) and in countries where it is weakest (East Germany). In countries which are in between (Britain and West Germany) magic seems to have the strongest appeal.

The Northern Irish, both Catholic and Protestant, are significantly higher on the magic scale than the Southern Catholics and are not significantly different from one another. Among the university educated Catholics, the difference between Northerners and Southerners disappears, though not among the young. The difference between Southerners and Northern Protestants is not affected either by youthfulness or education.[13]

On the matter of sexual morality (premarital, extramarital, same-sex sexuality) Northern Catholics are more like their Southern coreligionists; indeed, they are more orthodox than the Southerners and than their Northern neighbors. A group under pressure might well elect to emphasize those aspects of a religious culture that the leaders have most strongly proposed as essential. The Vatican is more likely to be concerned about abortion than about fortunetellers.[14]

The Irish Catholics however have one of the highest rates of opposition to the death penalty of any country in the world and the Northern Irish are even more likely to oppose it than their Southern neighbors, perhaps because they see some of their young men as potential targets for the death penalty or perhaps because they have less confidence in the legitimacy of the criminal justice system (table A). Thus on a factor which combines support for the death penalty and for harsh sentences for criminals, Irish in the North are significantly more tolerant than Irish in the South and Protestants are significantly less tolerant than are Catholics in either community. Among university educated Catholics, there is no significant difference between Catholics and Protestants. Ireland, incidentally has one of the lowest murder rates in Europe and Northern Ireland has the lowest rate of non-political crimes in the United Kingdom.

However, Irish Catholics in both regions are more likely to approve of cheating on taxes and government compensation forms and Northern Catholics are also significantly more likely to think it is all right to cheat the government than do Northern Protestants. Professor Liam Ryan explains this lack of scruple as a survival of the old feudal sense of community which distrusts the modern state. It is also possible that the consoling Catholic doctrine that tax laws are "purely penal" (bind in conscience only to accept punishment if one is caught) plays a part in this relaxed attitude. Well trained in casuistry that they are (especially by their Jesuit teachers) the Irish can be depended on to know about "purely penal" laws.

Table A
Ireland Compared to Other Countries

	South Catholics	North Catholics	Protestants	Britain	USA
Own Fate	71%	59%	59%	60%	63%
Predeterm	53%	55%	62%	21%	40%
Fortune Tellers	26%	30%	32%	41%	
Family Suffer (Disagree)	45%	44%	38%	43%	48%
Tax Cheat (Not Wrong)	34%	38%	21%	26%	17%
Abortion OK Defect	52%	43%	86%	92%	83%
Pro Death Pen	37%	19%	64%	33%	50%
Attend Weekly	71%	90%	26%	17%	44%
Church too much Power	36%	32%	33%	28%	23%
%Very Happy	40%	33%	39%	33%	37%
Job satisfaction	52%	48%	35%	19%	31%
God	97%	98%	95%	94$	71%
Obedient Children	35%	58%	51%	32%	39%
Nuclear Threat	44%	37%%	23%	21%	25%

Two variables serve as a short hand measure for FEMINSIM in ISSP 91:

- A husband's job is to earn money; a wife's job is to look after home and family.
- Family life suffers when a woman has a full time job.

On the FEMINSIM scale Irish Catholics in both regions are more likely to take a feminist position than are Northern Protestants who are significantly lower in their support for FEMINISM than are Catholics. Indeed (table A) there is no difference between Irish Catholics and Britons or Americans on this issue.[15] Neither youthfulness nor education have an impact on these differences.

Issp 91: Happiness, Work, Church, and State

It was claimed recently in *Society* magazine that Scandinavians report the highest levels of psychological well-being as measured by the "happiness" item; in fact the Irish of whatever religious persuasion in fact have the highest score, though it is lower among Catholics in Northern Ireland than in the South. As table A demonstrates, however, Northern Irish Catholics are slightly higher than Americans and significantly higher on this measure than Britons.

Despite their happiness (or perhaps because of it) Southern Irish work longer hours than members of the other two communities, almost forty four hours a week as opposed to slightly under forty for the Northerners. If number of hours worked is a sign of the Protestant Ethic, then Irish Catholics are the last Protestants in Europe. These differences disappear among the young and the well educated, one of the rare times in the present analysis that we discover that youthfulness and education do lead to a convergence in behavior.

Finally a series of items attempted to measure attitudes towards church-state relationships:

- Politicians who do not believe in God are unfit for public office.
- It would be better if people with strong religious beliefs held public office.
- Do you think that churches and religious leaders in this country have too much power?

Catholics are more likely than Protestants to think that church leaders have too much power. Neither education nor youthfulness diminish this cross-border difference. Moreover (table A) on the third item Southern Catholics are more likely than Britons or Americans to think the churches have too much power—arguably because the do.

A Fourth Irish Religion?

In the above analysis I combined all Christians who were not Catholic in the North into one category as a preliminary strategy. The question remains, however, whether there might be a fourth Irish religion, Northern Church of Ireland. Therefore I compared Presbyterians (217) and Anglicans (167) on the variables in table one. On two of them was there a statistically significant difference: Presbyterians were fifteen percentage points higher on the DEVOTIONAL scale and, not surprisingly, eleven points higher on the CALVINIST scale. If one compares Northern Anglicans with Southern Catholics[16] one will find inevitably, given the previous analysis, that the two groups differ significantly on many of the measures available in the ISSP data. Catholics are more DEVOUT, less MORAL, more satisfied the relationship between CHURCH and state, more PELAGIAN, more tolerant of CRIME and of those who CHEAT.

On the measures used in this project therefore there does not appear to be a fourth religion in Ireland.[17] Yet devotion and worldview might be considered the most important of the religious measures in table 8.1. Northern Anglicans are on both measures different from both Southern Catholics and Northern Protestants, less devout than either Catholics or Presbyterians, less Pelagian than Southern Catholics and less Calvinist than Presbyterians. If devotion and worldview are defining characteristics of religion, then Ireland indeed has a fourth religion—Northern Anglican.

Finally I compared Northern Anglicans and Southern Anglicans and found only one significant difference: Southern Anglicans are significantly more likely to have high scores on the FEMINISM scale than are northern Anglicans—58 percent versus 33 percent.

ISSP 91 Summary

Protestants in the North differ systematically from Catholics in the South on all items except personal happiness. Clearly then, as these indicators measure religious differences, there are two different religions on the Island, not completely different, but different enough. Southern Catholics are more PELAGIAN, less CALVINIST, more faithful, more devout, less superstitious more sympathetic to criminals, more likely to approve of cheating the government, more likely to be strict on sexual morality, more feminist, more likely to work longer, and more opposed to the power the church. They do not however differ from Protestants in the proportion who are very happy. Only in hours of work do education an age seem to diminish the difference.

Northern Catholics are somewhere between the two. In worldview faith, superstition, and hours of work, they are more like their Protestant neighbors. However they are stricter morally and more "faithful" than the Southern Catholics and even more sympathetic to criminals. They do not different from Southerners in their devotion, their propensity to cheat the government, their feminism and their views on church and state.

There does not appear to be a fourth religion in Ireland because Presbyterians and Anglicans in the North differ from one another only in their levels of religious devotion and in adherence to a Calvinist worldview.

Tentatively we may conclude that this "third" Irish religion is the result of tension between the culture in which northern Catholics live as a hated minority and the religious culture they are taught in their churches and schools. Does this greater similarity with Northern Protestants suggest they might be more open to accommodation? Or is it more probable that the culture conflict might increase their hostility?

The data do not enable us to make a choice. If I were forced to speculate I would lean to the latter alternative.

EVS 1990

In the Value study many scales were administered to respondents which might be interpreted as linked somewhat to religion. The most obvious is the FAITH scale which replicates the finding reported about the FAITH scale in the ISSP study: Northerners are more FAITHFUL than Southerners.

The EVS however presented a different measure of MORAL ABSOLUTISM:

Here are two statements which people sometimes make when discussing good and evil. Which one comes closest to your point of view?

- There are absolutely clear guidelines about what is good and evil. These always apply to everyone, whatever the circumstances.

- There can never be absolutely clear guidelines about what is good and evil. What is good and evil depends entirely upon the circumstance at the time.

Southern Catholics are not different from Northern Catholics in their moral absolutism as measured by this item. However, Northern Protestants are more absolutist than Southern Catholics on this measure.

Northerners of both religions are more likely to want children who are obedient and hard working than are Southern Catholics. In fact as table A shows Southern Catholics are similar in this respect to Americans and Britons and Northerners, Catholic and Protestant are very different. This seems to be a case of the minority group absorbing the values of the majority group through psychological processes of emulation mixed with dislike. Catholics in the South are under no pressure to do the same thing.

There are more protests (petitions, lawful and unlawful demonstrations, boycotts, occupation of buildings) in Northern Ireland than in the Republic, a finding which can hardly be called surprising. Moreover when demonstrations are considered separately, there are also more likely to be found in the two Northern Communities. As noted earlier, protests and demonstrations are more frequent in the North than the EVS average and less frequent in the South.

The EVS provides a twelve-item list of people a respondent would not like to have as neighbors:

People with a criminal record

People of a different race

Left-wing extremists

Heavy drinkers

Right-wing extremists

People with large families

Emotionally unstable people

Muslims

Immigrants/foreign workers

People who have AIDS

Drug addicts

Jews

Hindus

Southern Catholics are more TOLERANT than both Northern Catholics and Protestants. There is no difference between the two Northern groups on this tolerance measure. Irish Catholics (in the South) continued to be the most tolerant people in the English speaking world, as Ward and I reported of the 1981 EVS study, and Northern Irish among the most intolerant, whether Catholic or Protestant.

There were three "morality" factors to be found in the EVS data set. On only one were there differences among the three Irish communities, a factor I call CIVIC VIRTUE:

Please tell me for each of the following statements whether you think it can always be justified, never be justified, or something in between:

- Taking and driving away a car that belongs to someone else
- Taking the drug marijuana or hashish
- Someone accepting a bribe in the course of their duties
- Buying something you knew was stolen
- Sex under the legal age of consent

Northern Catholics are more likely to reject approval of these activities (as represented by the factor score) than are Southern Catholics, though there is no difference between Northern Protestants and Southern Catholics. It is possible that is a phenomenon which represents an over-adjustment of the minority group to the perceived norms of the majority.

One item in the long morality battery may have special implications for an island in which civil unrest seems endemic, a question which asks whether political assassination is ever moral. Nineteen percent of Southern Catholics think that it may on occasion be moral as opposed to 11 percent of the Northerners of both denominations. In Britain 30 percent think it may be moral as do 23 percent of Americans. The average support for assassination in the EVS is 22 percent. If this item be taken as a measure of support for political violence, the Southern Catholic percentage is not particularly high, but the Northern percentage, for both Catholics and Protestants, is exceptionally low—perhaps because both communities have had the chance to see the impact of political assassination. The gunmen patently do not speak for the people.

The final four items in table 8.2 are based on responses to questions about work. The first two deal with what makes a job attractive, the second two with why one works. The questions which create the first two factors are:

Which one of the following do you personally think are important in a job:

- Pay
- Security
- Interesting
- Opportunity for promotion
- Useful
- Responsibility
- Respect

The first two cluster on a factor that is called SECURITY and the remaining five on a factor called CHALLENGE.

Table 8.2
Religions of Ireland (EVA)
(%Different from Southern Catholic)

	All		Higher Education		Under 35	
	North Cath.	**North Prot.**	**North Cath.**	**North Prot.**	**North Prot.**	**North Cath.**
Faith	17%	07%	14%	07%	22%	07%
Moral Absolutism	04%*	06%	00%	06%	00%	05%
Docile Children	21%	24%	27%	26%	23%	27%
Protests	09%	05%	07%	08%	03%	09%
Demonstrate	11%	09%	07%	12%	09%	16%
Tolerance	-05%	-07%	-06%	-07%	-05%	-09%
Civil Laws	13%	00%*	20%	00%	10%	04%
Challenge	-08%	02%*	04%	-04%	-11%	04%
Security	10%	05%*	15%	08%	-15%	11%*
Must Work	11%	05%*	13%	00%	15%	06%
Like Work	-10%	05%*	-13%	00%	-15%	.06%

*Not significantly different from Southern Catholics
**Significantly different from both Southern and Northern Catholics,

Irish Protestants do not differ on these factors from Southern Catholics but Northern Catholics are more likely to reject challenge and opt for security. As is perhaps not untypical of a minority, they want to take no chances.

Finally, a number of items seek to determine why people work:

- The more I get paid the more I do.
- Working for a living is a necessity.
- I will always do the best I can regardless of pay
- I enjoy my work.

The first two items form a cluster called MUST WORK; The second two constitute LIKE WORK.

As we would now come to expect with regard to the EVS data, Northern Catholics are higher than the other two communities on the MUSTWORK factor and low on the LIKEWORK factor; and there are no differences between Southern Catholics and Northern Protestants.

The pattern in the Value Study data seems to be that the Northern Catholics are either more like the Northern Protestants than Southern Catholics or at least tend to be unlike Southern Catholics. Only on MORAL ABSOLUTISM are they not significantly different from Southern Catholics. Moreover on most variables they are significantly different from Southern Catholics even when Northern Protestants are not significantly different from Southern Catholics. This pattern strongly suggests a values system which has been heavily influenced by minority status, by the experience of a group which has been "on the bottom" for a long time as opposed to a group which has been "on the top" for a long time. One might argue that these variables are graphic proof of the impact of the Northern Ireland polity and culture on its Catholic citizens. Since virtually none of the variables are affected either age or education, the data do not present a very hopeful picture for the future. Contrary to the dictum of the character in Roddy Doyle's *The Commitments*, the Negroes of Europe are not those who live on the North Side of Dublin, but rather Catholics who live in the North.

ISSP 94—The Environment

Attitudes towards the environment may be an important effect of religious because they may represent a stance towards life and its purpose. A series of fifteen questions about the threat of chemical pollution, industry, water pollution, and nuclear energy and the dangers of these to one's family generated four factors of which three differentiated among the three Irish communities: CHEMICALS, TEMPERATURE, and NUCLEAR.

On all three factors (table 8.3) Southern Catholics are substantially more concerned than Northern Protestants, and on CHEMICALS Southern Catholics are also more concerned than Northern Catholics. Northern Catholics are also more concerned that their Protestant neighbors about the dangers of nuclear energy. Table A establishes that concern about the nuclear threat among Irish Catholics (of North and South) is notably greater than not only of the Protestant community but also of the citizens of the United States and Great Britain. Indeed the concern of Irish Catholics about nuclear power is the highest in the world[18]—and this in a country where there are no such stations.

Table 8.3
Environmental Concerns (ISSP 93)

	All		Higher Ed		Young	
	North Cath.	Prot	North Cath	Prot.	North Cath.	Prot.
Chemicals	-22%	-29%	-06%	-08%	-12%	-13%
Temperature	-01%*	-10%	-09%	-19%	-06%	-10%
Nuclear	00%*	-22%**	09%	-31%	09%	-31%

*Not significantly different from Southern Catholics
**Significantly different from both Southern and Northern Catholics,

It may be that the liberal wing of the Irish Church has scored points with its people by insisting on the danger of nuclear energy, an insistence which is cost free in a country that doesn't have any nuclear energy—just like attacks on the policies of the United States in Latin America are cost free. Moreover the Catholic respect for nature as sacramental may account in part for the Irish horror of meddling with the power of the atom. Finally a well-publicized nuclear incident in Britain and fear of what would happen if there would be an incident across the Irish Sea in Wales may be of considerable importance in explaining the intensity of Irish feelings on the subject.

One should also note than in the South both education and youthfulness predict greater differences than they do in the North. In the more relaxed and open society of the South (in recent years very open indeed and becoming more so) the usual demographic variables have a substantially greater impact than they do in the more constrained society of the North.

Summary and Conclusion

There can be little doubt that there are two different religions on the island of Ireland. Northern Protestantism and Southern Catholicism are not completely different. They are both Christian, European, Western, English speaking (though there is an Irish–speaking element among Southern Catholics). Yet of the twenty-six variables we used in trying to trace out rough outlines of religion and religiously related culture, only on the "happiness" measure is there no significant difference between the two communities. One supposes that this finding surprises no one, though it might be deemed worth while to have documented it. Moreover, there is no indication that the differences are diminishing among the university trained and those under thirty-five.

The third religion of Ireland presents a more complex and intricate picture. It is Catholic (in the sense of being like Southern Catholicism) in its faith, devotion, morality, and some of its attitudes (feminism, sympathy for criminals, tolerance for cheating, two attitudes towards the environment), but it is not like Southern Catholicism in its worldviews or much of anything else. It is significantly different from Southern Catholicism on twenty of the twenty-six variables. It is significantly different from Northern Protestantism on DEVOTION, CRIME ATTITUDES, FEMINISM, and CHEATING. On the various work values it is different from the Catholicism of the South in matters on which the Northern Protestants are not different from Southern Catholics. The religion of Northern Catholics fits nicely into the model of a (repressed) minority group torn between its traditional heritage and the cultural environment in which it finds itself. To test this thesis I compared Catholics in the North with Catholics in the counties which border the North, which includes the three counties of historic Ulster which are not part of the North. There is no decline in the differences between Catholics in the North and Catholics in the South when one limits the comparison to the border counties. Whatever the reason for the difference between the two Catholic religions in Ireland it is limited to the Six Counties and the experiences within their border.

Finally one might argue that Northern Anglicans constitute yet a fourth Irish religion, different from their Presbyterian neighbors and Southern Catholics in that they are less DEVOUT and in that they are less PELAGIAN than the Catholics and less CALVINIST than the Presbyterians.

In terms of the theory that religion is a story (or a collection of stories) which explain the meaning and purpose of life there are four important conclusions to this chapter:

1. There are three (or perhaps four) religions in Ireland, all of them Christian, which have rather different stories.

2. Two of these religions are Catholic. Thus it is clear that the raw religious materials of a religion, especially one as luxuriant in its metaphors as Catholicism, can be shaped into rather different stories, depending on the circumstances in which groups of Catholics might find themselves.

3. Apparently the experience of being a minority religion, and one that is, to state the matter mildly, under cross pressures, accounts for the different Catholic story in Northern Ireland.

4. There is no evidence that the differences among the religions of Ireland are being substantially affected by either age or educational attainment.

One can deny reality indefinitely of course, especially in Ireland. One can pretend that there is not a third religion on the island, a religion of a repressed minority and be none the worse for such a pretense. But then one ought not to be surprised that peace efforts are less than successful.

Notes

1. For reasons that escape me Akenson ignores analysis of large data sets pooled from surveys in the United States which explore the continuing differences between Irish Catholics and Irish Protestants, which in fact reverse the conclusions of many of those who write about religious differences in Ireland. Irish Protestants (equal in number to Irish Catholics) are more likely to be rural and southern and less likely to be economically, socially, and educationally successful. Irish Catholics are now the most successful gentile group in America. They exceeded the national average of college attendance for those of college age in the first decade of the present century. It is remarkable indeed, is it not, the impact of sea air on the alleged deficiencies of the Irish Catholic character?

Akenson is not the only scholar to ignore these findings. So do most American scholars. Economist Thomas Sowell dismisses the findings with the airy comment that no American Protestant would admit to being Irish!

2. I use these terms without any political connotations. I do note however that the latter governmental unit includes only six of the nine counties of historic Ulster.
3. The ISSP will repeat its religion study in 1998.
4. Calvin, like most of the Protestant leaders was in fact an Augustinian. Augustine in his later life took a profoundly pessimistic view of human nature. Humankind could do nothing by itself. It was utterly dependent on God's mercy. He sharply divided nature and grace, saying that God owed humans nothing. Pelagius saw a much smoother development of nature into grace and was far more optimistic about humankind. The Greeks defended Pelagius (and have never considered Augustine a saint). Thomas Aquinas leaned more in the Pelagian direction than in the Augustinian. It is fascinating that, insofar as our scales measure the two strains of the Western Catholic heritage, Ireland is divided between the Augustinian North and the Pelagian South. As we shall see, the old debate between the North African and the Irishman continues to be live in Ireland today, with the border between the six and the twenty six counties also marking the border between the two theologies In fact, the Irish score higher on the PELAGIAN scale than any other population in the ISSP.
5. Factor names are in caps to remind the reader that they nothing more than labels for a cluster of intercorrelations.
6. The convention is followed in the tables of using an * to indicate the absence of statistical significance between either of the two Northern groups and Southern Catholics. Two ** indicates a significant difference between Northern Protestants and both Catholic groups.
7. The factor scores were first computed for the entire sample and for the three communities. There were no basic differences in the various calculations. PELAGIUS and CALVIN did not correlate and hence could not be combined into one scale.
8. The percentages are the B statistic in dummy variable multiple regression analysis in which Protestants and Northern Catholics are compared with southern Catholics. Statistical significance is generated by the regression equation.
9. Numbers representing the "left hand" bars are omitted for the sake of making an already complicated chart less confusing than it might be. The issue is not differences among the older and the less educated, but among the younger and the more educated.
10. Table A enables the reader to compare the three Irish communities in the context of percentage responses to individual questions in other countries, Britain and the United States. Thus the Southern Irish would seem to be the most Pelagian and the Northerners the Most Calvinist not only in Ireland but in all three countries.
11. This does not mean that younger Catholics are more faithful or devout than their elders, but only that the differences persist even among the young and educated, though in all three groups their levels of faithfulness persist even though the absolute levels may have declined. Younger Catholics are somewhat less likely to go to church regularly than older Catholics, but they remain more likely to attend than younger Protestants and at the same level of difference. . .
12. Table A shows that in the five communities being considered Irish Catholics are more likely to attend Church regularly than Irish Protestants and than Americans and British. Nine out of ten in Ireland and the United States believe in God as opposed to seven out of ten in Britain, Far from being the result of faith, magic seems incompatible with it.

13. Britons are, as previous research would lead us to expect, more likely (Table A) to believe in fortune tellers than any of the three Irish communities.
14. Table A shows that barely half of Southern Catholics support abortion in the case of a defective child as opposed to 43% of Northern Catholics, almost seven eighths of Northern Protestants . In Britain the rate is 92% and in the US (in this survey) 83%. In the US Catholic attitudes towards abortion are indistinguishable from the National average. Attitudes towards premarital sex in Ireland are a ten year cohort behind those in the United States – the rate of approval among Irish in their thirties, is the same as that of Americans in their forties.
15. Many years ago, British Gallup did a study of attitudes towards the role of women in the then nine Common Market countries. On the more than thirty variables, the Irish and the Danes were in either first or second place on every one. It does not follow, I hasten to add, that Irish feminists have no just grounds for complaint. It only follows that matters were worse in other countries.
16. One cannot add the thirty southern Anglicans to the northern Anglicans because, as explained earlier, they would not represent a valid sample of all the Anglicans in Ireland, save if a complicated weighting process were used. Such a process, given the small number of southern Anglicans, would be at best precarious.
17. I excluded the 30 Anglicans in the South so as to hold "country" constant in the analysis described in this paragraph.
18. At least in the twenty three nation world studied by the ISSP

9

A "Secularized" Ireland?

with Conor Ward

"The many priests and nuns who had been defiant in an age of state persecution and who became so numerous and conspicuous over the following two centuries are an aging, dwindling and even disrespected profession."

—Editorial, *History Ireland,* Autumn 2000

Introduction

Many voices have been raised recently to argue that Ireland has become "secularized," that the social, economic, and religious changes of the past decade have turned Ireland away from its traditional faith and made it indistinguishable from the other materialist, secularist, consumerist, neo-pagan countries of Europe.[1] Ireland, once the most religious country in Europe and the most Catholic country in Europe, is fast becoming—if it has not already become —a secularized country. Thus His Eminence the Cardinal-Archbishop of Dublin has announced that Ireland is now a "post-Catholic" country. Writer Mary Kenny has proclaimed "The End of Catholic Ireland."

This description of contemporary Ireland is proposed both by those who lament the decline of traditional faith in Ireland and those who celebrate it. Surely the decline of vocations to the priesthood and religious life suggest a sea change in Irish piety? Moreover the various sexual and physical abuse scandals of which the clergy and religious have been accused have shattered the public image of those who once were so deeply respected.

The International Social Survey Program's second survey module on religion, administered in Ireland and in some twenty-five[2] other countries during 1998 provides an opportunity to measure the extent and direction of religious change in Ireland since the first such module, data for which was collected in 1991. The ISSP study has the distinct advantage over other longitudinal studies in that it asks the same questions at both points in time, making it possible to measure precisely the change in attitudes and behavior during the 1990s.

Briefly, to the question of whether Ireland is "secularized" four answers may be given:

> In terms of basic religious belief, there has been little change.
>
> In terms of attitudes towards sexual behavior there continues to be a drift away from acceptance of traditional sexual teaching, a drift which has occurred in all other countries in the International Social Survey Program surveys.
>
> In terms of confidence in and respect for the church organizations, there has been a dramatic decline among the Irish in the last seven years. Confidence in the local priest, however, is relatively high especially among the younger adults.
>
> The young birth cohort, disaffected as it patently is in many ways, is in other ways the most traditional in Ireland.

If sex and authority attitudes are important indicators of Christianity, then religion among the Irish is in decline. If acceptance of core teachings is the ultimate test of the survival of religion in Ireland, then the Irish continue to be deeply religious.

Faith

Table 9.1 compares the Irish responses in 1991 to those in 1998 on eight measures of religious faith. On only one measures is there a statistically significant change through the decade, the proportion who say that they have no religious affiliation, which has increased from 2 percent to 6 percent. On all other items—belief in God, belief in life after death, belief in miracles, belief in heaven, weekly church attendance, and monthly activity in a religious organization, there

Table 9.1
Religious Attitudes and Behavior in 1991 and 1998

	1991	1998
Life After Death	80%	78%
God	96%	94%
Heaven	87%	85%
Miracles	73%	71%
No Religion	2%	6%*
Activity Monthly	16%	17%
Feel Very Religious	14%	13%
Attend Once a week	65%	63%

*Difference statistically significant

has been no statistically significant change.[3] Figure 9.1 shows the proportion of Irish believing in God by birth cohort and year. The only major change is in the belief in God of the birth cohort of the nineteen seventies whose belief in God, while still high (at 85 percent) is nonetheless significantly different from that of all the other cohorts, even when the younger age of the cohort is taken into account. If the youngest cohort shapes the future of Irish religion, belief in life after death (figure 9.2) will be lower among the Irish though still higher than in all other European countries studied by the International Social Survey Program. However, the youngest birth cohort—those born in the nineteen-seventies is as likely to believe in life after death as all previous cohorts with the exception of those born before 1930.

Note that these and subsequent figures do not take into account the effect of age on behavior cohorts. Whether lower scores among those born in the 1970s and higher scores of those born in the 1920s are merely the result of the fact that the former are younger and the latter are older remains to be seen in subsequent surveys which measure a longer period of time. However, (table 9.2) the fact that there

Figure 9.1
Belief in God in Ireland by Cohort and Year

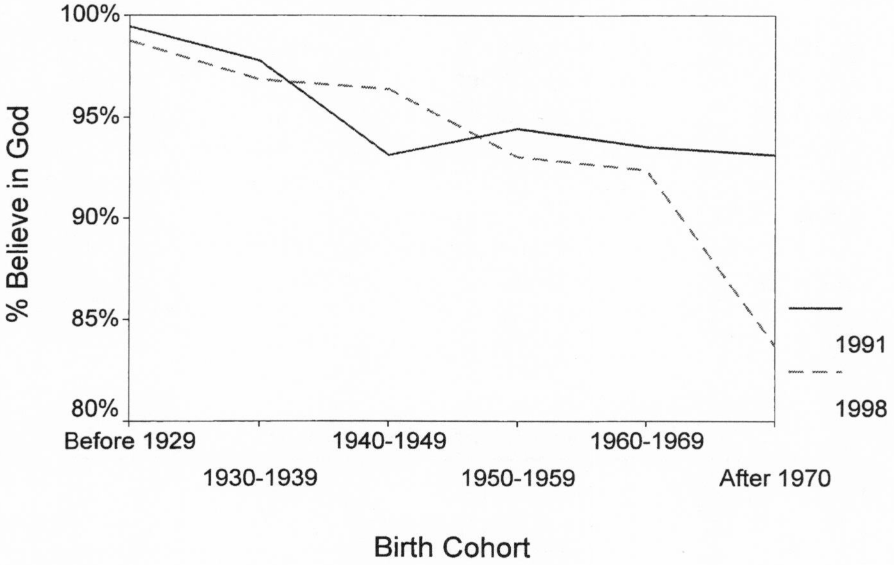

Figure 9.2
Belief in Life After Death in Ireland by Cohort and Year

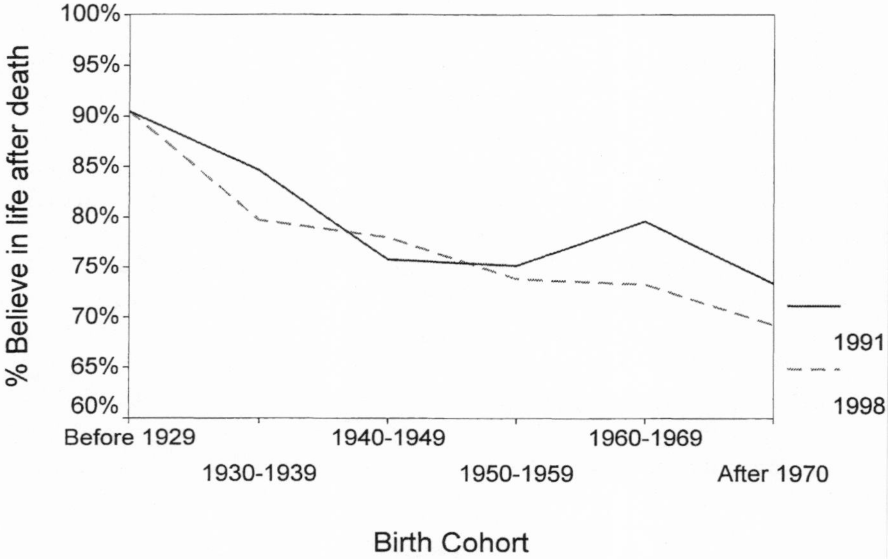

is little short run change among the cohorts since 1991 suggests that the cohort differences may to some extent relate to life cycle. Church attendance among the Irish has not changed in the nineteen nineties. (figure 9.3) The decline from much higher levels presumably occurred before the nineties. In 1974 Irish church attendance was reported as 91 percent, and 87 percent in 1983.

While there has not been a significant change in involvement in church related activities during the nineties (figure 9.4), it is interesting to note a slight increase among those in their middle years of life. For those born in the fifties and sixties this increase is in fact

Table 9.2
Attitudes Towards Church by year

	1991	1998
Confidence in Organization	46%	27%*
Too Much Power	38%	46%*
Voting	26%%	44%*
Government	28%	45%*

*Difference statistically significant

Figure 9.3
Weekly Mass Attendance in Ireland by Cohort and Year

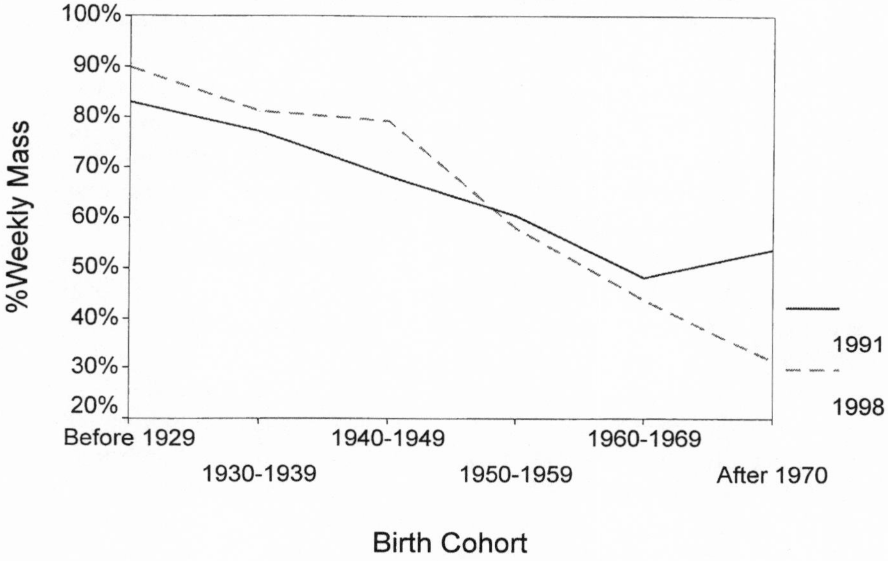

Figure 9.4
Church Activities in Ireland by Cohort and Year

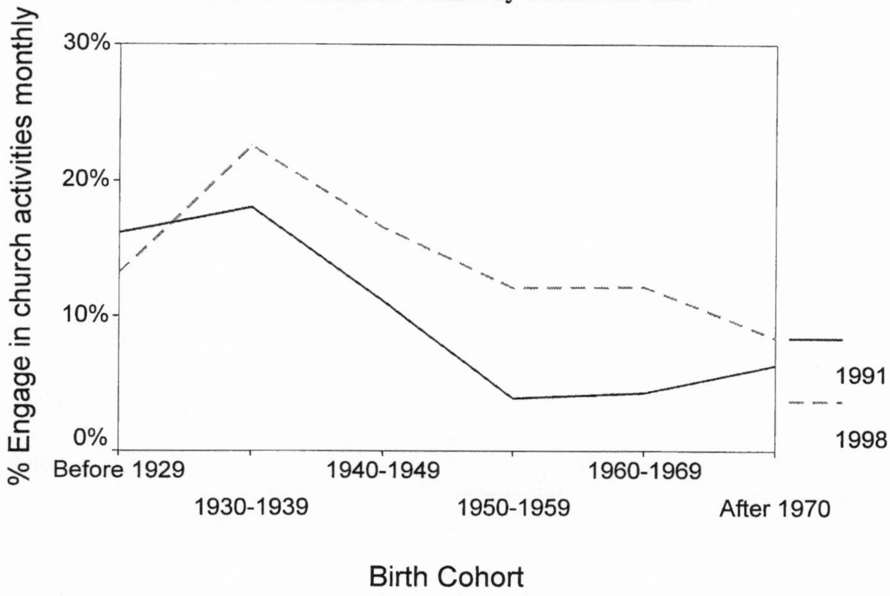

statistically significant, perhaps reflecting increased efforts on the part of the Irish Church to reach out to younger adults. (Activity here may be artificially low due to the fact that the order of the question excluded "Charitable activities, helping the sick, elderly, poor, etc.")

It is precisely in those two birth cohorts as well as those born in the seventies that there has also been an increase in the proportion having no religious affiliation (figure 9.5) in the decade. While even among those born in the 1970s 7/8 of the Irish population do claim a religious affiliation, the increase in non-affiliation among the younger cohorts during the nineties has been dramatic. If the increase in church-related activities during the nineties is the church's response to its current problems with its younger members, it is clear that much more reaching out is in order.

Thus the Irish continue to believe in God and life after death and attend weekly Mass at the highest rates in Europe and their church-related activities have increased marginally among the birth cohorts of the fifties and sixties. However, the very youngest birth cohort is somewhat more likely to reject both God and religious affiliation – though the overwhelming majority of this cohort do not share that rejection.

Figure 9.5
No Religious Affiliation in Ireland by Cohort and Year

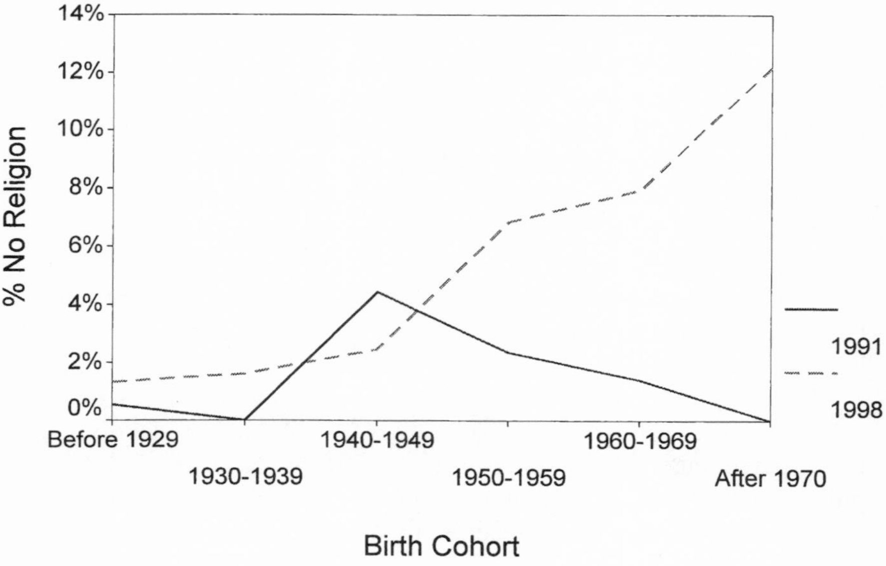

Leadership

Although the Irish are relatively firm in their religious faith and still by the criteria of faith available in this project, the most religious people in Europe, they have much lower levels of confidence in their religious leadership (as measured by their confidence in the church organization) at the end of the 1990s than they did at the beginning. This decline in confidence is widespread in Europe, even among the former socialist countries which are experiencing a revival of religious faith.

Thus (table 9.2) the proportion having a "great deal" of confidence in the church has fallen from 45 percent to 28 percent, those who think the church has too much power has increased from 38 percent to 46 percent, those who disapprove of the clergy trying to influence voting has gone up from 26 percent to 43 percent and those who disapprove of their influence on government has increased from 22 percent to 39 percent. While this decline of approval for the religious organization in the nineties has occurred in most European countries, it is particularly precipitous in Ireland. Indeed Russians have more confidence in their religious leaders than do the Irish. Moreover, in Ireland, confidence in the Dail and in the schools and educational system has increased in the nineties (and confidence in the courts and the legal system has remained unchanged) so the decline in confidence in church leadership cannot be attributed to some society-wide collapse of confidence in institutions.

Figure 9.6 shows that the decline in the church organization in Ireland between 1991 and 1998 has affected all birth cohorts. Even among those born before 1930 there has been a ten percentage point decrease in confidence. Among those born in the middle cohorts the decline has been in the neighborhood of twenty percentage points and among the youngest closer to thirty percentage points. Unless there is some change in the perception of church leadership in Ireland, the long-term outlook is for an Ireland in which less than a fifth of the population have a "great deal" of confidence in the ecclesiastical organization.

Figure 9.7 reveals the massive increase in the conviction that the church ought not to try to influence voting behavior in elections, a thirty percentage point change in most cohorts. It is impossible to judge whether this is a spontaneously dramatic change in attitudes in Ireland or whether it is a reaction to specific attempts to influence voting on, for example, specific referenda. Clearly, however, the

Figure 9.6
Confidence in Church Organization in Ireland by Cohort and Year

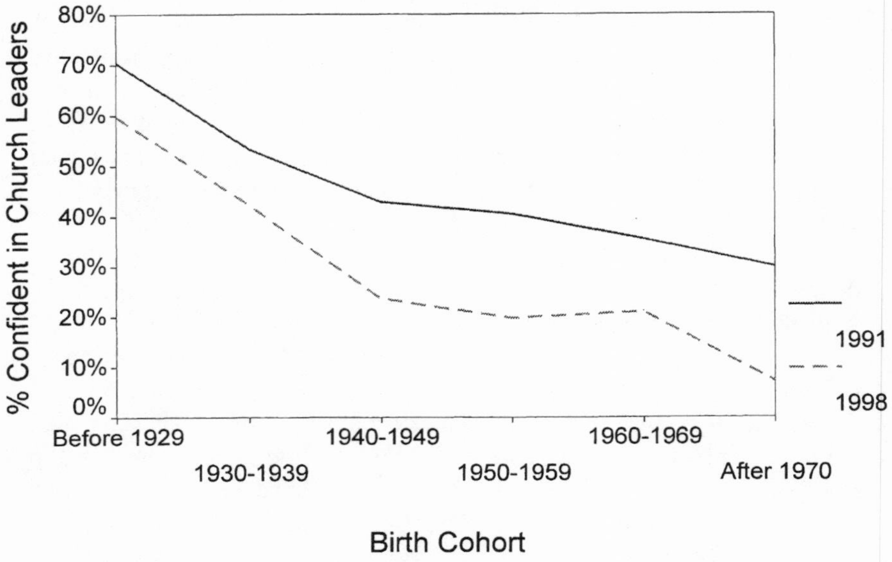

Figure 9.7
Religious Leaders Not Influence Voting by Cohort and Year

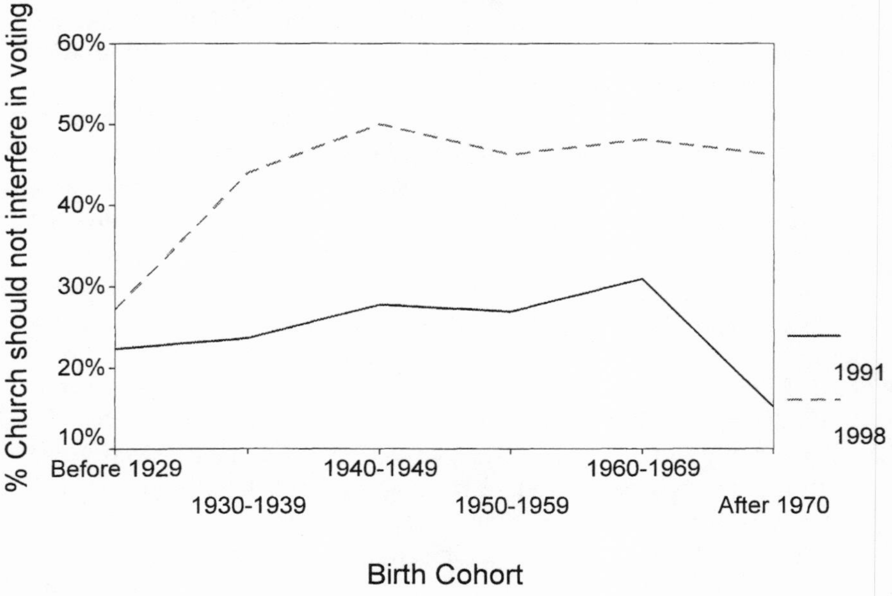

change in attitudes is a warning to the church leadership that such attempts can prove counterproductive. Since this attitude does not correlate with age (save for the decline among the respondents from the oldest cohort) holding age constant will not change the pattern of apparent resentment.

Finally, figure 9.8, the increase in the conviction that the church has too much power in Ireland has occurred especially among the younger two cohorts, in both of which disapproval of church power has affected a large majority. In the other cohorts (except the oldest) at least half disapprove of the power they perceive the church to possess. It would not be an exaggeration to suggest that the leadership of the Irish church may be faced with considerable resentment among its entire population, especially among those born since 1950.

Religious leaders in many countries respond to similar finding by blaming the laity for succumbing to various vaguely defined cultural trends—consumerism, secularism, materialism, capitalism, humanism, pan-sexualism. Such explanations are satisfying because, implicitly at any rate, they explain all the variance and are not subject to empirical validation. Moreover, they do not require the insti-

Figure 9.8
Religious Leaders Have Too Much Power by Cohort and Year

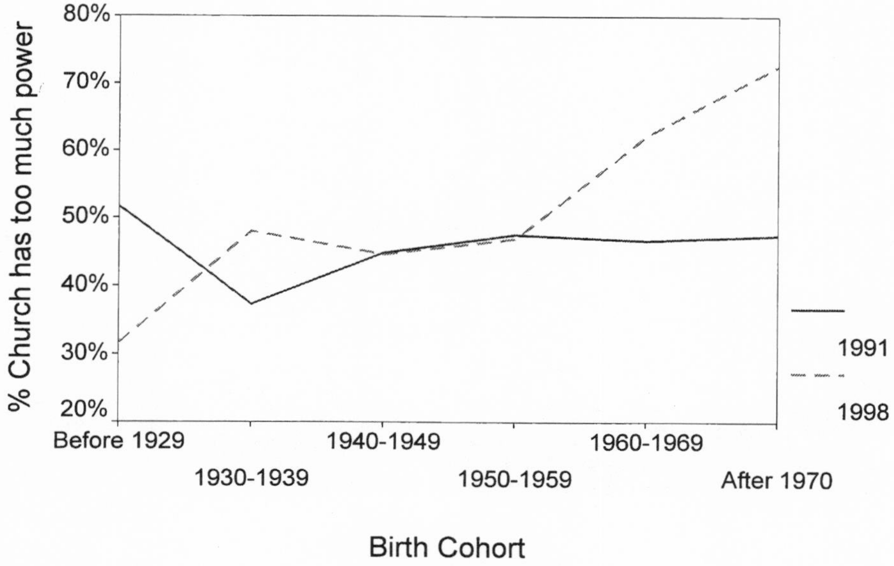

Figure 9.9
Attitiudes Towards Premarial Sex in Ireland by Cohort and Year

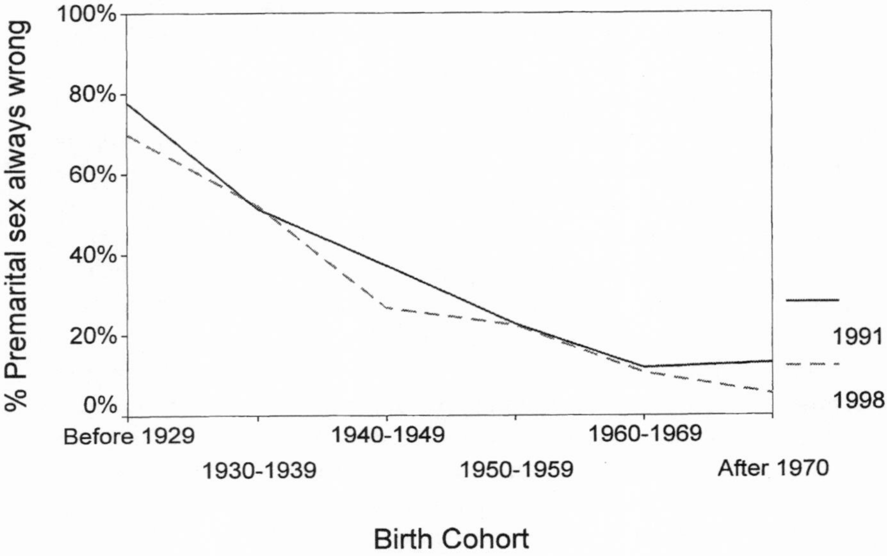

Table 9.3
Attitudes on Sex and Abortion by Year
% Always wrong

	1991	1998
Premarital	36%	30%*
Extra Marital	71%	63%*
Homosexual Relations	68%	60%*
Abortion (Serious Defect)	48%	41%*
Abortion (Poor)	67%	59%*

*Difference statistically significant

tutional leadership to examine its own behavior and attitudes, much less to ponder the possibility that it might change at least the style of its response if not the substance.

Sexuality

The so-called sexual revolution appears to have increased its effect. (table 9.3). The proportions of the Irish people thinking that premarital sex, extramarital sex, same sex relationships and abortion when there is a danger of serious defect in the child are always wrong have all declined significantly in the seven years between 1991 and 1998. While these changes are more modest than the changes in attitude towards the church as organization, they affect most of the birth cohorts and not merely those born in 1970. The shift away from acceptance of the traditional teaching (figures 9.10, 9.11, and 9.12 is rather evenly distributed in the Irish population. Clearly condemnations from church leadership have not been able to avert the drift. Despite opposition from Rome and the local hierarchy sexual attitudes continue to change.

Education, Cohort, and Attitude Change

It is often claimed that the increase in prosperity in contemporary Ireland is the cause of the disaffection of the Irish with some dimen-

Figure 9.10
Homosexual Relations Always Wrong By Cohort and Year

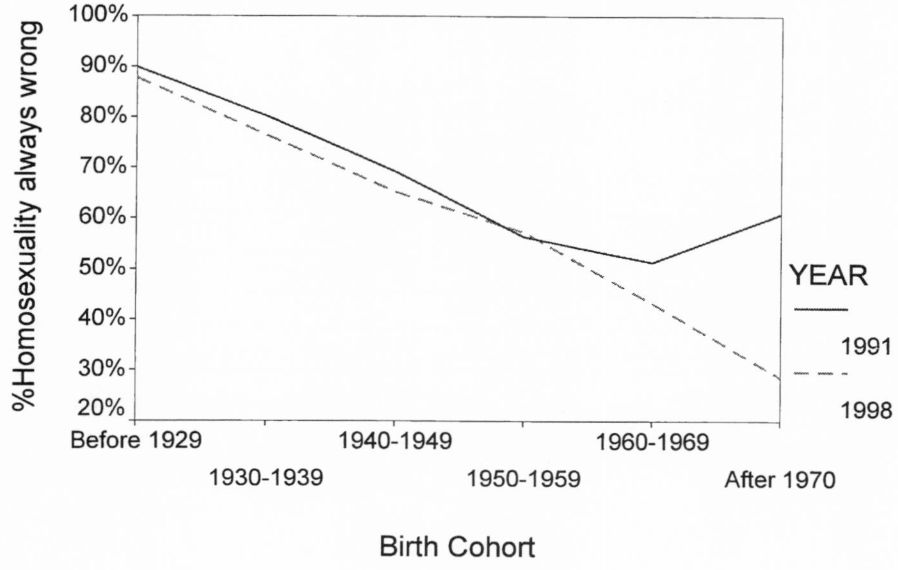

Figure 9.11
Extramartital Sex Always Wrong by Cohort and Year

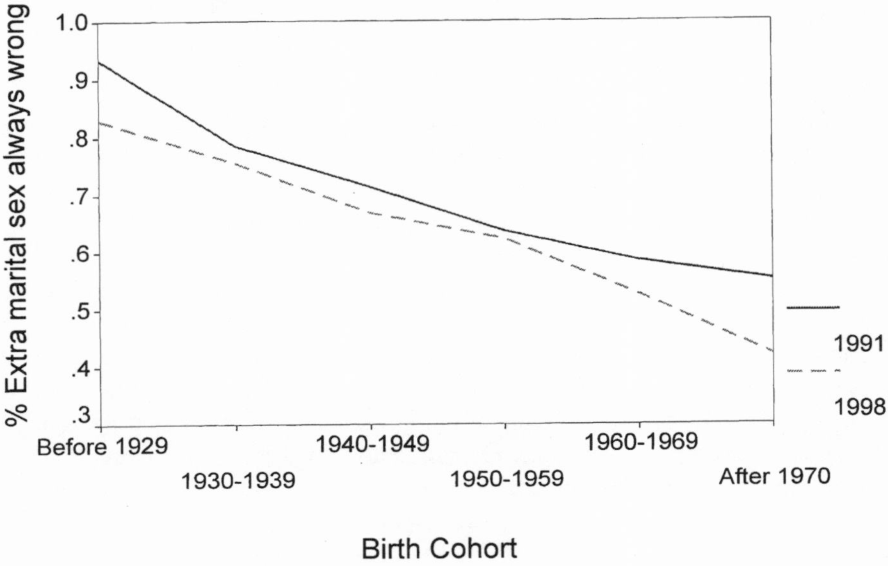

Figure 9.12
Abortion Legal if Danger of Defect by Cohort and Year

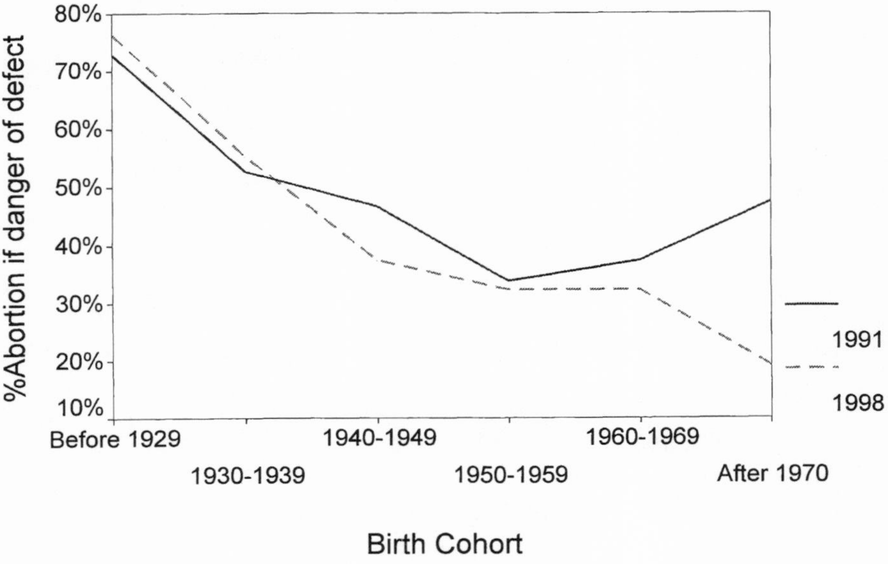

sions of their religious heritage. If this were the case, those who have been particularly likely to have benefited from the prosperity would be the most likely to have anti-clerical attitudes and to reject traditional sexual teaching. Surely those who attended university would be the most disaffected. However, if one enters both birth cohort and attendance at university in regression equations, the influence of university education is minor in both authority and sexual attitudes.[4] Thus when the issue is critical attitudes, years of education correlate at the .07 level and cohort at the .28 level. For sexual attitudes the coefficients are .07 and .41. It is the young people, educated or not, who are most responsible for the changing sexual attitudes.

This phenomenon is neatly demonstrated in figures 9.13 and 9.14: in every birth cohort there is little difference in attitudes between those who have attended university and those who have not. The "prosperity" argument, so satisfying to many who thought that Ireland was a better country when its people were both poor and uneducated, is not supported by the data. Finally even those who attend mass every week are inclined to reject the church's traditional

Figure 9.13
Anti-Clerical Attitudes by Cohort and University Attendance

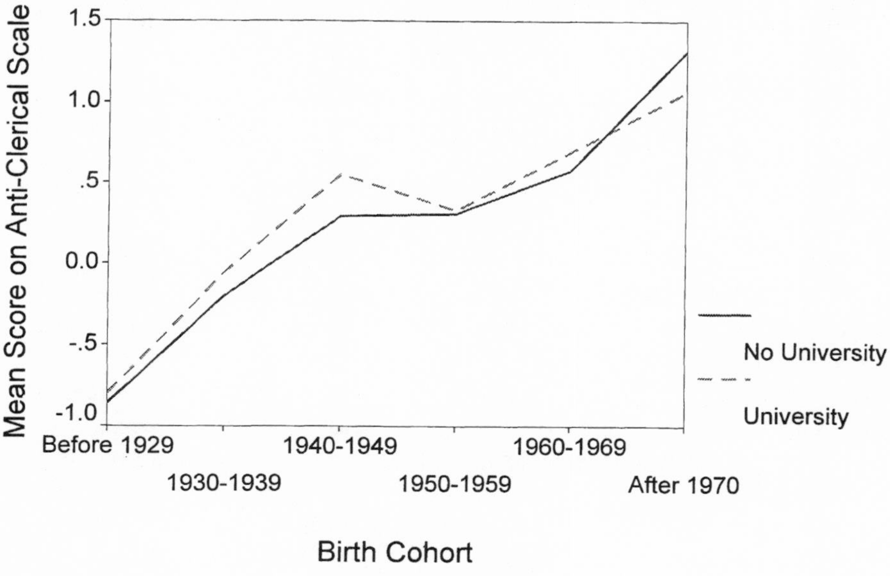

Figure 9.14
Sexual Attitudes in Ireland by Age and University Attendance

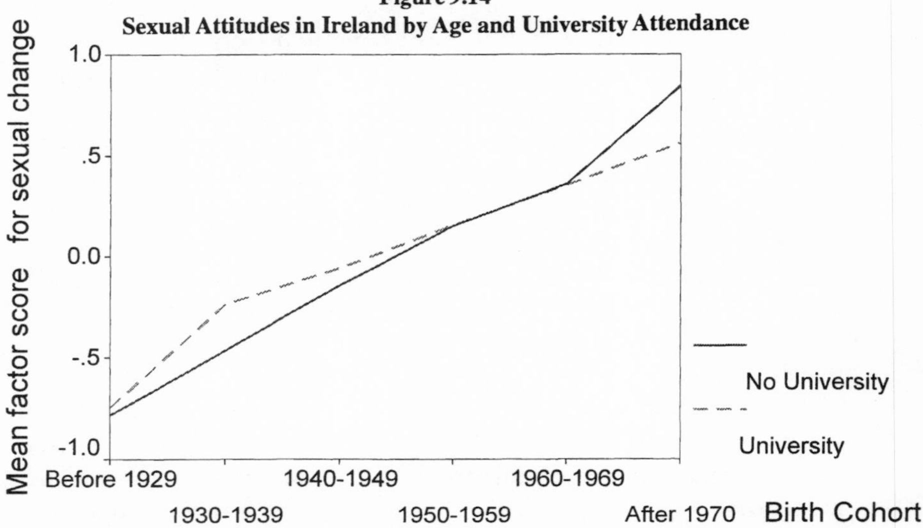

sexual ethic. Thus (figure 9.15), while those who attend Mass every week are more likely than those who do not to think that premarital sex is always wrong, only about a fifth of those born in the sixties and the seventies who attend mass every week think that it is always wrong and only about two fifths of those born in the forties and fifties think it is always wrong. Thus the drift from the church's sexual teachings is happening even among the] those who attend Mass every week.

Four Studies of Religion in Ireland

Using data from the first two waves of the European Values Study (Fogarty 1984, Whelan 1994) one can stretch the present analysis back into the past and, very tentatively into the future. These two studies, administered in 1981 and 1990 provide benchmarks against which the 1991 and 1998 International Social Survey Program studies may be compared. Slight differences in question wording, however, must be taken into account when one compares the percentages in table 9.4. Thus the European Values Study questionnaire provides as its top three mass attendance responses "once a day," "once a week," and "once a month." About four out of five Irish respondents replied that they went to church at least every week. The International Social Survey Program questionnaire added a response of "two or three" times a month, providing an alternative

Figure 9.15
Premarital Sex by Cohort and Church Weekly Mass

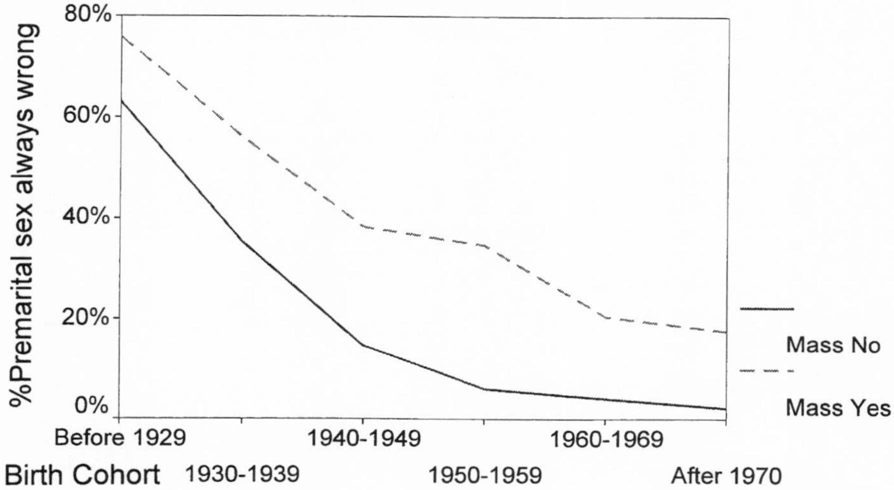

answer for those who attended regularly but not every week. In 1991, the year after the second European Values Study the proportion saying they attended weekly was only 65 percent. In all probability, this difference was the result of variation in the wording of the question. "When two or three times a month" was added to "weekly," the responses of the 1990 European Values Study and the 1991 International Social Survey Program were relatively similar. Because of this and other variant question wording, table 9.4 must be studied with a focus on the statistically significant response differences within the two research traditions. On two of the five items are such differences found—opinions on abortion and on confidence in the religious organization. On the other items—belief in God, belief in life after death and church attendance—one cannot with confidence say that there has been appreciable decline in the faith of the Irish in God or in life after death or in church attendance over the two-decade period. Thus the findings of the research on International Social Survey Program data can be cautiously extrapolated into the past—acceptance of basic religious truth and practice, increased rejection of reproductive ethics, and decline in confidence in the church organization. One might also extend very cautiously into the future these findings. The problems that the Irish experience are not with faith but with sex and authority.

The item on personal happiness has been added to table 9.4 to show that when questions are worded the same way there is conti-

Table 9.4
Attitudes and Behavior in International Social Survey Program and European Values Study by Year.

	EVS*[A]*	EVS*[A]*	ISSP	ISSP
	1981	1990	1991	1998
God	97%	98%	96%	94%
Life After Death	84%	83%	80%	78%
Abortion (*serious* defect)	74%	68%*	48%	41%**
Church (2 or 3 times a month)	82%	81%	76%	73%
Confidence in Church	51%	40%*	46%	27%**
Very Happy	41%	44%	41%	44%

*Significantly Different from 1981
** Significantly different from 1991

nuity across all four surveys: more than two-fifths of the Irish say that they are very happy (the highest proportion in the world).

Irish Religious Imagination

Greeley (1996) has argued that religion is story before it's everything else and after it's everything else, that is to say, religious imagery is essential to religion and the understanding of religious imagery is necessary to the understanding of religion. Four items were used in the ISSP to measure religious imagination, items on which the respondents were asked what images came to mind when they heard the word God. They were asked to choose on a seven-point scale[5] which measured the distance in images of God between Mother/Father, Master/Spouse, Judge/Lover, and Friend/King. In Ireland during the 1990s there has been an increase of emphasis on the Celtic spiritual direction which might be reflected in changing imagery of God. Whether this "Celtic revival" is responsible or not, there have been significant changes in Irish imagery on two of the four items—God as Mother and God as Spouse (table 9.5) The former has increased from 32 percent to 39 percent and the latter from 33 percent to 42 percent. Two out of every five Irish people see God as either equally Mother and Father or more Mother than Father and equally Spouse and Master or More Spouse than Master. Figure 9.16 shows that this change in the Irish religious imagination has occurred in the cohorts born after 1940, which are twenty percentage points more likely to score high on the Mother/Spouse scale in 1998 than they were in 1991.

Table 9.5
Religious Imagination in Ireland by Year
% Equally or More

	1991	1998
Mother (versus Father)	32%	39%*
Spouse (versus Master)	33%	42%*
Lover (versus Judge)	46%	49%
Friend (versus King)	79%	78%

*Difference statistically significant

Figure 9.16
GRACE Scale by Cohort and Year

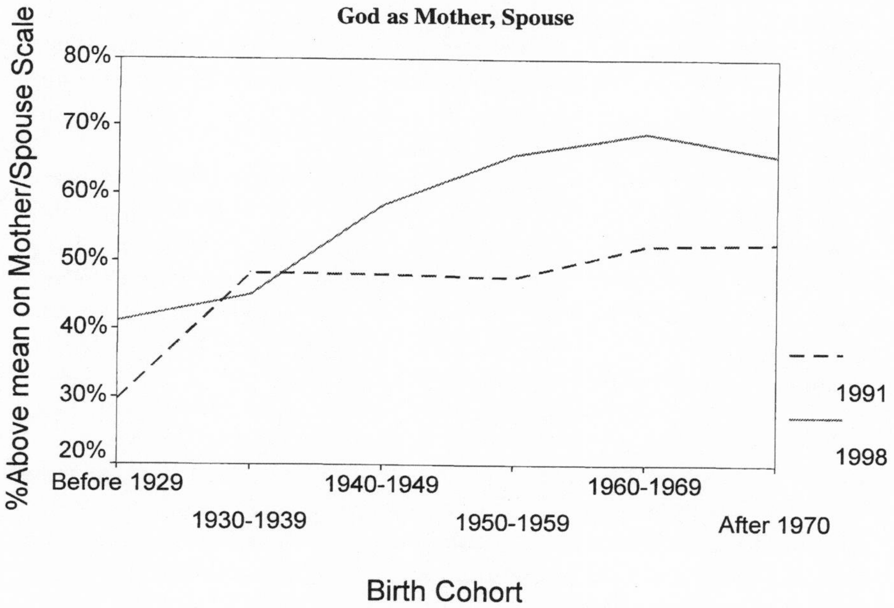

Moreover, (table 9.6) the Irish were more likely than all Americans and than all American Catholics to image God as Spouse and Friend and more likely than the American average (though not American Catholics) to picture God as mother.

This dramatic change in the direction of a more loving and gracious image of God may represent a major religious shift in Ireland both towards more ancient imagery of God as Love. Contrary to the expectations of many, however, these changes do not account for the changes in sexual and authority attitudes in Ireland.[6]

Ireland and Other Countries

Are the trends presented in this chapter limited to Ireland or are they taking place among in other countries? In many of the former socialist countries, the rates of religious faith presented in table 9.1 have actually increased, though they have not risen nearly so high as the Irish rates. In virtually all countries with substantial Catholic populations studied in the International Social Survey Program there have been declines in the acceptance of the traditional sexual ethic and in confidence in church leadership, though the decline in the latter has been more abrupt in Ireland.

In table 9.7 comparisons are made between the Irish and American Catholics and between the Irish and the Polish and the Irish and the Italians. American Catholics are more likely to believe in life after death, less likely to attend Mass regularly, engage more often in church-related activities, are less critical towards religious leaders, more likely to approve premarital sex (at least as not always wrong) and less likely to oppose extramarital sex (as always wrong). There are only small differences on abortion and homosexual rela-

Table 9.6
Religious Imagination in Ireland and United States (1998)

	Ireland	USA	Catholics USA
Mother	39%*	32%	38%
Spouse	42%**	35%	36%
Lover	49%	47%	49%
Friend	78%**	68%	68%

*Significantly Higher than all Americans, but not higher than American Catholics
**Significantly Higher than all Americans AND American Catholics

Table 9.7
Religion in Ireland and Other Countries
(1998)

	Ireland	USA (Catholic)	Poland	Italy
God	94%	96%	95%	87%
Afterlife	72%	78%	78%	73%
Heaven	87%	86%	76%	68%
Miracles	73%	76%	60%	72%
Mass Weekly	63%	43%	42%	29%
Church Activity	16%	24%	15%	7%
Religious Leaders	28%	43%	22%	33%
Too Much Power	46%	20%	61%	41%
Premarital Sex	30%	19%	18%	17%
Extramarital Sex	63%	77%	70%	58%
Same sex relations	60%	62%	74%	56%
Abortion (defect)	41%	37%	31%	12%

tionships. Polish Catholics are less likely to believe in heaven and miracles and attend weekly mass, have less confidence in religious leaders and are more likely to think the leaders have too much power and are less likely to think that abortion and premarital sex are always wrong. On virtually all the measures, Italians are less likely to be orthodox than are the Irish. Thus if the Irish are post-Catholic, so are Poland and Italy, only more so.

Young People and Priests

The data reported thus far in this chapter seems to confirm the popular impression that Irish young people tend to be alienated from the churches. While they continue to believe in God and to identify themselves as religious, they have little confidence in the ecclesiastical institution, attend church services infrequently and ignore its sexual ethic. Two explanations are often advanced to account for this dissatisfaction—the well-publicized cases of sexual and physical abuse by clergy and religious and a hostile reaction to the authoritarianism of priests and bishops.

Tip O'Neill, the onetime speaker of the American House of Representatives, remarked that all politics are local. So too, we believe, religion is usually local. We added to the standard International Social Survey Program questionnaire a series of questions about reactions to local officials. It provides and opportunity to test these explanations for the decline of religion among the youngest Irish.. Respondents were asked successively: *Do you have complete confidence, a great deal of confidence, some confidence, very little confidence, no confidence at all in local TDs, County Councilors or Corporation members, local industrialists and business people, local trade unionists, local Gardai, local priests, local teachers?*

Political, business, and labor leaders did not fare nearly so well as priests, guards and teachers. Fifteen percent answered that they had either complete confidence or a great deal of confidence in the local TD, 15 percent in the county councilors, 24 percent in local business leaders, 15 percent in local union leaders, 54 percent in the local Gardai, 60 percent in local teachers, and 42 percent in local priests. While Guards and teachers outrank local priests, the local clergy enjoy substantially more confidence than does the church *as an organization (*28 percent). Interestingly enough there is no correlation between evaluation of the church as an institution and evaluation of the local priests. The Irish do not judge the church as an organization based on their evaluation of the local priests and vice versa.

Only 7 percent of those born after 1970 have a high level of confidence in the church. Although there is no correlation between the confidence measures, it would not be unreasonable to assume that the "alienated" young have relatively little confidence in the local clergy either.

Figure 9.17 astonishingly[7] presents the exact opposite finding. Irish women born since 1970 have the *highest* level of confidence in the local priest and young men born since 1970 are virtually tied with men born before 1929 in their confidence in the local priests. The lines on the chart are in effect a "U" curve in which confidence in the clergy seems to be highest among young adults and those who could be their grandparents with those of the parental generation having less confidence than either.

Perhaps the older respondents maintain the historic respect for the local priests, the respondents in the middle years may be affected by the resistance of their generations to clericalism, and the younger respondents may live in a post-clerical environment, and one affected by the post-Vatican II changes, and more effective communication and cooperation in the parishes.

Figure 9.17
Confidence in Local Priest by Birth Cohort and Gender

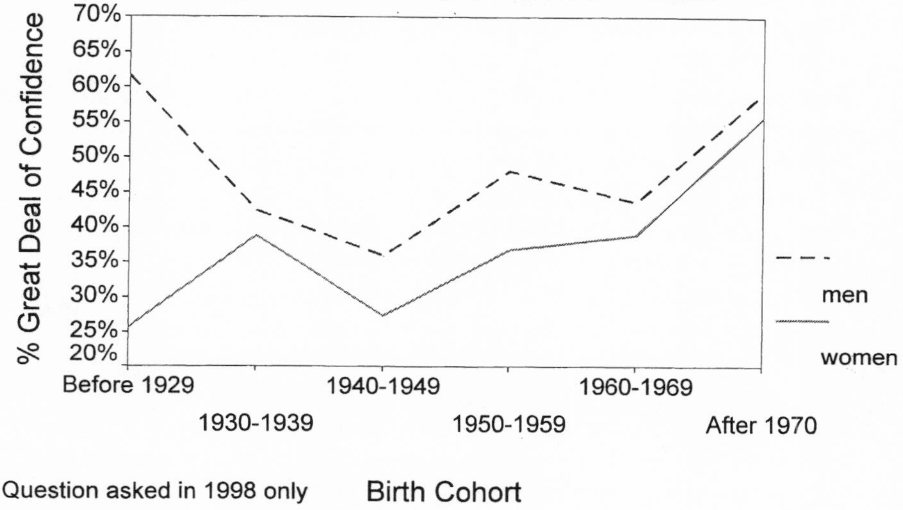

Moreover (figures 9.18 and 9.19) the relative advantage of teachers and Gardai over the local priest in confidence ratings declines sharply among the youngest birth cohort. Perhaps young Irish people see their local priest (as opposed to their bishop) through very different lens or from very different perspectives than do their parents. They may not like the "church" very much but they trust their parish priests. Finally, figure 20 demonstrates that higher education does not have the slightest negative impact on this confidence, not only among the young but in all age cohorts.

Patently this finding suggests the need for further research. What exists in the chemistry between the local clergy and young Irish men and (especially) young Irish women which engenders such high levels of trust (three fifths) in priests. What are the local priests who are in contact with these young people doing that is so effective? Given the problems in Irish Catholicism—which the present report has documented—the answer to this question is crucial for the future of Irish Catholicism.

Young People and Religious Identity

A second way to measure the religious condition of Irish young people is to investigate their religious identity. A question, adapted

Figure 9.18
Confidence in Gardai and Priests by Cohort and Gender

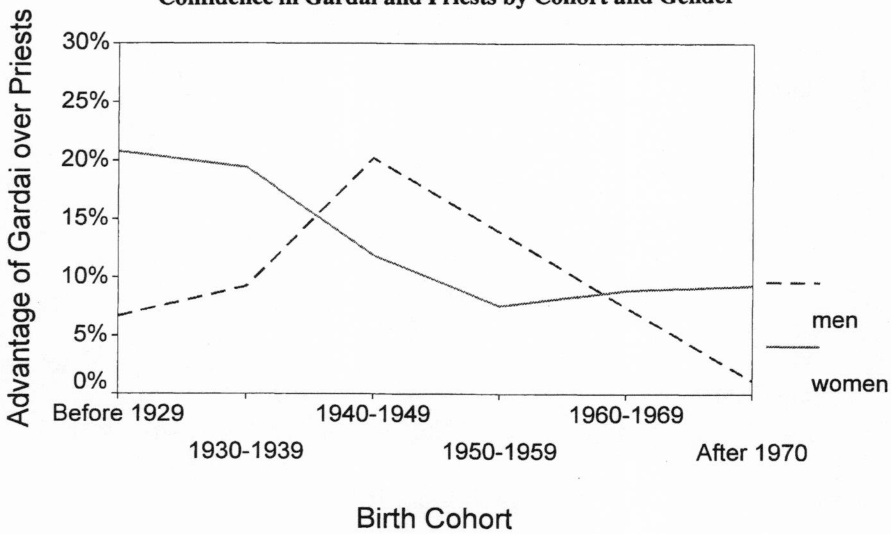

1998 only

Figure 9.19
Confidence in Priests and Teachers by Cohort and Gender

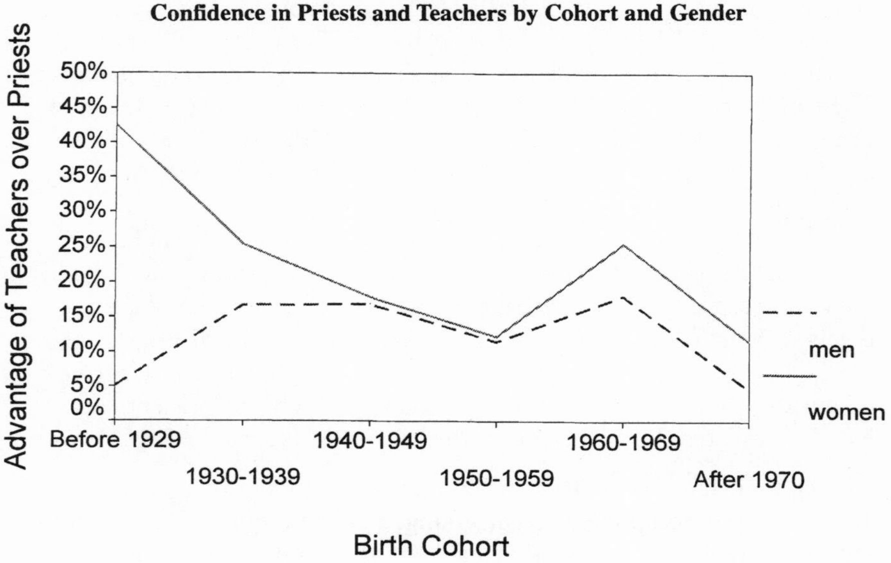

1998 only

Figure 9.20
Confidence in Clergy by Birth Cohort and Education

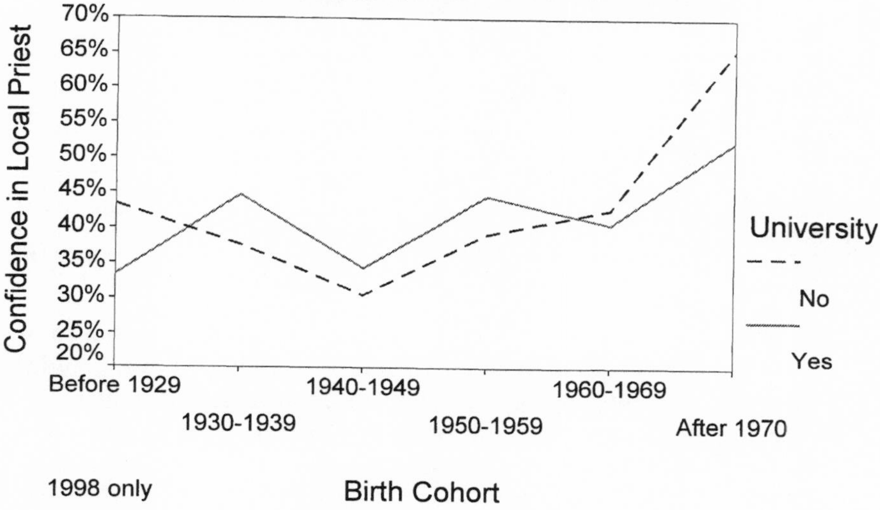

from an American survey, asked, "I *have a few questions about different elements of the Catholic faith. Some of these elements may be more important to you than others. As I read them out please indicate how important they are to your sense of what your faith is.*" (Responses on a seven point scale from *not essential at all* to *absolutely essential*)

In the United States the four most important components of Catholic identity (all endorsed as absolutely essential—6 or 7 on the scale—by more than half the respondents) were the presence of God, the sacraments, service of the poor, the real presence of Jesus in the Eucharist, and Mary the Mother of Jesus. In the United States, "Pope as head of the church" fell just under the 50 percent mark. The findings in Ireland are essentially the same (table 9.8), though Irish respondents rated the Pope above 50 percent.

For the purpose of evaluating the young people of Ireland, however, the striking finding in table 9.8, is that on each of the five components of Catholic identity the most recent birth cohorts scores *higher* than the rest of Irish respondents, significantly higher on all but the papal component. Irish young men and women are, if anything, more likely to say that each of the components are "absolutely essential" than their older compatriots. If "sacramentality," "community," and "hierarchy" are the essential components of the

Table 9.8
Catholic Identity by Birth Cohorts

	Seventies Cohort	All Other Cohorts
Christ in Eucharist	74%	65%
Help for the Poor	71%	62%
God in Sacraments	70%	62%
Mary, Mother of Jesus	68%	53%
Pope	64%	58%*

*Difference not statistically significant

Irish heritage, then the Irish are surely an orthodox Catholic community and the younger Irish even more orthodox than the older Irish. Thus it would appear that younger Irish men and women, as disaffected as they certainly are on some matters, have a strong and clear notion of what it means to be Catholic.

Figure 9.21 illustrates dramatically the higher levels of Catholic Identity for the younger birth cohorts—those of the nineteen seventies for women and those of the 1960s and 1970s for men. In figure 9.22 we note that those Irish people who have attended university have higher scores on the Identity scale than those who have not attended until the youngest cohort when the position is reversed. Among those born since 1970 those who did not attend university scored higher than those who did.

Might there be a relationship between scores on the Identity Scale scores and trust in priests? In fact a multiple regression equation suggests that there is indeed such a connection. When trust in priests is entered into the equation, the relationship between cohort and Identity scores goes to zero and statistical insignificance. Does a stronger Catholic identity among the young lead to more trust in priests or do those who trust in priests acquire a stronger Catholic identity. Either explanation is possible, but the latter seems more likely, giving a hint perhaps of the role priests can play in working with the dissatisfied young. More orthodox than their parents in their sense of orthodoxy and more trusting of their clergy, young Irish, hardly seem to be "secular" in any ordinary meaning of that word.

Mary and the Young Irish

In a recent issue of *History Ireland* James Donnelly (2000) celebrates in a kind of reverse triumphalism the decline of religion in

Figure 9.21
Catholic Identity by Cohort and Gender

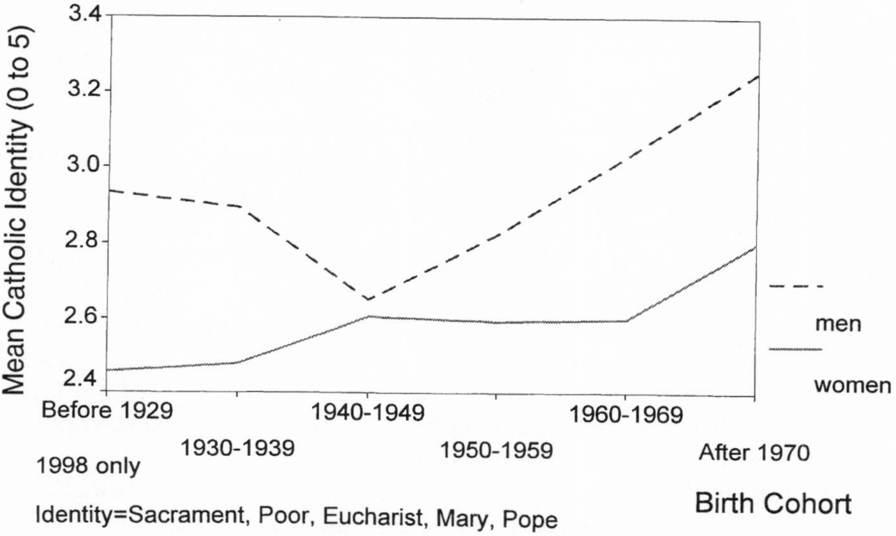

Figure 9.22
Catholic Identity by Cohort and University Attendence

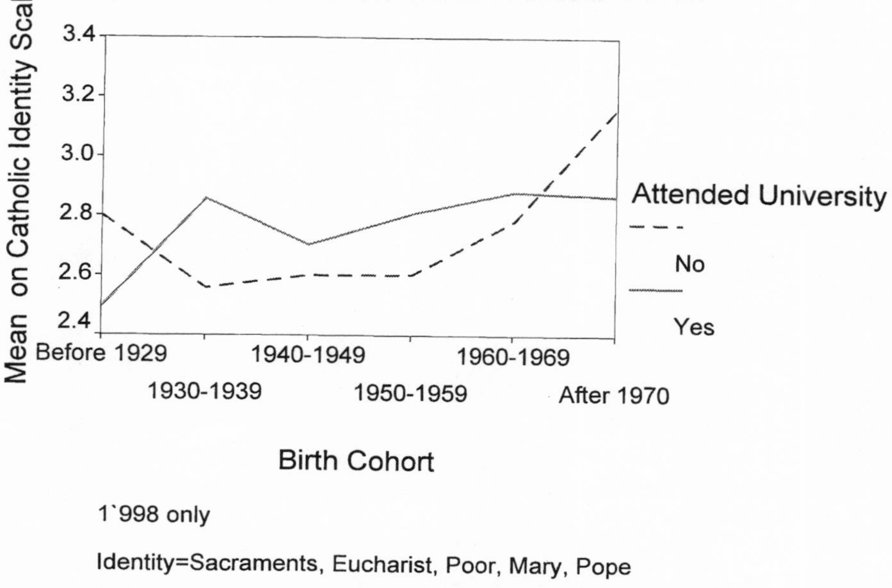

Ireland. He is particularly pleased, it would seem, by the decline of "Marianism" and describes with some relish the collapse of "Marian" organizations "within a decade." A reader might wonder if a historian so distinguished as to be on the faculty of the University of Wisconsin thinks that one of the most powerful symbols (if not the most powerful) in the history of Europe can be wiped out in a mere decade. Moreover, a reader might also wonder whether the collapse of certain organizations, for whatever reason, indicates the definitive end of this symbol.

We have already noted that the role of "Mary the Mother of Jesus" as an essential part of a person's religious faith was especially important to the cohort born during the nineteen seventies (and hence between eighteen and twenty eight at the time of the survey). Figure 9.23 demonstrates vividly the importance of the symbol of Mary the Mother of Jesus to this cohort, chosen by almost 70 percent of its members as opposed to 50 percent of previous cohorts.

Moreover (figure 9.24) shows that despite its low level of religious practice, its massive distrust of the church organization (though in keeping with its high opinion of local priests), and its almost total

Figure 9.23
Mary Essential of Catholic Faith by Birth Cohort

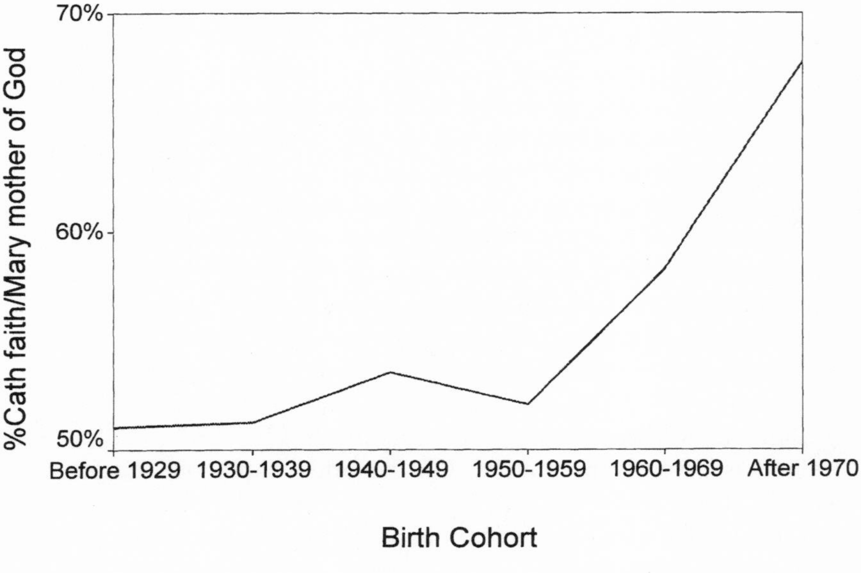

Figure 9.24
Closeness to Catholicism by Birth Cohort

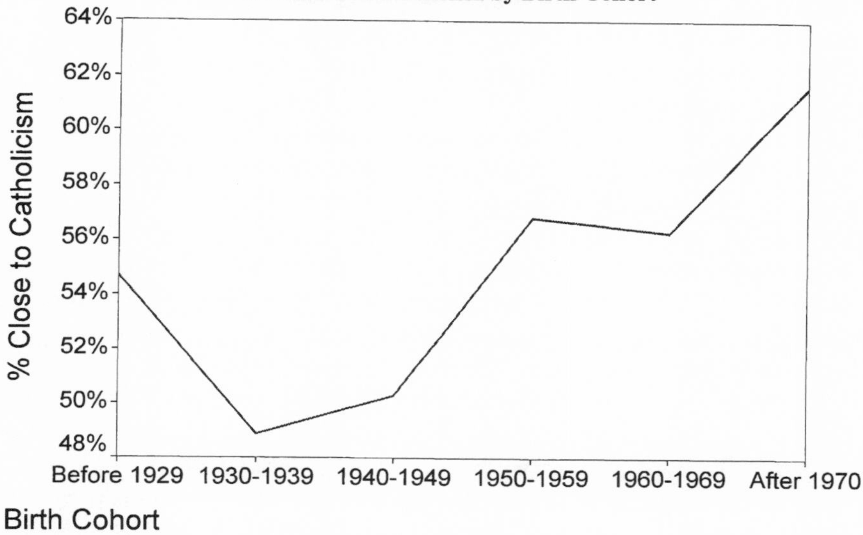

repudiation of the traditional sexual ethics, the same cohort is more likely to say that it is "close" or even "very close" to the church. Clearly the religious orientation of younger Irish is very complex. In this context perhaps "church" means one's religious heritage.

The question arises whether the heightened valuation of Mary among younger Irish (a reality which will strike many as so impossible as to merit dismissal out of hand!),[8] which seems to follow a curve similar to that of the curve for closeness to the church, may account for the heightened sense of closeness to the church of the young Irish. Figure 9.25 suggests this is the case. When the Mary variable is taken into account the lines of closeness to the church flatten out. In a dummy variable multiple regression equation (the 1940s cohort as the comparison group) the nineteen seventies cohort describes itself as significantly closer to the church than all the other cohorts. (r=.17). However, when the Mary variable is entered into the equation, the relationship between cohort and closeness to the church falls to .00 and (obviously) statistical insignificance.

Donnelly's happy assumption of the death of the Mary symbol in Ireland is patently premature. On the other hand, one might well wonder if the leaders of the Irish Church including its intellectual and theological elite) appreciate the power of that symbolic resource, or have the slightest idea how to relate to it.

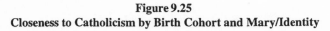

Figure 9.25
Closeness to Catholicism by Birth Cohort and Mary/Identity

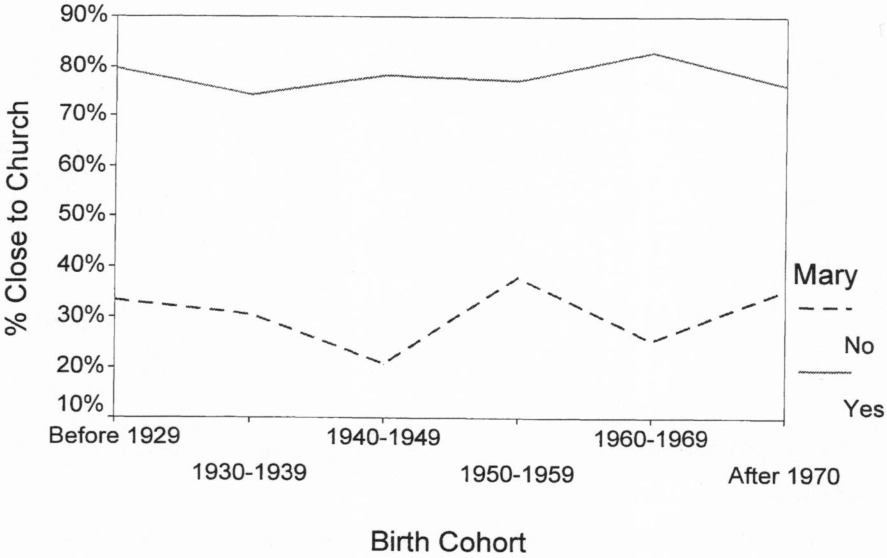

A similar exercise can be performed about the approval of local clerics, producing similar graphs and regression equations. Favorable attitudes towards the local clergy, a sense of closeness to the church, and a high valuation of the Mother of Jesus are important elements, one would think, in the traditional Irish Catholic heritage. They also correlate strongly with one another in the International Social Survey Program data. Indeed they constitute a single factor. In figure 9.26 we observe that Irish young people born in the 1970s are almost twenty percentage points more likely to be above the mean on this heritage scale. One would write the young Irish off as "post-Catholic" only at considerable risk.

RAMP

A group of European scholars carried out a study in 1995 of Religious And Moral Pluralism in Europe. The Irish version of RAMP was included in the 1998 Irish International Social Survey Program questionnaire. Unfortunately, the data from this project are still unavailable even to those who participated in the project.[9] However, those who presided over the project agreed that two nations could share data and publish it. Moreover, a Scandinavian report has already been pub-

Figure 9.26
Catholic Heritage by Birth Cohort

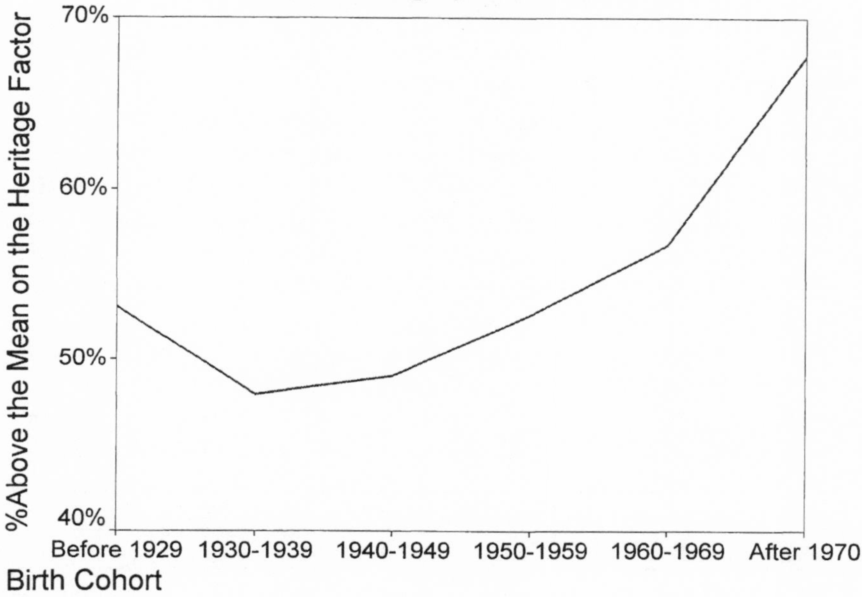

lished. Comparisons are therefore made in table 9.9 between the Irish, the Scandinavians and the Americans on the subjects of the causes of human suffering, the influence of religion in their lives, the sources of personal morality, qualities which are important in children.

The Irish are more likely than the Scandinavians to blame suffering on social injustice, accidents, fate, and God's punishment confirming perhaps the belief that there is a fatalistic strain among the Irish. They are also more likely to endorse obedience in children and less likely to emphasize independence and creativity.

However, they put much greater emphasis on the importance of religion in daily-life decisions, in important decisions and as a basis for morality. Moreover, when charts are created to show the relationship between birth cohort and Irish attitudes towards these emphases on religion, they look very like figures 9.17, 9.24, and 9.26 —the youngest Irish cohort (those born in the nineteen seventies and hence between eighteen and twenty eight at the time of the data collection) have the highest scores on the importance of religion for decision making. In fact these three variables combine neatly with confidence in the local priest, Mary as an important part of Catholic identity, and closeness to the church. The factor loadings average is

.8 which indicates that all the variables are highly inter-correlated, they cluster as if they were one dimension of response. This phenomenon is particularly impressive because the items come from two separate studies. Figure 9.27 shows the relationship of this scale to year of birth.

As striking as is this creation of a scale from separate studies, it is even more surprising the youngest cohort has the highest score on the scale (in a shape not unlike those of figures 9.17, 9.24, and 9.26). On an empirically derived scale of some of the most important characteristics[10] of the Irish religious heritage, the youngest Irish would appear in these respects the most Catholic of all birth cohorts.

Table 9.9
RAMP measures by country
(%High 6-7)

Human suffering:	**Ireland**	**Norway**	**Sweden**	**USA**
People behaving badly	60%	60%	65%	
Unjust Society	53%	45%	48%	
Lack of Natural Resources	54%	48%	55%	
God's Punishment	13%	3%	2%	
Accidents	32%	16%	13%	
Fate	24%	8%	9%	
Religion Influences				
Daily life	40%	12%	11%	
Important decisions	38%	13%	10%	
Morality Sources				
Conscience	73%	72%	75%	
Others will think	18%	14%	13%	
Upbringing	64%	62%	59%	
Law	63%	53%	56%	
Religion	48%	20%	13%	
My own happiness	55%	48%	52%	
Other People Happy	33%	38%	41%	
Teach Children				
Independence	62%	79%	69%	
Obedience	58%	52%	32%	
Creativity	61%	79%	69%	

Figure 27
Catholic Heritage From Two Studies by Birth Cohort

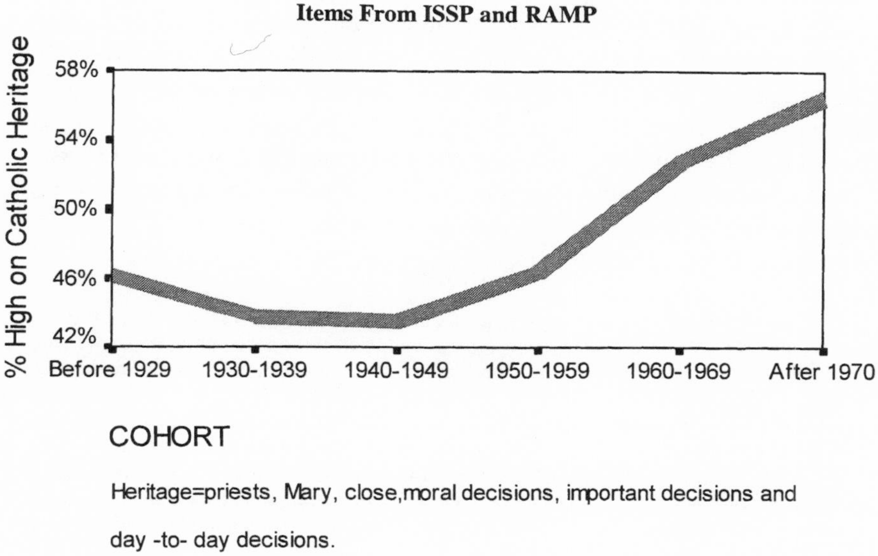

The complexity of this finding becomes apparent when one considers that this cohort, more likely than the others to say that their religion is important in their moral decision making, dissents from Catholic sexual teaching. Thus three quarters of the young people who say that their religion is important in their moral decisions also think that pre-marital sex is not always wrong.

The resolution of this seeming contradiction is beyond the scope of this chapter. However, it presents a considerable challenge to future social research in Ireland.

Conclusion

Whether the Irish are "secularized" depends on how one defines "Catholic." If faith in the central religious teachings make a people religious, the Irish are vigorously religious, still the most religious people in Europe. If, on the other hand, it is required for a people to have confidence in the religious organization to be defined as religious, the Irish are indeed rapidly becoming secular. If adherence to traditional sexual ethics is required, then the Irish are indeed post-

Catholic, as are virtually all the other Catholic populations. One doubts, however, that a people can really be called post-Catholic when those between eighteen and twenty-eight, despite all the scandals, have such high regard for their local priests and such clear notions about their Catholic identity, especially the role of Mary in that identity, and see religion as more important than do respondents in the other cohorts in shaping their moral decisions. Irish religion has indeed changed. The secularization model, however, fits the change badly. Ireland continues to be Catholic, though now on its own terms.

Notes

1. This study is limited to the twenty six counties, of whom 93% are in the present survey Catholic. Separate surveys were conducted of the six counties in the north by National Centre for Social Research in London. For a comparison between the two regions see Greeley (1999). Note that fact the data refer to all the Irish in the republic. There seemed to be no valid reason to exclude those who are not Catholic, they too being Irish. Moreover, there are not enough of them and they are not different enough from Irish Catholics in the matters under study to effect percentage distributions and not enough of them to permit comparative analysis. Thus no responsible social scientist would generalize to the membership of the Church of Ireland from 69 respondents.
2. Of the predominantly Catholic countries in Europe only Croatia and Lithuania were not in the sample.
3. One would liked to have more measures of religious faith – belief in the divinity of Jesus for example. However the ISSP module lasts only fifteen minutes and the questionnaire must be hammered out in dialogue with colleagues who have interests of their own – and in many cases considerable suspicion about religion.
4. Factor scales constructed from the variables discussed in the last two sections.
5. Called the GRACE scale.
6. When the image of God as Mother and Spouse is entered into a regression equation, it does not diminish the relationship between year (1991 versus 1998) and either sexual or authority attitudes.
7. So surprising was the finding that we recalculated it several times to make sure there were no mistakes.
8. Let them get their own money and do their own survey to refute this finding!
9. The reason for this restrictive policy is fear that someone will beat you with their book or articles. In fact, this fear, while understandable, is groundless. No two scholars will ever approach the same data sets with similar interests and predispositions. However, by burying the data till they has become obsolete, such a policy damages of the possibilities of useful analysis.
10. Obviously not all of the important characteristics.

Appendix 1: Area Differences

For demographic purposes Ireland was divided into three different areas—cities; suburbs and rural. One would expect that the people in countryside would be the most "Catholic." Table A-1 demonstrates that is the case except for the three RAMP decision-making items, the responses to which do not differ across the three areas. "Suburbanites" are less likely than urbanites to attend weekly mass, to believe that the church has too much power and to have confidence in the local priests. However, they agree with urbanites on life after death, premarital sex, and abortion. Both are less "orthodox" and "clerical" than the rural people.

Table A-1
Attitudes and Behaviors in Different Regions of Ireland

	Cities (35%)	Suburbs, Towns, County seats (19%)	Rural (46%)
Life After Death	79%	77%	82%
Weekly Mass	62%	51%	73%
Church too much power	39%	47%	32%
Premarital sex always wrong	41%	42%	55%
Abortion wrong	41%	43%	55%
Mary important for identity	45%	44%	58%
Confidence in local Priests	45%	31%	51%
Religion in daily Decisions	40%	40%	39%
Religion in important Decisions	39%	32%	37%
Religion in moral decisions	50%	43%	47%
% Very Happy	42%	42%	42%

10

Religious Markets in Norway

Introduction

Supply-side theories of the sociology of religion contend that the demand for products in the marketplace of religion is relatively constant and that the different levels of religious practice in various countries is the result of variance in religious supplies. Established churches are "lazy monopolies" (or in some cases such as the Federal Republic "lazy duopolies") which result from state regulation of the religious marketplace. In countries where a free religious marketplace exists, competition between various religious "firms" increases the supply of religious products available and leads to higher levels of certain kinds of observable religious behavior such as church attendance.

At first consideration such a claim seems absurd. It is not clear, for example that many European countries are so "secularized" that religion is almost invisible? Are not the Scandinavian countries classic examples of the decline of religion in Western Europe?

Stark and Iannaccone (1994) have challenged these assumptions with the considerable vigor that marks the "supply-side" contribution to the current debate in the sociology of religion. They deny that most European countries are, in fact, unreligious, question the assumption that church attendance is the only valid measure of religious behavior and, on the basis of an analysis of religious behavior in Sweden, they argue that at least 65 percent of Swedes and perhaps all Europeans could be attracted by an increase in the supply of firms in the religious marketplace. While the supply-side approach was subject to strong criticism in the late 1990s, it provides some useful perspectives for examining European religion, especially in countries where there seem to be "lazy monopolies."

Data from the Norwegian International Social Survey Program study of religion provides and opportunity to replicate the Glock and Iannaccone findings. In fact 59 percent of Norwegians believe in God and only 10 percent firmly believe that God does not exist. 60 percent say that life after death is certain or probable and 58 percent say that in some fashion Jesus is their savior (a question asked only in the Norwegian version of the ISSP). It is difficult to dismiss a country with those rates as totally "secularized, " especially since there is evidence (Greeley 1995 p. 87) that Norwegian belief in life after death has not changed in the last five decades. Hence it seems appropriate to ask what the condition of the religious market place in Norway might be and whether an increase in the supply of religious firms could leave eventually to a resurgence of observable religious practice.

Religious Markets

We devised a typology of possible Norwegian religious market places. At the low end were the Atheists and the Agnostics who either rejected God firmly or said that they did not know about God's existence. 22 percent of the respondents fell into this category, 9 percent in the former and 13 percent in the later. The next level consisted of the "marginally" religious, those who did not attend church services but expressed some kind of belief in God. 33 percent of the respondents fell into this category. The fourth level – which we call "Private" was occupied by those who believed in God but did not attend church services often, a quarter of the Norwegians. Finally there was a group we call Devout which both believed in God and attended church services regularly. This group included 20 percent of the respondents. Thus, almost half of Norwegians are religious in some fashion, and only a fifth are either firm atheists or agnostics.

However, a surprising proportion of those who are atheists and agnostics acknowledge that God is loving, believe (at least probably) an afterlife, and that in some fashion Jesus is their savior. While these two groups could hardly be considered as prime religious markets in Norway, they are not without some religious inclinations.

Those who are marginally religious constitute a marketplace that might be more ready to listen to new religious entrepreneurs. Al-

Table 10. 1
Beliefs of Norwegian Marketplaces

	Atheist	Agnostic	Marginal	Private	Devout
Afterlife	8%	18%	48%	78%	95%
Loving	18%	27%	71%	85%	99%
Savior	4%	14%	39%	81%	99%
Miracles	4%	7%	32%	57%	85%
Heaven	3%	3%	27%	73%	94%
Hell	3%	3%	10%	23%	69%
Devil	4%	4%	13%	23%	71%

most half of them believe in life after death, two-fifths acknowledge Jesus as savior, and seven out of ten believe that God is loving. Large majorities in the "private" marketplace endorse these convictions and believe in the existence of heaven.

Similar patterns exist for religious practices in table 10.2. Some Atheists attend services occasionally and some engage in the ceremony of lighting a candle on the grave. More than two-fifths contribute money to church organizations which in Norway is more of a civic than a religious practice. The Agnostics have certainly not cut themselves off completely from religion. 43 percent attend church services at least some times and 37 percent light a candle for the dead. The majority of the Marginals (58 percent) attend church services and light a candle for the dead (62 percent) and 21 percent of them have said prayers with a child at bed time. Thirty percent of the Private group pray at least once a week, 77 percent attend church services regularly, and 30 percent have prayed with a child at night. In the Private and Devout groups the custom of lighting a candle for the dead is reported less frequently than in the Marginal group, perhaps because it is considered a folk custom.

Finally in table 10.3 we observe that there are differences in sexual attitudes among the five religious market places with the devout being less tolerant than the other groups. However, while most Norwegians are willing to admit an occasional exception to the judgment that extramarital sex is always wrong, four out of five believe that it is almost always wrong. On the other hand, very large majorities of all groups save for the Devout are tolerant of pre-marital sex. Hence the image of Norway as a sexually liberated country whose mores

Table 10.2
Religious Behavior in Norwegian Marketplaces

	Atheists	Agnostics	Marginal	Private	Devout
Pray Weekly	1%	3%	7%	30%	74%
Attend Several Times a year	29%	43%	58%	77%%	100%
Pray with Child	2%	9%	21%	30%	62%
Candle on Grave	32%	37%	62%	44%	42%
Money	43%	55%	58%	73%	94%
Religious publication	3%	5%	8%	14%	64%
Contact with the Dead	4%	6%	13%	19%	13%
Mystical Experience	2%	5%	10%	12%	24%
TV Pray	5%	12%	22%	43%	87%

Table 10.3
Attitudes in Religious in Norwegian Marketplaces

	Atheists	Agnostics	Marginal	Private	Devout
Death Penalty (favor)	24%	18%	21%	17%	10%
Extramarital always wrong	38%	40%	50%	61%	79%
Extramarital always or almost always wrong	80%	80%	85%	92%	92%
Premarital never wrong	94%	89%	83%	73%	20%
Abortion for Poor	50%	37%	39%	32%	4%

are pagan and where anything goes hardly survives in the face of the data. The Devout and the Private, on the other hand, are less likely to support the death penalty for a convicted murderer.

The religious picture of Norway which appears in these three tables indicates that the image of the country as being in the final stages of a secularization process is, to say the least, much too simple. Even the "social differentiation" dimension for the secularization theory is hardly compatible with the financial contributions all groups make to church organizations. Religion has not disappeared from the public or private lives of Norwegians. There are traces of religion to be found among both the Atheists and Agnostics and strong residues of religion among the Marginals. The differentiation between the Devout and the Private is what one might expect in a society where there is a lazy monopoly and no great effort to reclaim to the Private to say nothing of the Marginal.

Are the Norwegians religious? Thirty-seven percent of them say they are, while only 16 percent say that they are not; the rest equivocate by saying that they are neither religious nor non-religious. Seventeen percent of the Marginal and 53 percent of the Private assert that they are religious. To assert that such a country is thoroughly secularized is to deprive the word of all meaning.

Norway is not as religious a country as Ireland (many of whose citizens are distant relatives of the Norse). However, religion persists in Norway. Moreover, the recent research on the social history of religion in the middle ages raises serious questions about how religious any country in Europe was in ages past. Perhaps Norwegians are less devout than they used to be, but that fact remains to be proven. Hence it remains to be proven that there is not a religious demand in Norway to which the religious supply has not responded.

It may well be that the relatively religious Private segment of the population finds that the "lazy monopoly" of the Established Church does not respond to its religious needs (demands) save on certain highly specific situations (marriage, baptism) and hence sees no point in more frequent church attendance.

In terms of the supply side theory, there would appear to be some excellent markets available for firms to enter—particularly among the Private and the Marginal. If one excludes the Devout, who are already religious, and the Agnostics and the Atheists, more than half of the Norwegian population manifest what might well be a demand for religious services to which the lazy monopoly is not responding.

In the perspective of Stark and Iannaccone, the available market in Norway would seem to include the 80 percent of Norwegians who are not Agnostics or Atheists, a larger figure than the 65 percent they estimate for Sweden and other "secularized" European countries. It does not follow, however, that Norwegians are sufficiently dissatisfied with the religious monopoly in their country that they would welcome competing "firms" which might try to break the hold of the State Church's lazy monopoly. Indeed they may not be dissatisfied at all. My impression as an outsider is that many Norwegians like their religion the way it is. They are rather embarrassed to find that they are as religious as they are, but are content too with that embarrassment.

A Changing Marketplace?

Does the picture presented thus far in this analysis represent a decline from previous religious conditions in Norway? Is it a snapshot taken out of a continuing film of Norwegian religious change? Or is it a portrait of a blend of faith and unbelief that is relatively stable? As mentioned earlier, levels of belief in life after death in Norway have not changed for several decades. Nor has the proportion of Norwegians who describe themselves as atheists increased (Jagodzinski and Greeley 1996) during the decade of the 1980s.

Moreover, a single factor accounts for almost half the variance (r=.67) in the Norwegian religious market place as represented by tables 10.1 through 10.3: it consists of the conviction that Jesus is savior, Jesus is a good person, God is loving, prayer with a child, belief in life after death, frequency of personal prayer, and lighting a candle on a grave.

The question then becomes one of whether this factor which seems to account for the variety of Norwegian religious pluralism is stable. The factor in its turn seems to be shaped in part by a socialization process: about a quarter of the variance on it can be accounted for by a combination of the respondents church attendance when twelve years old, and parental church attendance at that time.

The question then becomes how stable church attendance rates have been across generational lines. Are respondents as likely to attend church today as their parents were? The data available are not sufficient to enable us to answer that question.

Conclusion

One of the merits of the supply-side approach to the sociology of religion is that it has forced researchers to consider the complexity of religious beliefs and behaviors in countries which had previously been written off as "secularized." Leaving aside the metaphor (model) of the religious market place, one is still forced to conclude from a closer look at a country like Norway, where religion might first appear to be quiescent, that God is still alive and well (and living in Oslo and Bergen) and that hope in life after death is still strong. Norway may be a more religious country than many Norwegians realize. Minimally, such analytic exercises should persuade one that, whatever the merits of the "secularization" theory, it leaves many phenomena unexplained as well as much variance unaccounted for.

Cheerful predictions that religion will "continue" to diminish in Norway on the basis of church attendance figures ignores the large group involved in Private religion and the persistence of basic beliefs and practices among most Norwegians. These predictions also assume that there was a time of greater religious devotion in some unspecified golden age in the past, when one could just as well argue that the present situation in Norway is typical of the human condition.

Excursus: The Search for New Religious Measures in Norway

As the International Social Survey Program prepared for the 1998 modules, there was considerable discussion about whether there might be measures which would enable us to tease out traces of religion in a supposedly non-religious population. I'm not sure what the word meant to everyone. To me it meant not so much the survival of a traditional religious faith (though that too might be present) as a vague notion that life has meaning and purpose. I proposed three items which might tap such a dimension, roughly corresponding to faith, hope, and love. Our Norwegian colleagues were willing to try to administer them in a pre-test and ask the interviewers whether the respondents had any trouble answering them. The referred to the questions as "poetic" which is fine with me because I think religion is poetry before it becomes prose and after it has become prose.

The three items were:

- There is reason for hope
- Good is stronger than evil
- Love is as strong as death

The readers of this note will doubtless remember that the final item is a direct quote from the Song of Songs (which is in the TNK or the Hebrew bible). I would call them together a minimum religious faith, in the same sense that one can be minimally pregnant. Or to put he matter another way, beyond these insights all religion is commentary and explication.

I ask the reader before the next paragraph is read to estimate and write down the responses. Don't cheat.

26 percent of the Norwegian respondents (n=153) said they strongly agreed that there is reason to hope and 93 percent either

agreed or strongly agreed. 27 percent strongly agreed that good is stronger than evil and 90 percent either agreed or strongly agreed. 8 percent agreed strongly with the lovers' song that love is as strong as death and 63 percent either strongly agreed or agreed. The difference between the response to this item and first two is in the proportion who neither agreed nor disagreed (20 percent). Only 17 percent disagreed or disagreed strongly.

84 percent of the interviewers said that the item was easy or very easy to administer. Only 5 percent found it difficult.

The responses form a cluster. 90 percent of the Norwegian respondents strongly agreed or agreed with at least one of the items, 44 percent with all three and 44 percent with two out of three. If one considers only those who strongly agree, 39 percent strongly agree with at least one item and 15 percent with two or more items.

Thus the "poetry" items are easy to administer, form a single dimension, and display sufficient variation. There is also some variation on a range of demographic variables, especially if one uses the "strongly agree scale." Those (seven) respondents in their teens are less likely to agree, but there no significant difference among other age groups. Women are more likely than men to have a score above the mean. Married people have higher scores as do among the unmarried those who do not have a permanent partner. The university educated have higher scores than those who did not attend university—perhaps because education inclines people to reflect more seriously about what life means.

Despite the success of the Norwegian pretest, the proposed items were rejected by the International Social Survey Program board, not without some ridicule. Instead the previously discussed "village atheist" items were chosen to replace. Such for innovation!

11

Orange Exceptionalism

Introduction

Sociologists are not immune to the temptation which afflicts everyone to think that what is happening in their own country is both typical and predictive. Either we are setting the standard for the present or at least leading the way into the future. Thus, sociologists from both Britain and the Netherlands, well aware of the near collapse of religion in their own countries and also aware of the persistence of religion in the United States have, on occasion, usually informally and often without malice, dismissed the American religious situation as one more example of (perhaps peculiar) "American exceptionalism." Just as the United States never produced a strong socialist party or a comprehensive welfare state, so it has not (yet) experienced a "secularization" phenomenon. That which is happening in their own countries (and France and Belgium too) is typical and perhaps even normative.

Enough data has been assembled so far in this book to call into question the assumption that the dramatic and rapid decline of religion in these two countries where the House of Orange has provided (in England under other names) monarchs since the seventeenth century is not typical. Similar events are not happening in most Catholic countries and certainly not in Eastern Europe. Professor Michael Hout was therefore well within the boundaries of accuracy when he said that the Netherlands and Britain constituted a case of "Orange exceptionalism."

There are, therefore, two research questions which are perhaps different sides of the same question: why has religion declined so sharply in these two countries (as well as in France) and not in other countries. The data available to this project do not permit us to answer either question with any precision. However, it is possible to test some tentative explanations.

The Netherlands: The End of a "Pillarized" Society

The usual explanation for the collapse in a single generation of the once flourishing Dutch religion is that religion was sustained in the Netherlands by a complex social structure (*Verzuiling*) that divided the country into three "pillars"—Catholic, Protestant, and socialist. Each group had its own schools, its own newspapers, its own universities, its own theological faculties, its own radio and television stations, even its own football leagues. This social structure continued in existence long after the political and economic realities which brought it into being had ceased to exist. After the war there was considerable dissatisfaction with it (Coleman 1978) but it lingered. As Coleman points out, since the Catholic "Pillar" was the largest, Dutch social structure could not change until Catholics were ready to change. Ecumenism and the Second Vatican Council swept away the weakened pillars and the edifice of Dutch religion crumbled over night.

Before 1960, Catholicism in the Netherlands seemed to be the strongest in Europe, highest rates of church attendance, lowest defection rates, highest vocation rates, highest birth rates—a model for postwar Catholicism. All changed once the social structural supports for this intense "missionary" Catholicism were removed. The problem for Dutch Catholicism was that it was supported by a political structure and not by a deeply Catholic religious culture such as existed in other countries.

There is no reason to question this analysis, though one may well wonder why it happened so quickly and how strong Protestantism and Catholicism were in the Netherlands in the era immediately before the collapse. All the vigorous organizational activity might well have concealed how thin support for religion really was. The house of cards may have needed only the slightest push. However, the outside observer in the 1950s and early 1960s would have had a hard time detecting such weakness.

Writing in 1978, Coleman was optimistic about the future of Dutch Catholicism. He noted that Catholics were still 39 percent of the population, only one percentage point below the 40 percent of the 1950 rate. However, Eisinga et al. (1992) report that affiliation rates were already declining. In 1979 the rate was 31 percent; in 1985, 28 percent; in 1990, 24 percent; and (according to International Social Survey Program data), 22 percent in 1991 and 19 percent in 1998. Dutch Catholicism lost half of its "market share" in twenty-five years.

Granted that Vatican II provided the ideology for the Catholic abandonment of *verzuiling* and granted too that the Vatican has been consistently unperceptive and insensitive in its interventions in the Netherlands, it seems likely that the outcome would have been the same whenever the "pillarized" social structure came to an end.

Both Protestant and Catholic affiliations today have fallen in half compared to the affiliation when the respondent was growing up and the affiliation of the respondents parents (table 11.1). Thirty-one percent of the Dutch were Protestants when they were growing up, only 17 percent are Protestants now. Forty percent were Catholic, now only 19 percent are Catholic. The proportion with no affiliation has increased from 23 percent to 59 percent. In the space of a single generation, the Netherlands has become a country where a substantial majority of its people have no religious affiliation. The Dutch may have become a pagan people almost overnight.

Table 11.1
Religion by Life Cycle in the Netherlands

	Father	Mother	Growing up	Now
Protestant	33%	36%	31%	17%
Catholic	40%	40%	38%	19%
Islamic	1%	1%	1%	1%
None	17%	15%	23%	58%
Other	9%	8%	5%	5%

Table 11.2
No Religious Affiliation by Birth Cohort

Birth Cohort of Self	Father	Self
Before 1929	19%	38%
1930-1939	12%	42%
1940-1949	14%	55%
1950-1959	18%	61%
1950-1969	23%	64%
After 1970	19%	72%

That this phenomenon is of the present generation is patent from table 11.2. There is little change by birth cohort in the proportion of fathers with no religious affiliation but a huge change among the respondents, so that 72 percent of those born during the 1970s are unaffiliated. The most striking change between father and child occurred in the cohorts born after 1940, the men and women who grew up during and after the religiously and politically troubled nineteen sixties. It may be that the phenomenon of the sixties was the push to the house of cards of Dutch pluralism.

It is proper to wonder whether the house would have collapsed if it had not been for the legitimization of ecumenism at the second Vatican Council, the disillusionment after the council, the birth control encyclical and John Paul II's heavy-handed reform of Dutch Catholicism in the 1980s. However, Coleman's (1978) study of religion in the Netherlands after 1954 suggests that the dynamisms which tore pillarized religion apart were at work before the Council. Moreover, while lack of confidence in the church and rejection of sexual teachings account for about a third of the variance in religious affiliation in the Netherlands (with the former twice as powerful a predictor as the latter), they have less predictive power for Catholic disaffiliation than for Protestant. Nevertheless, it is clear that both denominations suffered huge losses of confidence among their faithful in recent decades. Confidence declined from almost 50 percent among those born before 1929 to 20 percent among those born in the 1940s (who came of age during the tumultuous sixties) and then leveled off among subsequent cohorts of Protestants. Among those raised Catholic, however, it continued to decline until in the seventies cohort it reached 10 percent. Clearly both churches were perceived as failing in the Netherlands in recent decades. Whether they could have been more responsive to the religious crises among the people is another question.

Sociological analysis requires comparison. Thus, one must find another nation which is in some ways similar to the Netherlands to determine whether we can account in part for the collapse of religion in recent decades. The most obvious choice is Switzerland, a choice which may cause many Dutch scholars to cry out in protest that they are not at all like the Swiss. One may concede the point and still say that both countries are small, tri-polar (in language in Switzerland), almost equally divided between Protestants and Catholics, very much part of international economics, politics, and religious ecumenism. One could reasonably expect a similar religious result in Switzerland if the Netherlands phenomenon is either typical or a predictor. Should the Dutch protest that the Swiss are "conservative," one must reply that the Netherlands looked pretty conservative not so long ago. Moreover, there is not a statistically significant difference between the two countries in judging that premarital sex is always wrong. Finally, if Dutch sociologists wish to make a comparison with another country, they are certainly free to do so.

In fact, as figure 11.1 shows, religious disaffiliation increases across cohort lines in the Netherlands from 40 percent to 70 percent and never rises about 10 percent in Switzerland. This does not prove that the Swiss are better people (or worse) only that in two relatively similar countries, the response to religious crises can be very different.

Figure 11.1
No Religious Affiliation by Cohort and Country

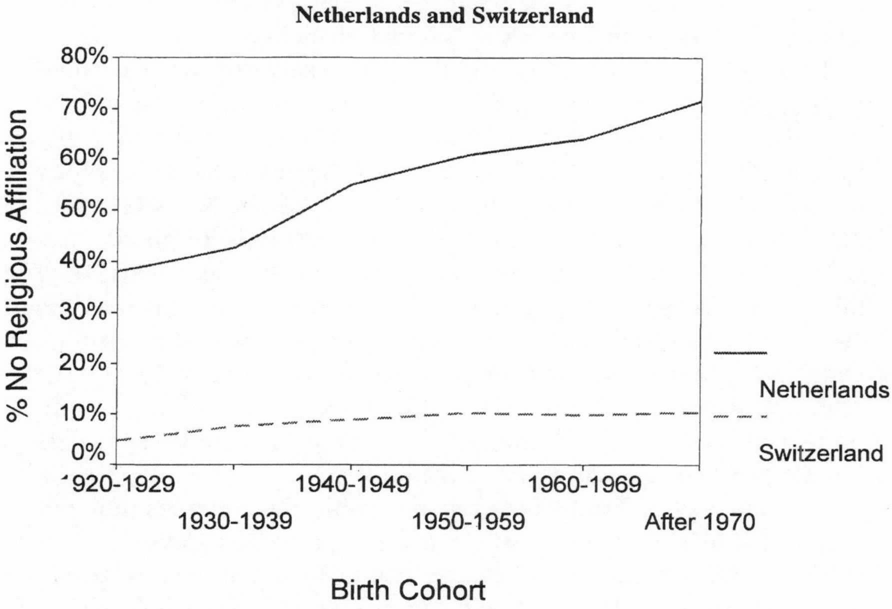

We can account for about a quarter of the correlation between disaffiliation and country in a model (table 11.3) in which the predictors are mother's religious behavior, confidence in the church

Table 11.3
Explanation of Difference between Netherlands and Switzerland in Absence of Religious Affiliation

	Beta	Decline in Beta for country
Country		.48
Mother (Church attendance and no religion)	.15, .16	.45
Confidence in Church	.31	.40
Lost Faith	.17	.36

and loss of faith. These four variables reduce the correlation between the Netherlands and disaffiliation from .48 to .36. (Education, age, gender and many other variables were in the original equations but did not contribute to an explanation). The strongest beta (correlation net of the other three) is for confidence in church. The Swiss in other words, while not deliriously happy about their churches, are not as displeased as the Dutch and this in part explains why they are less likely to decamp from their original affiliation.

This partial explanation of the difference between the two countries is as far as we can go. Obviously the question remains as to why the Swiss have more confidence in their churches especially the Catholic Swiss who have on occasion been treated as shabbily by the Roman Curia as have the Dutch. One has to be content with the conclusion that people in the two countries have responded differently to the political and religious crises of the latter decades of this century because of deep differences in their social structure and culture. Swiss religion is supported by a strong religious culture. Dutch religion was supported by what turned out to be a very fragile social structure. To sort out these differences would be a very important exercise in the sociology of religion, but the present data sets do not permit such an investigation.

The minority of Dutch who remain within the religious denominations (table 11.4) are devout, Protestants more than Catholics, and believe firmly in God and life after death (Protestants more firmly than Catholics). As for those with no affiliation, almost half are either atheists or agnostics, but half believe in life after death. Seven out of eight of them never attend church. There is no trace of a religious revival in the Netherlands (save for the increase in belief in life after death among the young). The prospects for organized reli-

Table 11.4
Attitudes and Behaviors of Religious Groups in the Netherlands

	Protestant	Catholic	None	All
Believe in God	98%	89%	28%	89%
Atheist/Agnostic	3%	4%	48%	29%
Life After Death	89%	69%	45%	60%
Church Several times a month	51%	25%	1%	18%
Church Never	22%	26%	87%	60%
Pray Several times a month	85%	60%	13%	38%

gion do not look too good with three out of four of the youngest cohort rejecting religious affiliation. The Netherlands, then, is not quite a pagan country, not yet anyway. However, the churches have their work cut out for them if they hope to turn the tide.

Britain: The End of the Reformation?

For a couple of generations, British sociologists have been celebrating the decline of religion in their own country. They explain the decline as the result of "modernization" which involves "urbanization," "industrialization," "bureaucratization," and the collapse of a religious inspired cultural worldview because of competition from other worldviews. There is little inclination among these social scientists to test their assumptions against data from other countries (except the Netherlands!), apparently because if these processes are at work in causing "secularization" in Britain, then patently they will do the same in other countries, if not now then in due course.

There is no thought of comparing religion in Britain with that of Italy which has recently passed Britain in economic wealth or that of Ireland which has surpassed Britain in per capita income. Both are, nonetheless, backward countries, it would seem. If religion survives there the reason would be that neither country is as "modernized" as Britain.

Recently the most vigorous and persuasive advocate of the "modernization" theory is Steve Bruce of the University of Aberdeen. Bruce argues, based on the work of Eamon Duffy, that pre-reformation England did indeed have a "unified world view" that was religious, however much it may have been mixed with superstition. Then he traces the decline of religion in nineteenth- and twentieth-century Britain and refutes the notion that Britain is more religious today than was Catholic England before the reformation. I suspect he's right, though it's hard to compare the fifteenth century with the twentieth.

However, he seems to miss one important variable: the Reformation itself. Might the present collapse of religion in England simply be the last act in the play that began with Henry VIII's break with Rome? Might the Reformation have destroyed the religious culture of England and begun the long downhill process which culminates today in 80 percent of the cohort born in the 1970s and raised Protestant have no religious affiliation and a quarter of all Britons classifying themselves as atheists or agnostics?

Bruce himself can find little but decay in the nineteenth century, save among the Free Churches, and especially the Methodists. Others, however, place the beginning of secularization back at the reformation itself. C. John Sommerville (1992) summarizes the difference between the middle ages and early modern times in his book, *The Secularization of Early Modern England,* by saying that before the Reformation, England had a religious culture and after the Reformation a religious faith. In the former era, religion, a mix of orthodoxy and animism, permeated all of life. In the latter era, in the absence of the support of religious culture, intellectually grounded religious commitment and devotion became possible and necessary. He does not add, as well he might, that it is harder to sustain a religious heritage when there is little religious culture to sustain it. He does point out, however, that a really powerful and determined modern monarch like Henry VIII could stamp out a religious culture in thirty years.

Just as the socialists did in East Germany and as they failed spectacularly to do in Russia. Might the religious culture have been reborn after Henry as it was in Russia under Gorbachev. Perhaps it might, but it never really had a chance.

In this study of Devon and Cornwall, Robert Whiting (1989) argues that the Reformation owed its success in these areas to "obligation to authority, xenophobia, the urge for social or sexual self-determination, the hope of material gain, the fear of material loss, the pressure of secular financial demands, the dread of social isolation, of corporal punishment or death."

He adds,

> Those factors were in themselves insufficient to create an intelligent commitment to the Protestant faith, and indeed must frequently have operated as deterrents against it. Together they help explain why, for the average man and woman, the reformation was

less a transition from one form of religious commitment to another than a descent from relatively high level of devotion into conformism, inactivity and even disinterest.

If, as R.H. Tawney claimed, Karl Marx was the last of the Schoolmen, then Henry VIII, was the first of the secularists.

If secularization in England is the result of the failure of the Church of England to sustain enough of the residual Catholic subculture to support an intellectual commitment to religion, then the last half century may suggest that an end time is near. Thus in table 11.5, only 10 percent of British respondents had no religious affiliation when they were growing up (the opposite of which often meant a tentative commitment to the Church of England for life cycle ritual purposes), 46 percent have no religious affiliation now. Sixty-eight percent were "Protestants" (which in the International Social Survey Program coding means Anglican in Britain) when they were young only 43 percent are now.

British sociologists note that the era after the Second World War seems to have been a turning point for British religion. The increase in disaffiliation in table 11.6 that becomes dramatic with the 1940s birth cohort seems to support this notion. It was no longer quite enough for those who grew up in the postwar years and after to

Table 11.5
Religion by Life Cycle in Great Britain

	Father	Mother	Growing up	Now
Protestant	60%	69%	68%	43%
Catholic	11%	13%	12%	9%
Islamic	1%	1%	1%	1%
None	12%	7%	10%	46%
Other	14%	10%	9%	1%

Table 11.6
No Religious Affiliation by Birth Cohort in Britain

Birth Cohort of Self	Father	Self
Before 1929	4%	26%
1930-1939	6%	28%
1940-1949	6%	40%
1950-1959	11%	50%
1950-1969	18%	57%
After 1970	25%	71%

maintain a nominal affiliation with Anglicanism. They had to declare themselves free from all religion.

I do not intend to impeach the enormous religious, devotional, intellectual, and ecclesiological riches of the Anglican tradition. Moreover some two-fifths of the Britons still identify with it. However, the dramatic losses of the last half century might suggest that its energies are spent.

What would have happened if Charles II had been able to finesse a reunion of the Anglican and Roman Church as he apparently planned? What if James II had won the Battle of the Boyne? What if Bonny Prince Charlie had won at Culloden Moor? Was there still a possibility of a revival of the religious culture of England? What would the religion of Catholic England look like today?

Such questions are for fantasy fiction and not for serious sociology. Yet they do suggest a possible analytic strategy. What if there were a Catholic component of England today that had kept alive some of the communal and ritual traditions of the Catholic past? How would it survive the pressures of secularization?

There is such a group, mostly Irish in origin, and living especially in the west of England and in Liverpool and Manchester. Figure 11.2 suggests that this group has largely resisted the increase in dis-

Figure 11.2
No Religious Affiliation by Religion Raised by Birth Cohort

Great Britain

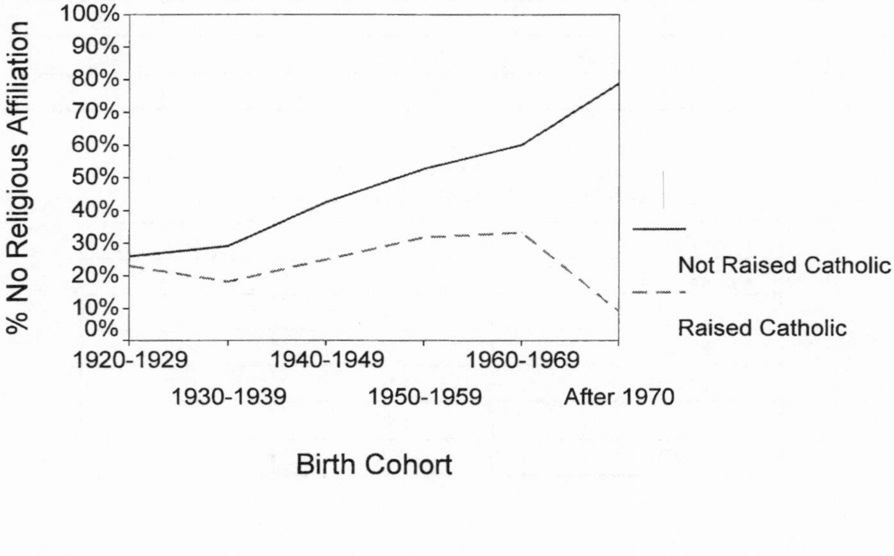

affiliation that has occurred across cohort lines during this century. The Protestant (Anglican) disaffiliation rate has increased from thirty percent in the first cohort to almost eighty percent in the most recent cohort. Among Catholics however there has been no statistically significant change. The negative correlation between Catholic and disaffiliation is -.15. When parental church attendance is entered into the equation, the relationship becomes statistically insignificant. Thus it is at least possible that the Catholic communal heritage facilitates continued Catholic affiliation through the traditional Catholic strategy of the family acting for the church.

Obviously this whole argument highly speculative. However, it would appear that at least in this century "secularization" in Britain is a "Protestant" (i.e., Anglican) phenomenon and has not affected Catholics at least so far as it implies leaving the church. Thus such scholars of secularization as the worthy Steve Bruce might consider that what is apparently destroying religion in England is not "modernization" but the last and perhaps final effects of the Reformation.

The Catholic subculture in England is small and often not quite respected. It may have a hard time sustaining its distinctiveness, though it seems to have succeeded so far despite the articles some Catholic writers submit to the London *Tablet*. (One might add that the American Catholic subculture might also find it difficult to maintain its own distinctiveness, especially if it abandons Catholic schools.)

If Catholic culture had survived in England and adjusted, as it has in other cultures, to the changes in the world, would English religion today look all that different from the Catholicism of the Irish immigrants and their descendants? It is a question worth pondering.

Catholics are more likely than surviving Protestants to remain religiously active (table 11.7)—to believe in God and life after death, to attend church regularly and to pray several times a month. They are also less likely than their Protestant counterparts to never attend church (26 percent versus 37 percent).

While half of the unaffiliated are either atheists or agnostics, half also believe in life after death. Eighty-four percent of them, however, never go to church.

It is beyond the scope of this book to prognosticate or prescribe for the future of religion in England. However English sociologists might well consider that in addition to "modernization" they might ponder that what they are observing is the end of the Reformation.

Table 11.7
Attitudes and Behaviors of Religious Groups in Britain

	Protestant	Catholic	None	All
Believe in God	90%	95%	36%	68%
Atheist/Agnostic	7%	3%	46%	25%
Life After Death	71%	82%	43%	59%
Church Several times a month	24%	38%	1%	17%
Church Never	37%	26%	84%	54%
Pray Several times a month	53%	64%	15%	37%

France: The Church's Eldest Daughter Decamps

Of the traditional Catholic countries in this study—Poland, Slovakia, Ireland, Italy, Spain, Austria, and Portugal—only France shows marked effects of secularization. Indeed (table 11.8), although three quarters of the French respondents were Catholics when they were growing up only half are Catholic today. Once more (figure 11.3) the decisive change seems to have occurred in the cohort born in the 1940s. In that cohort the proportion disaffiliated increased from 30 percent in the previous cohort to 50 percent.

Thus in all three "secularized" countries the churches do not seem to have been able to sustain the allegiance of those who grew up during and after the "postwar" world. Yet among the Catholics in England and among the Swiss no such effect seems to have occurred.

Nor as we see in figure 11.3 does the effect occur in Italy. It does not seem unreasonable to compare the two countries. Both had strong anti-clerical experiences in nineteenth and twentieth centuries—the *Resorgimento* and the Third Republic. Both suffered under Fascist regimes which were linked to reactionary elements in the church.

Table 11.8
Religion by Life Cycle in France

	Father	Mother	Growing up	Now
Catholic	75%	83%	77%	49%
None	15%	8%	15%	47%
Other	10%	9%	8%	4%

Figure 11.3
No Religious Affiliation by Cohort and Country

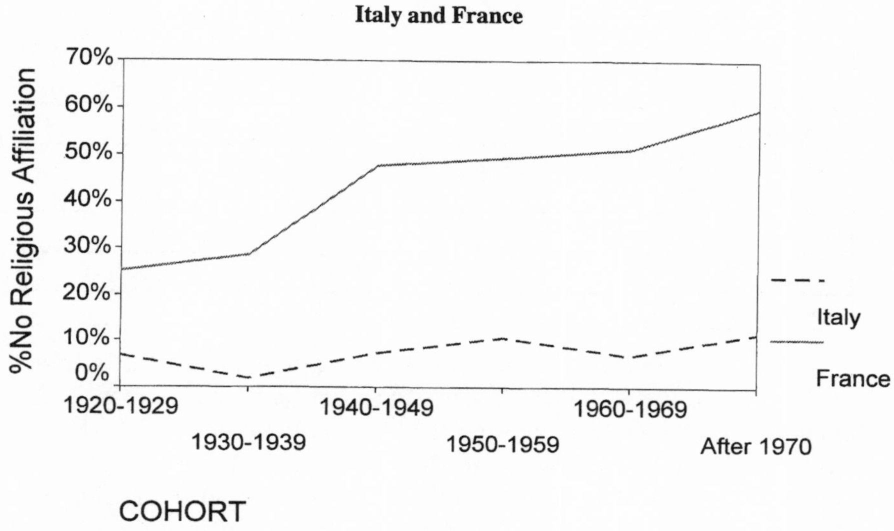

Both have experienced economic and political instability in the years since the War. Both have strong regional differences. Both are major industrial nations. Both suffer from ecclesiastical interference in politics, Italy more so that France because of the intrusive eye of the Vatican. If France represents a trend that will affect the other traditional Catholic countries, the same energies ought to be at work in Italy. But as figure 11.3 shows the disaffiliation rate in France has doubled across cohorts while in Italy it has not changed and remains below 10 percent.

The model we used for the Netherlands and Switzerland accounts for half the difference in disaffiliation between Italy and France (table 11.9) The Italians are less likely to disaffiliate from Catholicism because their parents are more religious, because they have somewhat more confidence in the church institution, because they are less likely to have abandoned belief in God and because they are somewhat less resistant to the church's sexual teaching.

This model may be less impressive than would at first seem to be the case. All it really says is that Italians are somewhat more reli-

Table 11.9
Explanation of Difference between France and Italy in Absence of Religious Affiliation

	Beta	Decline in Beta for country
Country		.42
Parents (Church attendance and religion)	.15. .13 .07 .06	.28
Confidence in Church	.27 .	.25
Lost Faith	.19	.22
Sex mores	.06	.20

gious than the French, that in effect their religious culture is more impervious to the religious shocks of the last half century than is the French religious culture and this for historical and structural reasons that are difficult to specify with the available data. More important for the purposes of this book, however, is the fact that the disaster that has affected French Catholicism has not spread to Italy, not yet anyway. Might it? Perhaps and perhaps not. However, such a contagion is not inevitable unless one believes, as some sociologists do, in irresistible social forces, a belief for which there is little support in the data analyzed in this book.

Some years ago, Roberto Cipriani described Italian Catholicism as diffuse, that is, spread so subtly through Italian culture that it is impervious to the effects of external forces—such as, for example, ecumenical councils, encyclicals, and disappointments and disillusions. There is nothing in the present analysis to refute such a suggestion. On the contrary something like it also seems to apply to Spain and Portugal in the Mediterranean Catholic countries.

Although 30 percent of the unaffiliated French believe in life after death, two thirds of them are either atheists or agnostics (table 11.10) only 7 percent pray with any frequency and more than four fifths never go to church. The divide between those who are Catholic and those who are not is sharper in France than in the Netherlands and may be harder to cross.

In both the models from Switzerland/Netherlands and Italy/France, lack of confidence in the institutional church is the most powerful variable. However, this lack of confidence could just as well be an effect of disaffiliation as a cause. One might judge that the church

Table 11.10
Attitudes and Behaviors of Religious Groups in France

	Catholic	None	All
Believe in God	91%	13%	69%
Atheist/Agnostic	6%	66%	24%
Life After Death	74%	30%	61%
Church Several times a month	39%	1%	27%
Church Never	15%	84%	35%
Pray Several times a month	61%	07%	46%

had been more effective in Italy and Switzerland in maintaining the confidence of the laity than it had been in the Netherlands. Or one might also judge that the Swiss and the Italians are more immune to those ecclesiastical behaviors that shake one's confidence in the church.

Conclusions

1. Among the European countries, the British, the Dutch, and the French are the exception in that they seem to fit the "secularization" model.

2. However, other and roughly similar countries (and British Catholics) do not fit the model though the theory of inevitable modernization ordains that they should. The argument that secularization will inevitably catch up with most Catholic cultures therefore begs the question. If one cites Ireland as an example of a "rapidly secularizing" Catholic country one has changed the definition and ignored the data reported in previous chapters.

3. It may well be that the sudden collapse of affiliation with the Church of England in the last half century is the end of a process begun long ago with the Reformation itself.

4. An important issue which is raised by the findings in this chapter is the relationship between cultural support and religious belief. The Reformation tended, perhaps implicitly, to treat the medieval religious culture as interfering with the pure exercise of faith. Catholicism has almost emphasized that faith, while ultimately an individual responsibility, is also a communal act support by an enveloping religious culture with metaphors and stories and devotions which incline the whole human person to religious assent. It would be wrong to suggest that Catholic religious culture in, let us say, Italy, Switzerland and Ireland has not changed since the years before the Reformation. The

subculture (perhaps imperiled, perhaps not) of British Catholics is not the same as that of pre-Reformation England as described by Eamon Duffy. It is not, however, completely discontinuous with it either. The data analyzed in this book suggest that in the Catholic and Orthodox countries a supporting religious culture (or subculture) might be a firewall which resists "secularization" which does not exist in Protestant countries.

12

Conclusion

Let us consider the condition of European religion at the end of the First Millennium. The most likely scenarios for the future at that time would have been that Europe would become Muslim or Nordic or Slavic pagan or Byzantine Christian.

The Danes (Norse) were attacking Britain, Ireland, and Northern France. The Arabs had swept away the Christian countries of the Middle East and Northern Africa and occupied most of Spain (where they had built a civilization which was matched nowhere in Western Europe). The Saracens (as Christians called them) had occupied Sicily and periodically sacked Rome. The Papacy was dominated by the women of the Theophylact family and was in its worst condition ever. The "Franks" had not been able to hold together the empire of Charlemagne and were having a difficult time imposing Catholicism on the Wends, the Lithuanians, and the North Slavs. Byzantine Orthodoxy had enjoyed some progress among the South Slavs and had established an outpost in the vast steppes of Eurasia in Kiev under Vladimir. No one would have bet on the survival of Western Christianity, save perhaps in far-off Ireland where the Danes were becoming Christian. (Fletcher 1998)

Vast areas of Western Europe were covered again with forests. There was no network of local parishes. Most priests were illiterate, barely able to say the key sacramental words. The laity were either warrior lords who were only a step above barbarians and for whom murder and mayhem were a vocation or peasants converted by force (save where the Irish monasteries had introduced a less violent form of Christianity to the Continent). In both cases Christianity was a veneer which overlay paganism and was itself infected by superstition. Catholicism lacked the resources to do any more than teach the central doctrines and a few prayers.

Western Europe would improve in the next couple of centuries, even flourish and religion would improve too. My point, however, is that at the end of the first millennia the outlook for Christianity did not seem promising. The Danes, the Arabs, the Wends, the Sarcens, the Bulgars: all seemed at least as serious threats as does "modernization" today. Somehow religion survived.

So it still survives today. And flourishes? Has it ever flourished? Was there ever a golden age? Perhaps in some places, some of the time. Nothing much more than that.

Many social scientists assume that "organized religion" is in its last days, that the prophecies from Voltaire to Durkheim about the end of religion are at long last about to be fulfilled. One might remark that this expectation has been advanced before and religion somehow continued. If it turns out that the expectation is valid today, one might remark that it took a hell of a long time for the corpse to stay dead. A minimum conclusion from this book is that, if futures in religion were available in commodity markets, one would be ill-advised to sell short. Only when a majority of European humankind (unlike some academics and intellectuals) no longer need something to believe in, something to pass on to their children, and something to belong too, should the bugler begin to play taps for religion.

The following general observations seem pertinent at the end of the book.

1. The decline of religion in Britain, the Netherlands and France is not necessarily paradigmatic for the rest of Europe.

2. Whether the resurgence of religion in Eastern Europe is a return to the status quo ante or an actual revival is a question which ought not to obscure the point that the Orthodox and Catholic churches and heritages outlived Socialism.

3. While their peoples dismiss the church's sexual teachings, the traditional Catholic countries (with the exception of France) continue to be Catholic, one might almost say stubbornly so: Ireland, Spain, Portugal, Italy, Austria, Poland, Slovakia, Hungary, Slovenia, Switzerland. While it may be possible for some Orange sociologists to dismiss them as backward, that appears to be a hasty judgement.

4. Protestantism has on the whole fared less well, save in Switzerland. However, the Scandinavian countries are perhaps less un-Christian than they may seem.

5. The survival of Orthodoxy and Catholicism may in part be due to the rich cultural heritages which have supported belief in those traditions. Protestantism, almost as a matter of principle, is suspicious that these religious heritages verge on idolatry and perhaps thus gives away some of the game to the secularizers.

6. The Vatican's attempts to restore order in Slovenia, Hungary, and the Netherlands have apparently been counterproductive.

7. The most surprising finding is the increase in belief in life after death among the younger cohorts of most countries (and of new forms of Catholicism among the younger Irish). Perhaps this represents a return to levels of religious hope which existed before the world wars.

8. The terrible suffering of the world wars, the great surprise of postwar prosperity, and the sudden collapse of socialism are phenomena which have influenced religion—and everything else—in Europe enormously, but no serious attempt has been made to factor our their import much less to design a religious response to it. The propensity of religious leaders to bemoan materialism is little more than a revelation of their lack of creativity.

9. East Germany is the only country in Europe in which socialism effectively stamped out religion. Even there, the very youngest cohort is considerably more likely to believe in life after death. In France, Britain, and the Netherlands, religion has suffered considerable losses, but still has some claim on half the population. The division in the Czech Republic between Catholics and "Free Thinkers" seems to be historic.

10. No single, all-embracing model can describe the condition of European religion, much less predict its future. One must take refuge in Brown's paradigm cited at the beginning of the book.

It is fashionable for the social scientist to end by asserting that more research is needed. Some of the deficiencies of this book can be attributed, if one wishes, to the lack of skill of the writer. Yet the absence of much of what one would like to know about religion in Europe is the result of inadequacies of the data. The International Social Survey Program religion surveys may be the best data sets currently available on religion in Europe, but they are still not very good. They suffer from inadequate questionnaires and limitations of time. (They are, however, not locked up in archives like European

Values Study data or the RAMP data). Only an incurable optimist will expect that a better study or even a comparable study will be done anytime soon. No one should reasonably expect another International Social Survey Program religion module during the next decade.

Until then this profile of religion at the end of the Second Millennium in more than a score of European countries will have to defend itself on the ground that, while it is not very good, it is all there is.

References

Akenson, Donald H. 1993. *The Irish Diaspora.* Toronto: P. D. Meany Company.

Berger, Peter. 1968. *The Sacred Canopy*. New York: Doubleday.

Borowik, Irinia and Grzegorz Babinski. (eds.). 1997. *New Religious Phenomena in Central and Eastern Europe.* Krakow: TAIWPN Universitas.

Bossy, John. 1985. *Christianity in the West 1400-1700.* New York: Oxford University Press.

Brown, Callum. 1992. "A Revisionist Approach to Religious Change," in Steve Bruce (ed.). *Religion and Modernization.* Oxford: Clarendon Press

Bruce, Steve. 1992. Religion and Modernization. Oxford:Clarendon Press

—.1993. "Religion and Rational Choice." *Sociology of Religion*.54:193-205.

—.1995. "The Truth About Religion in Britain." *Journal for the Scientific Study of Religion.* 34:417-430.

—.1995b *Religion in Modern Britain*. New York: Oxford University Press

—.1996 *Religion in the Modern World.* New York: Oxford University Press.

—.1999. Choice and Religon. *A Critique of Rational Choice Theory*. New York: Oxford University Press.

Carroll, Michael. 1992. *Madonnas that Maim.* Baltimore, MD: Johns Hopkins University Press.

Casanova, Jose. 1994. *Public Religions in the Modern World.* Chicago :The University of Chicago Press.

Christian, William. 1981. *Apparitions in Late Medieval and Renaissance Spain.* Princeton, NJ: Princeton University Press.

Cipriani, Roberto. 1989. "Diffused Religion and New Values in Italy," in David Brikcford (ed.), *The Changing Face of Religion.* Beverly Hills CA. 24-48.

Coleman, John. 1978. *The Evolution of Dutch Catholicism, 1958-1974.* Berkeley: The University of California Press.

Dobbelaere, Karrel. 1987. "Some Trends in European Sociology of Relgion." *Sociological Analysis.* 48:107-137.

Duffy, Eamon. 1992. The Stripping of the Altars. New Haven, CT: The Yale University Press.

Eisinga, R. with A. Felling, J. peters and P. Scheepers. 1992. *Social and Cultural Trends in the Netherlands, 1979-1990.* Amsterdam: The Steinmetz Archive.

Ester, Peter, Loek Halman, and Ruud de Moor. 1993. *The Individualizing Society: Value Change in Europe and North America.* Tilburg: Tilburg University Press.

Flint, Valerie Irene. 1992. *The Rise of Magic in Early Medieval Europe.* Princeton, NJ: Princeton University Press.

Fogarty, Michael, Liam Ryan, and Joseph Lee. 1984. *Irish Values and Attitudes: The Irish Report of the European Values Study.* Dublin: Dominican Publications.

Gentilcore, David. 1992. *Bishop to Witch.* Manchester: Manchester University Press.

Ginzburg, Carlo. 1983. *The Night Battles: Witchcraft and Agrarian Cults in the Sixteenth and Seventeenth Centuries,* translated by John and Anne Tedeschi. Baltimore, MD: Johns Hopkins University Press.

Greeley, Andrew. 1994 "A Religion Revival in Russia." *Journal for the Scientific Study of Religion.* Vol. 33, No. 3 (September 1994) :253-272.

Greeley, Andrew. 1996. *Religion as Poetry*. New Brunswick, NJ: Transaction Publishers.

Greeley, Andrew. 1996. "In Defense of Surveys." *Society,* Vol. 33, 4. May-June. 1996.

Greeley, Andrew. 1999. "The Religions of Ireland," in Anthony F. Heath, Richard Breen, and Christopher T. Whelan (eds.), *Ireland North and South.* Oxford: Oxford University Press.

Husband, William B. 2000. *"Godless Communists:" Atheism and Society in Soviet Russia 1917-1932.* DeKalb: Northern Illinois University Press.

Jagodzinski, Wolfgang, and Andrew Greeley. 1997. "Hard Core Atheism, Socialism and Supply Side Religion." Unpublished paper. Köln: ZA.

LeRoy Ladurie, Emanuel. 1975. *Montaillou, Village Occitan* de *1294-1324.* Paris:Gallimard.

Luckmann, Thomas. 1967 *The Invisible Religion: The Problem of Religion in Modern Society.* New York: Macmillan.

Obelkevich, James. 1979. *Religion and the People 800-1700.* Chapel Hill: The University of North Carolina Press.

O'Connor, Fionnuala. 1993. *In Search of a State: Catholics in Northern Ireland.* Belfast: The Blackstaff Press.

Rubin, Miri. 1991. *Corpus Christi: The Eucharist in Late Medieval Culture.* New York: Cambridge University Press.

Stark, Rodney and Roger Finke. 2000. *Acts of Faith: Explaining the Human Side of Religion.* Berkeley: The University of California Press.

Schneider, Jane. 1990. "Spirits and the Spirit of Capitalism," in Ellen Badone (ed.), *Religious Orthodoxy and Popular Faith in European Society.* Princeton, NJ: Princeton University Press .24-54.

Sommerville, C. John. 1992. *The Secularization of Early Modern England.* New York: Oxford University Press.

Taylor, Lawrence. 1995. *Occasions of Faith: An Anthropology of Irish Catholics.* Philadelphia: The University of Pennsylvania Press.

Tos, Niko Peter Ph. Mohler and Brina Malnar. 2000. *Modern Society and Values.* Ljubljana: University of Ljubljana Press.

Tschannen, Oliver. 1991. "The Secularization Paradigm." *Journal for the Scientific Study of Religion.* 30 (December) :396-415.

Ward, Conor and Andrew Greeley. 1990. "Development and Tolerance: The Case of Ireland." *Erie-Ireland.* 25, no. 4 (Winter).

Whelan, Christopher T. (editor). 1994. *Values and Social Change in Ireland.* Dublin: Gill and Macmillan.

Warner, H. Steven. 1993. "Work In Progress Toward A New Paradigm For The Sociological Study Of Religion in The United States." *American Journal of Sociology.* 98.5 1044-1093.

Wilson, Bryan. 1976. *Contemporary Transformations of Religion.* London, New York: Oxford University Press.

—. 1969. *Religion in Secular Society.* Harmondsworth: Penguin Books

Zentralarchiv für Empirische Sozialsforschung 1993 *Religion. ISSP 92 Codebook (Preliminary).*Cologne.

—. 2000 Religion2 iSSp 98 Codebook Cologne : Die Universität zu.

Appendix

General Social Survey

CONFIDENTIAL

In this part of the survey we are interested in your opinions about politics, social issues and other things that affect our way of life in America.

We would like you to fill out this questionnaire on your own using a pencil. When you are finished please return the questionnaire to our interviewer.

HOW TO FILL OUT THIS QUESTIONNAIRE

To answer most questions you need only circle a number. Here are two examples:

Example A:

Do you think the government is doing a good job or a poor job?

A very good job 1
A fairly good job 2
A poor job 3
A very poor job 4

(IF YOU THINK THE GOVERNMENT IS DOING A "FAIRLY GOOD JOB", CIRCLE "2". CIRCLE ONE ANSWER ONLY).

Example B:

Do you agree or disagree with the following statements?
(PLEASE CIRCLE ONE NUMBER FOR EACH STATEMENT)

1. Strongly agree
2. Agree
3. Neither agree nor disagree
4. Disagree
5. Strongly disagree

	CIRCLE A NUMBER				
It is difficult to raise children	1	2	3	4	5
A woman should devote almost all her time to her family	1	2	3	4	5

(YOU WOULD CIRCLE "1" IF YOU STRONGLY AGREE WITH THE FIRST STATEMENT, AND "4" IF YOU "DISAGREE" WITH THE SECOND STATEMENT).

* * * * * * * * *

PLEASE READ EACH QUESTION CAREFULLY, REMEMBER THERE ARE NO RIGHT OR WRONG ANSWERS—WE JUST

WANT TO KNOW YOUR <u>OWN</u> PERSONAL OPINION.

1. If you were to consider your life in general these days, how happy or unhappy would you say you are, on the whole…

Very happy	1	07/
Fairly happy	2	
Not very happy	3	
Not at all happy	4	
Can't choose	8	

---

2. On the whole, do you think it should or should not be the government's responsibility to...

> 1. Definitely should be
> 2. Probably should be
> 3. Probably should not be
> 4. Definitely should not be
> 8. Can't choose

PLEASE CIRCLE A NUMBER

a. Provide a job for everyone who wants one	1	2	3	4	8	08/
b. Reduce income differences between the rich and poor	1	2	3	4	8	09/

---

3. Here are some measures to deal with crime. Some people are in favor of them while other people are against them. Do you agree or disagree that…

	Strongly Agree	Agree	Neither Agree nor Disagree	Dis-agree	Strongly Disagree	Can't Choose	
a. People who break the law should be given stiffer sentences	1	2	3	4	5	8	10/
b. People convicted of murder should be subject to the death penalty	1	2	3	4	5	8	11/

4. Do you think it is wrong or not wrong if a man and a woman have sexual relations before marriage?

Always wrong	1	12/
Almost always wrong	2	
Wrong only sometimes	3	
Not wrong at all	4	
Can't choose	8	

---

5. What about a *married* person having sexual relations with someone *other* than his or her husband or wife, is it…

Always wrong	1	13/
Almost always wrong	2	
Wrong only sometimes	3	
Not wrong at all	4	
Can't choose	8	

---

6. And what about sexual relations between two adults of the same sex, is it…

Always wrong	1	14/
Almost always wrong	2	
Wrong only sometimes	3	
Not wrong at all	4	
Can't choose	8	

---

7. Do you think the law should or should not allow a pregnant woman to obtain a legal abortion…

1. Definitely should allow it
2. Probably should allow it
3. Probably should not allow it
4. Definitely should not allow it
8. Can't choose

PLEASE CIRCLE A NUMBER

a. If there is a strong chance of serious defect in the baby	1	2	3	4	8	15/
b. If the family has a very low income and cannot afford any more children	1	2	3	4	8	16/

8. Do you *personally* think it is wrong or not wrong for a woman to have an abortion…

	Always Wrong	Almost Always Wrong	Wrong Only Sometimes	Not Wrong at All	Can't Choose	
a. If there is a strong chance of serious defect in the baby	1	2	3	4	8	17/
b. If the family has a very low income and cannot afford any more children	1	2	3	4	8	18/

9. Do you agree or disagree…

	Strongly Agree	Agree	Neither Agree nor Disagree	Dis-agree	Strongly Disagree	Can't Choose	
a. A husband's job is to earn money; a wife's job is to look after the home and family ..	1	2	3	4	5	8	19/
b. All in all, family life suffers when the woman has a full-time job	1	2	3	4	5	8	20/

10. Consider the, situations listed below. Do you feel it is wrong or not wrong if…

	Not Wrong	A Bit Wrong	Wrong	Seriously Wrong	Can't Choose	
a. A taxpayer does not report all of his income in order to pay less income taxes	1	2	3	4	8	21/
b. A person gives the government incorrect information about himself to get government benefits that he is not entitled to	1	2	3	4	8	22/

11. How much confidence do you have in...

> 1. Complete confidence
> 2. A great deal of confidence
> 3. Some confidence
> 4. Very little confidence
> 5. No confidence at all
> 8. Can't choose

	PLEASE CIRCLE A NUMBER					
a. U.S. Congress	1	2	3	4	5	8	23/
b. Business and industry	1	2	3	4	5	8	24/
c. Government departments	1	2	3	4	5	8	25/
d. Churches and religious organizations	1	2	3	4	5	8	26/
e. Courts and the legal system	1	2	3	4	5	8	27/
f. Schools and the educational system	1	2	3	4	5	8	28/

---

12. How much do you agree or disagree with each of the following...

> 1. Strongly agree
> 2. Agree
> 3. Neither agree nor disagree
> 4. Disagree
> 5. Strongly disagree
> 8. Can't choose

	PLEASE CIRCLE A NUMBER					
a. Politicians who do not believe in God are unfit for public office	1	2	3	4	8	29/
b. Religious leaders should not try to influence how people vote in elections	1	2	3	4	8	30/
c. It would be better for America if more people with strong religious beliefs held public office	1	2	3	4	8	31/
d. Religious leaders should not try to influence government decisions	1	2	3	4	8	32/

13. Do you think that churches and religious organizations in this country have too much power or too little power?

Far too much power	1	33/
Too much power	2	
About the right amount of power	3	
Too little power	4	
Far too little power	5	
Can't choose	8	

14. Please indicate which statement below comes closest to expressing what you believe about God.

I don't believe in God	1	34/
I don't know whether there is a God and I don't believe there is any way to find out	2	
I don't believe in a personal God, but I do believe in a Higher Power of some kind	3	
I find myself believing in God some of the time, but not at others	4	
While I have doubts, I feel that I do believe in God	5	
I know God really exists and I have no doubts about it	6	

15. How close do you feel to God most of the time?

Don't believe in God	1	35/
Not close at all	2	
Not very close	3	
Somewhat close	4	
Extremely close	5	
Can't choose	8	

16. Which best describes your beliefs about God?

I don't believe in God now and I never have	1	36/
I don't believe in God now, but I used to	2	
I believe in God now, but I didn't used to	3	
I believe in God now and I always have	4	
Can't choose	8	

17. Do you believe in...

	Yes, Definitely	Yes, Probably	No, Probably Not	No, Definitely Not	Can't choose	
a. Life after death	1	2	3	4	8	37/
b. The Devil	1	2	3	4	8	38/
c. Heaven	1	2	3	4	8	39/
d. Hell	1	2	3	4	8	40/
e. Religious miracles	1	2	3	4	8	41/

---

18. Which of these statements comes closest to describing your feelings about the Bible?

a. The Bible is the actual word of God and it is to be taken literally, word for word 1 42/
b. The Bible is the inspired word of God but not everything should be taken literally, word for word 2
c. The Bible is an ancient book of fables, legends, history, and moral precepts recorded by man 3
d. This does not apply to me.......................... 4
e. Can't choose 8

19. Do you agree or disagree with the following

1. Strongly agree
2. Agree
3. Neither agree nor disagree
4. Disagree
5. Strongly disagree
8. Can't choose

PLEASE CIRCLE A NUMBER

a. There is a God who concerns Himself with every human being personally	1	2	3	4	5	8	43/
b. There is little that people can do to change the course of their lives	1	2	3	4	5	8	44/
c. To me, life is meaningful only because God exists	1	2	3	4	5	8	45/
d. In my opinion, life does not serve any purpose	1	2	3	4	5	8	46/
e. The course of our lives is decided by God	1	2	3	4	5	8	47/
f. Life is only meaningful if you provide the meaning yourself ..	1	2	3	4	5	8	48/
g. We each make our own fate	1	2	3	4	5	8	49/

---

20. How often have you felt as though you were…

	Never in my life	Once or Twice	Several times	Often	Can't say	
a. Really in touch with someone who had died..............	1	2	3	4	8	50/
b. Close to a powerful, spiritual force that seemed to lift you out of yourself............	1	2	3	4	8	51/

21. Has there ever been a turning point in your life when you made a new and personal commitment to religion?

Yes 1 52/
No 2

---

22. What was your mother's religious preference when you were a child? Was it Protestant, Catholic, Jewish, some other religion, or no religion?

Protestant 1 53/
Catholic 2
Jewish 3
Orthodox (such as Greek
or Russian Orthodox) 4
Moslem 5
Other (Please Specify)
______________________________ 6
No religion 7
Don't know 8

If Protestant:
What specific denomination was that?

____

---

23. What was your father's religious preference when you were a child? Was it Protestant, Catholic, Jewish, some other religion, or no religion?

Protestant 1 54/
Catholic 2
Jewish 3
Orthodox (such as Greek
or Russian Orthodox) 4
Moslem 5
Other (Please Specify)
______________________________ 6
No religion 7
Don't know 8

If Protestant:
What specific denomination was that?

____

24. What religion, if any, were you raised in? Was it Protestant, Catholic, Jewish, some other religion, or no religion?

Protestant	1	55/
Catholic	2	
Jewish	3	
Orthodox (such as Greek or Russian Orthodox)	4	
Moslem	5	
Other (Please Specify) ____________	6	
No religion	7	
Don't know	8	

If Protestant:

What specific denomination was that?

____

If you are currently married or living as married, answer Q. 25:
If you are not currently married or living as married, go to Q. 26:

---

25. What is your husband's/wife's religious preference? Is it Protestant, Catholic, Jewish, some other religion, or no religion?

Protestant	1	56/
Catholic	2	
Jewish	3	
Orthodox (such as Greek or Russian Orthodox)	4	
Moslem	5	
Other (Please Specify) ____________	6	
No religion	7	
Don't know	8	

If Protestant:

What specific denomination was that?

____

26. When you were a child, how often did your mother attend religious services?

Never	1	57–58/
Less than once a year	2	
About once or twice a year	3	
Several times a year	4	
About once a month	5	
2–3 times a month	6	
Nearly every week	7	
Every week	8	
Several times a week	9	
No mother/mother not present	10	
Can't say/Can't remember	98	

---

27. When you were a child, how often did your father attend religious services?

Never	1	59–60/
Less than once a year	2	
About once or twice a year	3	
Several times a year	4	
About once a month	5	
2–3 times a month	6	
Nearly every week	7	
Every week	8	
Several times a week	9	
No father/father not present	10	
Can't say/Can't remember	98	

---

28. And what about when you were around 11 or 12, how often did you attend religious services then?

Never	1	61–62/
Less than once a year	2	
About once or twice a year	3	
Several times a year	4	
About once a month	5	
2–3 times a month	6	
Nearly every week	7	
Every week	8	
Several times a week	9	
Can't say/Can't remember	98	

Now thinking about the present...

29. About how often do you pray?

Never	1	63–64/
Less than once a year	2	
About once or twice a year	3	
Several times a year	4	
About once a month	5	
2–3 times a month	6	
Nearly every week	7	
Every week	8	
Several times a week	9	
Once a day	10	
Several times a day	11	

---

30. How often do you take part in the activities or organizations of a church or place of worship other than attending services?

Never	1	65/
Less than once a year	2	
About once or twice a year	3	
Several times a year	4	
About once a month	5	
2–3 times a month	6	
Nearly every week	7	
Every week	8	
Several times a week	9	

---

31. Would you describe yourself as...

Extremely religious	1	66/
Very religious	2	
Somewhat religious	3	
Neither religious nor non-religious	4	
Somewhat non-religious	5	
Very non-religious	6	
Extremely non-religious	7	
Can't choose	8	

32. In your opinion, should there be daily prayers in all public schools?

Yes, definitely	1	67/
Yes, probably	2	
No, probably	3	
No, definitely	4	
Can't choose	8	

---

33. Do you agree or disagree with the following statements

1. Strongly agree
2. Agree
3. Neither agree nor disagree
4. Disagree
5. Strongly disagree
8. Can't choose

	PLEASE CIRCLE A NUMBER						
a. Right and wrong should be based on God's laws	1	2	3	4	5	8	68/
b. Right and wrong should be decided by society	1	2	3	4	5	8	69/
c. Right and wrong should be a matter of personal conscience	1	2	3	4	5	8	70/

---

34. Some books or films offend people who have strong religious beliefs. Should books and films that attack religions be prohibited by law or should they be allowed?

Definitely should be prohibited	1	71/
Probably should be prohibited	2	
Probably should be allowed	3	
Definitely should be allowed	4	
Can't choose	8	

---

35. Would you say that you have been "born again" or have had a "born again" experience—that is, a turning point in your life when you committed yourself to Christ?

Yes	1	72/
No	2	

36. There are many different ways of picturing God. We'd like to know the kinds of images you are most likely to associate with God.

Below are sets of contrasting images. On a scale of 1–7 where would you place your images of God between the two contrasting images?

The first set of contrasting images shows Mother at 1 on the scale and Father at 7. If you imagine God as a Mother you would place yourself at 1. If you imagine God as a Father, you would place yourself at 7. If you imagine God as somewhere between Mother and Father, you would place yourself at 2, 3, 4, 5, or 6.

Where would you place your image of God on the scale for each set of images?

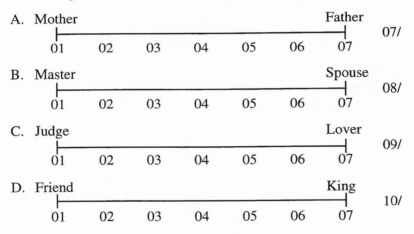

A. Mother — Father 07/

01 02 03 04 05 06 07

B. Master — Spouse 08/

01 02 03 04 05 06 07

C. Judge — Lover 09/

01 02 03 04 05 06 07

D. Friend — King 10/

01 02 03 04 05 06 07

37. People have different images of the world and human nature. We'd like to know the kinds of images you have.

Below are sets of contrasting images. On a scale of 1–7, where would you place your image of the world and human nature between the two contrasting images?

Look at the first set of contrasting images. If you think that "The world is basically filled with evil and sin," you would place yourself at 1. If you think "There is much goodness in the world which hints at God's goodness," you would place yourself at 7. If you think things are somewhere in between these two, you would place yourself at 2, 3, 4, 5, or 6.

Where would you place your image of the world on each of the scales below?

A. The world is basically filled with evil and sin. — There is much goodness in the world which hints at God's goodness.

1 2 3 4 5 6 7 11/

B. Human nature is basically good. — Human nature is fundamentally perverse and corrupt.

1 2 3 4 5 6 7 12/

---

38. Did you get any of your grade school or high school education in parochial schools or other schools run by religious groups?

Yes 1 13/
No 2

If "YES":

How many years did you attend religious schools? |_____| 14–15/

Index

Information appearing in a figure (or table) that is not also discussed in the text containing the figure (or table) is specified by an "f" (or "t") following the page number. For example: "14f" (or "14t") means that information in a figure (or table) on page 14 is not also discussed in the text there or in the text on surrounding pages. Information appearing in text, or in text and in a figure or table as well, is signified by a page reference or reference to a range of pages - e.g., "14" or "14-16," as appropriate.